JENNIE
And The Story of
Grossinger's

JENNIE
And The Story of
Grossinger's

by JOEL POMERANTZ

GROSSET & DUNLAP
A NATIONAL GENERAL COMPANY
Publishers/New York

To all Grossinger's employes,
past, present and future

JENNIE
And The Story of
Grossinger's

Chapter 1

Dawn comes early to the Catskills in June. On this late spring morning Jennie Grossinger was up only minutes after the first shafts of light shone over her sprawling resort hotel. Some inner time sense alerted her on days when a particularly heavy program or some special event was scheduled. This was to be one of those days. Jennie had been invited by her friend, Father George Francis Brennan, the pastor of St. Peter's Church in nearby Liberty, to attend the dedication of the new parochial school recently added to the parish church. Usually, in such cases, a bishop presides over the dedication formalities, but, today, Francis Cardinal Spellman was making the 100-mile trip from his Archdiocese office in New York City to do the honors. Although it would not be the first time in its 150-year history that Liberty, a pleasant township of some 5,000 persons, would play host to this prince of the Roman Catholic Church, the townspeople were eagerly looking forward to the ceremonies. So, in fact, was Jennie Grossinger. She had always admired the Cardinal for his contribution to interfaith and interracial causes, while his simple humanity had often inspired her.

There was a time, years back, when she was terrified at the prospect of meeting people of prominence. Her limited formal education and humble background made her feel shy in their presence. However, as years passed, her relentless pursuit of knowledge had long since enabled her to conquer her feelings of inadequacy. As owner and operator of one of the world's best-known vacation meccas, she had met a president of her adopted country, scores of senators, governors, and mayors, a small army of judges and cabinet officials, Nobel Prize winners, renowned writers and men of science, and virtually every important film and theatrical star in America. She brought to these meetings a sense of poise which never failed to astonish those who had known her in her difficult younger years. In turn, she was gratified to discover that notables liked meeting *her*, perhaps because she never compromised her natural warmth and unpretentious manner. No matter what, she was always just Jennie.

The Cardinal's much-heralded visit, Jennie knew, was a gesture of appreciation for the financial sacrifices made by members of the small St. Peter's parish to fulfill the dream of Father Brennan and his predecessors to add a school to their church. It was probably inspired, too, by a desire to thank the majority non-Catholic population of Liberty who had contributed so generously to the construction fund for the buff-colored schoolhouse.

Jennie spent the morning in her modest one-story, ranch-type house, named the Joy Cottage and located just opposite the Main Building of the hotel that bears her name. She attended to several pressing business matters and then chatted with her housekeeper, May Brown, about some of the religious details of the three P.M. dedication ceremony. At eleven thirty the phone rang. It was her son, Paul.

"Mom," he said excitedly, "Rocky just phoned. He's speaking near-by this afternoon and landing at the airport in about an hour. He asked if he could stop in to see you. Remember how he liked those egg rolls we served the last time he was here? I told the kitchen to have some ready and send them to your house right away."

Jennie was puzzled. Egg rolls? Rocky had been to her house more than a dozen times and he'd never asked for egg rolls.

"What do you mean he's landing at the airport in an hour? Where has he been? I saw him in the dining room just last night."

"Mom," Paul said, "I mean Governor Rockefeller."

"Oh, you shouldn't call *him* Rocky," she said reproachfully. "Of course, I'll be very happy to see the Governor. Will you and Elaine come over?" Paul and his wife, Bunny, live in a house fifty yards up the road. Just beyond is another house occupied by Jennie's daughter, Elaine, and her husband, Dr. A. David Etess.

"We'll try to make it" Paul told her. "But fifty people arrived this morning without reservations and Elaine and I are still trying to figure out what to do with them. We're completely filled."

Jennie's mistake was understandable. "Rocky" to her was Rocky Marciano, the former world's heavyweight champion who trained for each of his title fights at Grossinger's, and kept returning after his retirement as a faithful guest.

Ever since Barney Ross, the lightweight and welter-weight champion of the Thirties, broke precedent by pitching a training camp at Grossinger's, a succession of boxing champions had followed him to the Catskill Mountains retreat for their pre-fight workouts. Ingemar Johansson, who defeated Floyd Patterson for the heavy-weight title only a few nights before, also trained at Grossinger's and was now back celebrating at the hotel with Marciano. Even Governor Rockefeller had done some of his early training, in a sense, at Grossinger's. He came there during his maiden voyage into politics—his first campaign to wrest the Empire State governorship from Averell Harriman. He and Jennie hit it off from the start. She had a few qualms about this, because Harri-man was also a friend. Rockefeller re-assured her by confiding: "Averell and I are very friendly, too. There's nothing personal about our political battle."

After his election, Rockefeller returned many times to speak at Grossinger's. Occasionally, when he had an appointment in Sullivan County, he would fly from Al-bany to the hotel airport to see Jennie before continuing his trip by car. This visit was just such an occasion, but it presented a problem: the Governor's visit might delay her arrival at the school dedication. When she called Paul to discuss this, he convinced her there would be no conflict. Since Rockefeller's schedule called for him to speak in the early afternoon, he could only visit with Jennie a few minutes.

As it turned out, the Governor's plane was delayed

leaving Albany. It wasn't until one-thirty that Paul and Abe Friedman, Jennie's brother-in-law and the hotel's veteran maitre d', brought him over from the airport. Rockefeller greeted Jennie with a hug and a kiss and settled down on the sofa in Joy Cottage's spacious living room lined with autographed pictures of celebrities.

When a waiter brought in egg rolls and iced tea for the Governor, he smiled broadly. "I've been so busy lately, I haven't had much time to sleep and I was afraid I might doze off right in the middle of the day," he said. "These egg rolls are like pep pills."

A moment later, two other men, observing the informality of Jennie's place, walked into Joy Cottage without bothering to ring. "Hello, Jennie," they called out. It was the other Rocky (Marciano) and the new Swedish heavyweight champion, Ingemar Johansson. The two ringmen walked into the living room and looked surprised. Neither had expected to see Governor Rockefeller there. Rockefeller hadn't expected to see them either, but he was a sports fan, knew Marciano well, and appeared delighted. He slapped the former champion on the shoulder and said: "It's nice to see you, Rocco." The greeting certified the Governor's status as an authentic boxing aficionado: only deep-dyed ring enthusiasts knew that Rocco was Marciano's real first name.

Ingemar, whom the Governor had seen from a ringside seat at the championship tussle with Patterson, was now introduced to Rockefeller and bowed stiffly from the waist. The three men promptly talked boxing. A few minutes later, Milton Blackstone, the hotel's advertising and promotion consultant, dropped in and the discussion became even more animated. Soon, Blackstone reminded Marciano that his favorite baseball team, the Boston Red Sox, was playing the New York Yankees. The game was being televised. Marciano looked anxiously toward the Governor. "Turn the set on," the Governor urged, smiling brightly. "Let's see if the Yankees can improve against your team."

Jennie's guests continued to talk sports, interspersed with politics, while casting glances at the videocast from Yankee Stadium. Governor Rockefeller, plainly enjoying this respite from official headaches, informed everyone he didn't have to speak until four-thirty and wasn't in any hurry to go.

A good hostess is usually pleased when guests are enjoying themselves so much they forget to leave. However, Jennie, one of the world's great hostesses, found herself in a ticklish situation. A quick look at the clock told her that the dedication ceremonies would begin in fifteen minutes. Suddenly, the faint sound of sirens could be heard. As the sound grew louder, Jennie realized it must be coming from state trooper cars escorting Cardinal Spellman along Route 17 to Liberty. The Cardinal's car and his official escort passed within a hundred yards of Jennie's house. The Governor, intent on Ingemar's explanation of how he had developed his powerful right-hand punch, appeared not to hear the wailing sirens. Jennie looked about helplessly. The Governor would have excused her at once had she even hinted at an engagement. Jennie, as usual, decided it would be impolite to leave while a guest was still in her home. She slipped quietly out of the room and phoned Father Brennan, who was about to leave the rectory for the school. Jennie told him of the Governor's unexpected visit and of her regret at missing His Eminence. Father Brennan consoled her: "It's a pity, but I will tell him you phoned."

"I understand," Jennie said sadly. "Please be sure to explain why I wasn't there."

She went back to her guests who were still talking fights and baseball and drinking iced tea. Governor Rockefeller left the Joy Cottage a half hour later without knowing that his presence had prevented Jennie from meeting Cardinal Spellman. Yet, no one could have sensed her deep disappointment as she chatted brightly with the Governor.

Meanwhile, Marciano and Ingemar continued watching the ball game with Rocky trying (not too successfully) to explain the game to the new champion. Suddenly, for the second time that day, the scream of sirens filled the room. State troopers were escorting the Cardinal back to Route 17 and out of Liberty. But the sirens didn't fade away; instead, they grew closer and louder. Moving to the window, Jennie saw a large black limousine and four state troopers on motorcycles turn into the road leading to the hotel. The sirens stopped and a moment later her doorbell rang. She ran to the door, opened it, and stood face-to-face with a cherubic-looking, short man wearing a clerical collar. He was smiling sweetly.

"You're Jennie Grossinger," he said. "I'm Cardinal Spellman. May I come in?"

"This is a great surprise, Cardinal. I'm deeply honored to have you here," Jennie said excitedly. "I must apologize for not having been present at the dedication ceremonies."

9

"No apologies are necessary," the Cardinal said warmly. She escorted the prelate into the living room and introduced him to everyone present. Like the Governor, Cardinal Spellman didn't have to be introduced to Rocky Marciano.

"His hometown, Brockton, Massachusetts, is near mine in Whitman," the Cardinal told Jennie, with a grin. "I always say to him that at least one man from our part of the state made good."

"Let me turn the television off, Your Eminence," Rocky hastened to say.

The Cardinal shook his head. "No, no, I see you have a ball game on. What's happening?"

"The Yankees are clobbering the Red Sox," explained Rocky. "Whitey Ford has given up only two hits and Mantle hit a grand slam home run. They're ahead six to nothing."

The Cardinal smiled. "I never watch the Red Sox play the Yankees. I grew up rooting for the Red Sox, but I've been in New York twenty years now and I feel I ought not to root against the home team. So I try to remain neutral and that isn't easy for a baseball fan."

Cardinal Spellman quickly established an atmosphere of intimacy. He and Jennie found a number of mutual interests which they discussed with animation. The Cardinal showed skill at leavening the conversation with clever jokes. Finally, the Cardinal rose and announced regretfully that he had to leave. After shaking everyone's hand in the house, he stopped again on the lawn to pump the hand of each of the state troopers who had accompanied him.

Presently, the other guests were gone, too, and Jennie

was left to contemplate this remarkable day in her life. A prince of the Roman Catholic Church had come to visit with her, as had a governor—a Rockefeller, no less—and two of the most celebrated men in the sporting world. As a hotelier, she had also been playing hostess to 1300 guests, some of whom had come from as far off as Europe and South America, and many of whom were important figures in the worlds of industry, finance, science, medicine, and law. She could not help but reflect upon her remarkable good fortune and the long, sometimes painful road that brought her to this memorable day.

Chapter 2

Jennie's earliest memories were of her childhood in a small village called Baligrod in that part of the vast Austro-Hungarian Empire known as Galicia. Her father, Selig Grossinger, a tall, fine-looking man, was the youngest of four brothers whose father had left them a substantial estate. But by the time Selig was a young man, the large estate had been worked out. When the family was forced to sell, Selig accepted employment as the overseer of lands owned by others. Selig was a humble man and he accepted his fate as God's will. Because he loved the land, he was happy in his work.

Every day, he arose at dawn and said his morning prayers. After breakfast, he mounted his horse, lit his pipe, and made the rounds to check on the tenant farmers who were tending the master's livestock and tilling the soil. During the 19th Century, the overseer of an estate held considerable power over the peasants he supervised. But Selig Grossinger was a just man. He was respected not only for his fairness, but because he knew the land, and he knew what crops would or would not survive the hard winters. Traditionally, in this part of the world, Jews were tenant farmers, itinerant peddlers, or small shopkeepers in the larger cities. Seldom did they own land or become estate managers. All in all, Selig Grossinger should have been very satisfied with his lot, and for the most part he was.

He had a lovely wife, Malke, and two lively young daughters, Jennie and Lottie. Before their marriage, he and Malke lived about thirty miles from one another. It was the traditional traveling *shadchen* (matchmaker) who had arranged their marriage. A *shadchen* went from village to village searching for girls who wanted husbands and for young men who desired brides. He would seek out their parents—a custom hundreds of years old. It would have been unethical for him to deal with the prospective bride and groom until their families had sanctioned the proposed union.

Malke Grumet was lovely to behold and intensely religious. The daughter of a country innkeeper, she had been well trained in cooking and in the management of the inn. In every sense she was a fine catch. The *shadchen* realized he would have no trouble finding an eligible male and earning his broker's fee. By chance, his eye lit upon Selig Grossinger. After several discussions with the parents, he arranged a "chance" encounter at the home of mutual friends of both families. Malke and Selig, meeting for the first time, were, indeed, pleased with what they saw. Not too many days afterwards, while walking in the village square, she accidently spied the handsome young man who was to become her husband entering a shop. Acutely embarrassed, she fled without saying a word to him. The third time they saw each other was under the *chupah*—the ritual canopy over the marriage altar.

Six years later, although his home life left nothing to be desired, Selig Grossinger was a worried man. He knew that the era of large farming estates was coming to a close. They were uneconomical. The land itself was tired; it was never given a rest. The severe winters, with their heavy snows, washed topsoil away. Each year it seemed as if the land yielded less and less. And when, by some happy quirk of nature, the land gave forth a bumper crop, the markets in the villages and cities were glutted with vegetables and fruit and prices dropped. Worried estate owners began to liquidate their overtaxed land. Selig Grossinger did a good deal of thinking as he rode his horse and puffed on his pipe. Occasionally, he would receive a letter from a cousin, also named Selig, who some years before had gone to the New World to make his fortune. Cousin Selig had not actually made a fortune, but his letters from America were cheerful and optimistic. It was obvious that he liked the distant place called New York.

One could not enter a village in Galicia without hearing about a cousin or uncle who had emigrated to New York and become a "millionaire." Still, the shrewd peasants of *Mittel Europa* did not really believe that anyone willing to work hard enough would automatically amass a fortune. Once in a great while, however, someone who had gone to New York years before would send steamship tickets to relatives left behind, and again the legends of wealth would be heard and believed by the credulous.

Selig Grossinger was neither naive nor stupid. Above

all, he knew the land, and he knew that the land in Austria-Hungry was not capable of sustaining the rapidly increasing birth rate. What was the alternative? Farming was the only skill he possessed. He would be lost in the large cities of Poland, Hungary, or Germany. Learning a new trade meant years of unpaid apprenticeship. Again and again, he read the letters Cousin Selig sent from New York. The new American wrote proudly that soon he would be a citizen. He said that he lived in a place called the East Side, a predominantly Jewish neighborhood where the old customs still prevailed. But there was one difference, Cousin Selig wrote, between being a Jew in Europe and being a Jew in New York. Once they learned to speak English, he said, Jews in New York were accepted as part of the community. Their children attended school without paying even a penny for the privilege. In Galicia, schooling was expensive.

Selig was overwhelmed by the idea of free education for his children. It was still another inducement for leaving Galicia and emigrating across the Atlantic. But as a religious man, he would not make an important decision before many weeks of earnest prayer. Each morning he would drape his *tallith* (fringed prayer shawl) around his shoulders and attach the *tephillin* (two tiny boxes containing passages from the Holy Scriptures). He would bind one to his left arm and the other to his forehead by means of thin leather straps. Now symbolically, the Scriptures were close to his heart and his mind. He would turn toward the rising sun and chant the traditional hymn, *"Adon Olom,"* and thank God for the many blessings he received. It was during these devotions one morning in 1897 that he made the firm decision to leave and broke the news to Malke and his young daughters. He could not take them along, he explained, because he could not afford passage for everyone. He could barely manage the purchase of a steerage ticket for himself.

Malke listened, and, if she shed tears, they were shed in her heart where no one—least of all Selig—could see them. He would work hard, he said gravely, and as soon as he saved enough money he would send steamship tickets for his family. How long would that be? He shrugged his shoulders. That depended on God's will. But Cousin Selig would help him find work, and he would save every penny he could. It was true he didn't have a trade, but he was young and strong and willing to work as hard as the next man—harder, for he had a greater incentive than any other man. No one had such a family as he. Within a month, Selig sailed for the New World. It took the little family of three some time to adjust to the absence of a beloved father, but five-year-old Jennie and two-year-old Lottie finally accepted what was a new way of life for them.

Before he left, Selig rented a small farm for his family, where Jennie now did many of the chores. It was Jennie who helped her mother harvest and store the potatoes, carrots and onions against the long winter months when icy blasts and heavy snow plagued the Galician countryside. Through the kindly help of Christian neighbors, she even learned the skills of spinning, flaxing and weaving. These same friends would often bundle up the happy child and take her into their homes during the dark winter evenings.

Each morning, Jennie led the cow, Jhota, to pasture

and the geese out to run. It was puzzling to Jennie that the little yellow cow (Jhota means yellow in Polish) should give white milk. When the winter winds howled down through the foothills of the Carpathians and the cold turned the water in Jhota's trough to ice, Jennie would beg her mother to allow the gentle cow to spend the nights in the pantry adjacent to the kitchen. At first Malke hesitated, wondering if Selig would approve. Still, it was bitingly cold in the small cowshed and Jhota, in addition to being the youngsters' pet, was very valuable as the family's only source of milk, butter and cheese. She was also concerned about the inevitable sanitary problems an animal living in the house might create. A makeshift hole through one wall eventually solved that difficulty. "All right, bring the poor thing in," Malke would say, and with a squeal of delight Jennie, with Lottie following behind as usual, would hurry to the cowshed.

In the beginning, the cow balked at leaving the known chill of the shed for the unknown cold of the world outside, but Jennie was persuasive. When she supplemented her entreaties with sturdy tugs of the halter over the animal's neck, Jhota finally obeyed. She seemed to sense that Jennie would not lead her into harm and soon the cow, Jennie, and little Lottie actually looked forward to the bitterly cold nights. Jhota would lie down on the straw Jennie spread out on the hard pantry floor and bask in the warmth from the kitchen stove.

When spring came and the snow left, there was still another world for the children to enjoy. Not far from the small farmhouse ran a turbulent brook which, if one was clever enough, yielded delicious fish, a Galician version of perch. Every Friday, Malke would take the girls to the brook. Fishing poles and hooks were unknown in this part of the world. But Malke was wise in the ways of the fish. She knew that once the hot sun warmed the water, the fish would find shelter under the flat rocks which jutted out from the banks. They seemed to doze there. Momma Grossinger would wade into the brook and carefully approach the ledges. When she saw a fish, she would cup her hands together and with an incredibly swift motion scoop it up and into a wooden bucket. Each time this happened, the two little girls would shriek with delight.

Soon all three hurried home and the children watched fascinated as their mother cleaned the fish. She would boil part with onions and potatoes and prepare the rest in the traditional *gefullte* fish. Sometimes, especially during the winter months when the brook showed signs of freezing over, Momma Grossinger would make pickled fish. Every housewife in the nearby town of Baligrod had her own recipe for this delicacy, usually handed down from mother to daughter. Malke's formula was to place the pieces of fish in a saucepan with onions, salt, pepper, and water, allow them to simmer, and then place them between alternate layers of fresh onion. Bay leaves, vinegar, sugar, and pickling spices would then be added to the fish, followed by a boiling and cooling process. Years of helping in her father's kitchen at the inn had made Malke a superb cook, able to add a special succulence to any food.

The brook where Malke caught her fish almost became a setting of tragedy for the children one afternoon when she was away at the market. Normally, it was not very deep, but on this day, the water had risen danger-ously after a heavy rainstorm. When the storm subsided, Jennie decided to test a narrow plank which served as a bridge from one side of the brook to the other. Lottie followed her as she ran across. When the older girl reached the opposite side, she turned to see her little sister thrashing helplessly in the water, her head bobbing up and down frantically. Without a moment's thought, the horrified Jennie waded into the churning brook, grabbed the terror-stricken child by the hair, and pulled her to the bank. Less than twenty-five feet away, a whirl-pool, its flow accelerated by the storm, raged furiously. Only a super-human effort kept Jennie and Lottie from being swept into it.

That night, the two trembling sisters slept in the same bed with Malke, one in each arm. In the darkness, Malke held them tightly and intoned over and over again, "Thank God, Thank God," as tears streamed down her face.

Each Friday night, the eve of the Sabbath, was a joyous occasion in the small farmhouse. The floors had been freshly scrubbed, the brass candlesticks polished until they shone like gold, a newly washed and ironed cloth put on the table, and the *challah* (braided egg bread) freshly baked. By sundown Friday, everything was ready to welcome the Sabbath. No work would be performed by the family until sundown of the following day. Not even cooking would be done, but the ancient laws of ritual had been modified to the point where food could be warmed over a fire if the fire had been kindled on Friday before sundown.

It was on the Sabbath that the three missed Poppa

Grossinger most. Malke was very pious, but, in accordance with tradition, it was the husband and father who was the spiritual head of the house. It fell to Malke Grossinger to instruct her older daughter in the meaning of the Sabbath. Even at five years of age, Jennie knew enough Hebrew to follow the words of the hymns her mother read to welcome the Sabbath.

When Malke was married, her mother had given her a copy of the *Mishnah,* the collection of oral laws which forms the basis of the *Talmud.* Now, on Sabbath afternoons, she read the Scriptures aloud. Always on the Sabbath, too, Malke would say a special prayer for the safety of her husband and would speak of him at great length so that the girls would not forget their father. When he left, he promised he would send for the family within a year. The year had gone, and although there were letters every week, steamship tickets never fell from the eagerly opened envelopes. Selig's letters were couched not in despair, but in realism. The tales of easy wealth in New York were, he lamented, grossly exaggerated, but at least he had found work as a presser of coats. He was supporting himself and was able to put aside a little money each week for the tickets. Moreover, many of the good things that had been reported about the New World were, to be sure, quite true. Children of all faiths were allowed to go to the public schools. Jewish people could attain citizenship and vote in elections.

Months stretched into a year, then two, and now the image of the tall, dignified man with the wisp of a beard began to fade from the minds of Jennie and Lottie. They still joined their mother in prayers for his health, but by now "Poppa" was just a word vaguely associated with someone out of the past. It was different with their mother. Her thoughts were always with Selig. She went about the back-breaking farm chores almost mechanically. It was as though she were living in a vacuum that would never be filled until she and her husband were united again. And she had complete faith that this would come to pass. And finally, a little more than three years after Selig Grossinger had left, Malke opened an envelope, somewhat larger than the ones she usually received, and three precious steamship tickets dropped to the table. Her eyes could not stem the tears of joy. She, and she alone, had never doubted.

Eight-year-old Jennie and her five-year-old sister were wildly excited. Half-forgotten memories of their father returned. Now came a frantic period of preparations for departure: washing clothes, packing, and herding the geese, the chickens, and even Jhota to the nearby farm owned by Selig's sister. The two girls were saddened when their mother told them that they would have to leave the little yellow cow behind. It was as though they were deserting one of the family. Momma Grossinger told them that Jhota would have a good home. They knew this was so, but would their aunt allow the cow to sleep in the pantry on cold winter nights? Their mother reminded them their aunt had a fine strong barn that kept the icy blasts out and that she also had several cows. Jhota would not be alone.

And so in the first year of the newly arrived 20th Century, mother and daughters began the journey to America. It started with a wagon ride to Brunn, the nearest city on the railroad. Brunn (now Brno), Czechoslovakia, was not very large, but to Jennie and her sister the traffic of carts and carriages in the streets seemed overwhelming. They looked in awe at the hotels, the city hall and the churches, which seemed to tower dangerously high above the cobbled streets. Malke Grossinger took it all in stride, and because she was calm and unafraid, the two youngsters lost their fear.

Momma Grossinger led them directly to the railroad station where they were to board a train for Hamburg. Soon, a huge locomotive roared into the station and the two children pressed close to their mother. Again, her calm voice soothed them. They picked up their bundles of clothing and baskets of food and took their places on the hard wooden benches of a third-class car. Once the train was under way they found themselves racing across a new magic world of villages and towns and miraculous mountain passes. The excited children had never suspected the world was so large.

"Momma," Jennie said breathlessly, "this is like the words in the lullaby you used to sing to us. Remember?"

Malke remembered well. The lullaby was a very popular Yiddish folk song called, *"Rozinkas and Mandeln"* ("Raisins and Almonds"). Now, she sang it again for the children. It told of a time when iron trains would carry thousands of people over great distances. It was, of course, a prophetic song, and it ended as all lullabies do: "Sleep, my little one . . . sleep." And the two Grossinger children dozed.

It was another forty-eight hours before they reached Hamburg. The seaport was a huge, roaring, frightening place at first. The people talked with strange accents and wore strange clothes. None of them dressed the way Momma dressed. She, as always, wore a *sheitel*, the

22

headdress worn by pious Jewish women according to a tradition dating back to the Middle Ages. Jennie was amazed to see that not another woman on the street wore the head covering (actually a wig), which Jennie thought all women wore. But there was not much time to worry about the strange people who lived in Hamburg. Momma Grossinger hurried them to a Jewish-owned rooming house that had been recommended to her, and for the first time since leaving home, the children, hearing the familiar Yiddish phrases, felt really secure.

The next morning after breakfast the youngsters ran out to investigate the neighborhood. They joined a group of children playing with a ball. The children were laughing happily as they made the two newcomers welcome, and then a strange and terrifying thing happened. A stout woman, apparently the mother of one of the girls, emerged from the house in front of which they had been playing. In her right hand she carried a heavy wire rug-beater. She fixed her eyes on Jennie and Lottie. Hate and anger mingled in her piercing gaze. Suddenly, a curse erupted from the woman's taut lips. She seized the two girls and began beating them. Jennie eluded her grasp, grabbed Lottie's hand and ran down the street, more bewildered than hurt. Lottie began to cry.

When Jennie saw the woman was not chasing them, she stopped. She comforted her sister, wiping away her tears. "Don't tell Momma," she whispered. Lottie nodded obediently. Jennie wasn't sure why, but, somehow, she knew it would hurt her gentle mother to hear of this frightening episode. As the sisters walked back to the rooming house, Jennie tried to think of what they had done to earn the woman's animosity. Jennie remembered the woman's fierce, hate-filled expression. Never before had she seen the ugly face of bigotry or heard the scabrous accents of hatred.

Under the benevolent Emperor Franz Josef, violent anti-Semitism in the Austro-Hungarian Empire was unknown. There were pogroms in Poland and Russia at the time, but Jennie knew nothing of them. Her family's relations with their Christian neighbors had been warm and cordial. It would be many, many years before she would understand the chilling implications of what had happened that day.

Jennie as a young girl, with her father, Selig

The farmhouse in Ferndale, purchased in 1914, and called Longbrook House.

The family's second purchase, The Terrace Hill House, present site of the hotel.

Dancing on the lawn in the 1930s.

Jennie (left) with Milton Blackstone in Atlantic City.

Improvised skiing was on the golf course in the 30s.

An aerial view of the present-day Grossinger empire.

Jennie presides over a typical breakfast in the Grossinger dining room.

Grossinger's Olympic-size swimming pool.

Leonard Bernstein with the current skimaster, Tony Kastner.

Familiar faces: Danny Kaye (above), son Paul with Dean Martin and Jerry Lewis (bottom left), and (right) Jennie with Milton Berle and Johnnie Ray.

a.

b.

c.

d.

a. Toomler Lou Goldstein with guests.
b. Alan King, Moss Hart, and playwright Jerome Chodorov.
c. Red Buttons and Leonard Lyons.
d. Jennie with Eddie Fisher and Elizabeth Taylor.

Jennie with boxer Barney Ross and sportswriters, 1934.

Jack Dempsey working out with Rocky Marciano, 1953.

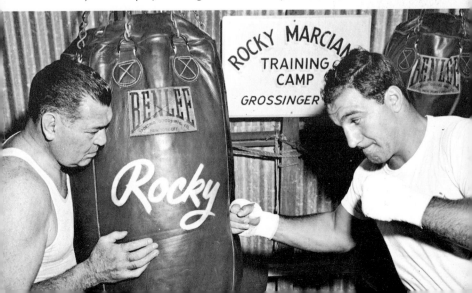

Jennie with notables: a. Eddie Cantor; b. Harry S. Truman; c. Frank Sinatra; d. Eleanor Roosevelt and Abe Friedman; e. Al Jolson; f. Jonas Salk.

g. Governor Nelson Rockefeller; h. Ed Sullivan; i. David Ben-Gurion (center); j. Mayor John Lindsay; k. Marion Anderson; l. Ted Kennedy and George Jessel; m. Irving Berlin.

Malke greeting Governor Thomas E. Dewey, 1948.

ie receiving her honorary doctorate from New England College.

Jennie with (left to right) son Paul, his wife Bunny, son-in-law Dr. A. David Etess, daughter Elaine and husband Harry.

Chapter 3

A few days later, they walked up the gangplank of the freshly painted *S.S. Potsdam.* The steerage quarters were crowded, but this did not bother Jennie or Lottie. It was as though they were now members of a huge, joyous family. Few tears were visible as the big liner slipped away from its dock and headed for the New World. These immigrants were looking forward to a new life. No one had any desire to look back at the hard, often tragic times of the past. Many of the very young, and the very old, literally believed that the streets of New York were paved with gold. Wise Malke Grossinger, ever the realist, listening to their awesome tales of the splendor that awaited them, could only pray that their disillusionment would not be too painful. For herself and her family, she hoped only for a better life—and to be reunited with her husband.

Malke had promised to deliver a favorite nephew to his family already settled in New York. With her cousin, Gershon Grumet, just a year or so older, Jennie explored the ship from deck to the engine room. When they got in the way, sailors told them to run along and bother someone else. It was a wonderful and exciting trip—if you were just eight years old—that is, until the turbulent Atlantic began to heave and hurl huge waves over the decks of the *Potsdam*. The terrified steerage passengers were immediately ordered below and the hatches closed. Now what had been a wondrous experience became a nightmare. The storm handled the *Potsdam* as though the mighty ship were a toy. She pitched and rolled in the mountainous waves. Frightened and trembling, the passengers huddled in the half-darkness of the steerage quarters; the constant rolling and pitching made nearly all of them sick. Officers refused to allow anyone on the wave-swept decks. The storm lasted three days and left the virtually airless steerage quarters heavy with a foul stench. Only at infrequent intervals of relative calm were the hatches opened to allow fresh air to penetrate below. Finally, the sea abated, waves flattened out, the sun shone, and the steerage passengers were allowed back on deck. Sailors, to whom this was an old story, hurried below decks with buckets of disinfectant.

Sometime during the storm, young Gershon Grumet had vanished. With the ingenuity of a ten-year-old boy, he managed to reach the deck, but now he couldn't be found. All that the officers could say was that the boy must have been washed overboard. The crew was about to give up its search when an excited cry came from one of them; he had found Gershon asleep atop a pile of coiled rope! Now that the sea had calmed, Jennie spent hours at the rail, hypnotized by the water below. She was fascinated as the sea changed from green to dark blue and then, if the sun was bright, to lighter hues.

JENNIE AND THE STORY OF GROSSINGER'S

Never having seen any ocean before this voyage, she stood transfixed for hours. It all seemed to her eight-year-old eyes like a mysterious, endless wonder. When, occasionally, a large fish broke the surface to leap into the air, Jennie would cry aloud in her delight. She was awake each morning long before anyone else, afraid she might miss some of the new magic provoked by the sea. One morning she arrived on deck to see a flock of gulls following the ship. "They're lost!" she cried, but a crew member explained the birds were a sure sign that land was near. The next morning, the *Potsdam* sailed proudly into New York Harbor to be greeted by a very tall lady holding something strange in her hand. A sailor announced they were passing the recently erected Statue of Liberty—a gift from France—and that she held the torch of liberty aloft.

Several hours later, the immigrants walked down the gangplank and stepped on to American soil for the first time. This was Ellis Island, a landfall of hope and a stage for drama and anxiety, opened in 1892 to meet the great tides of European immigration sweeping to America. The little Grossinger foursome was part of over sixteen million seekers after a new life who would pass through its gates in the next half century. This pin-point of an island in Upper New York Bay—no more than twenty-eight acres—would in time witness more raw human emotion than perhaps any other single piece of terrain in America. For it was here that the newly arrived immigrant learned if he might enter the beckoning "promised land" or be forced to return to the poverty, persecution and repression he had desperately left behind only weeks before. These displaced voyagers, who had staked everything on this great journey to an unknown new land of boundless hope, had now to pass a rigorous ritual of inspections and examinations, medical, financial, moral and mental.

For the immigrant, the Ellis Island experience was frequently an indignity and sometimes brutal. Only the poor, arriving by steerage, were required to stop here. The privileged—meaning those who traveled first or second class—were invariably processed right on board ship and taken directly to Manhattan. But the vast majority of the newcomers to America, like the Grossingers, were systematically tagged, put on barges and transported to the grim-looking island across from the Statue of Liberty. In the holding room, the frightened arrivals would be marked with chalk and then herded upstairs to a huge, two-hundred-foot-long room divided into twelve narrow alleys. Here, they were questioned. The processing often took as much as eight hours.

Before the turn of the century, many of the officials were disreputable types who openly abused the helpless immigrants, even stealing what little money they had. Ellis Island soon earned a sinister reputation. *Treren insel* (island of tears) was the label given the enclave by tens of thousands of Jewish immigrants who came through there before the 20th Century. It was not until 1902, when President Teddy Roosevelt appointed a reform-minded Commissioner of Immigration, that conditions were markedly improved. In 1900, when Malke set foot on the island, abusive, insensitive treatment was still commonplace. With the help of Yiddish interpreters, she first filled out several long forms and then answered many questions. And, for the first time, Jennie heard the unfamiliar words of the English language. Judged to be sound in mind and body and with a husband and father already in America awaiting them, all were readily certified as acceptable new arrivals. Soon, Malke, Jennie, Lottie and Gershon were ushered into a cubicle to wait until they were claimed.

Name after name was called. At each call, an immigrant family would rush joyously forward to be embraced by a waiting relative. Before long, they heard the name "Grossinger." Malke took up her baggage, giving each of her daughters small burdens to carry, left the cubicle, and passed through the barrier. There stood the tall, smiling man Jennie remembered as her father. When they saw Selig, the little band of travelers burst into tears. Quickly he gathered Malke, Lottie, Jennie, and Gershon in his outstretched arms and hurried them out of the building to a ferry which would take them to the Battery.

A half hour later, they set foot upon the mainland soil (except that it was hard pavement) of the New World. In her secret heart and sometimes in her dreams, Jennie saw America as a bright and shining fairyland. Now, faced with the drab reality of dirty paved and cobbled streets, the strident clanging of horse-drawn trolley cars, the frightening roar of elevated trains overhead, she felt her heart sink. Her father led them up steep stairs to the platform of the elevated railway. A long line of yellow-painted cars lurched into the station. Selig swept his little family into one of them. Lottie held tightly to Jennie's hand. Both girls were terrified as they looked out the window to the streets below, expecting this train on stilts to topple at any moment. They tried to gain confidence from the smile on their father's face and their mother's calmness. Selig reassured them repeatedly: "It is nothing. We are safe. The train cannot fall." Then the train started jerkily and picked up speed. After a while, their fear vanished as they imagined they were being borne over the city in some kind of magic vessel. The car was filled with fellow passengers from the *Potsdam*. Although many of the children screamed with fright, others, like Jennie and Lottie, were by now too exhilarated by this strange experience to feel any further terror.

It didn't take them long to reach the Allen Street Station where Selig hurried them out of the car and down the steep stairway to the street. "It's only a few minutes' walk," Selig said gaily, "and you will find your cousins and uncle and aunt waiting for us."

They walked through streets crowded with people and pushcarts, alive with the clamor of women bargaining with the peddlers of herring, whitefish, bread, cloth, dresses, shoes, pots and pans, vegetables, and fruit. Jennie was fascinated by the olives, bananas, and tomatoes. Because she had never seen any of them before, she found it hard to believe that these beautiful things could actually be eaten. The streets were never silent. People swarmed from one pushcart to another, jostling each other, crying shrilly, greeting a neighbor warmly, occasionally screaming invective at a peddler whose prices seemed too high. This was a sight they had never known in quiet Baligrod—not even on market day. But most of the talk and the cries were in Yiddish, and this took much of the strangeness out of it. It would be some time before Jennie would be aware that any other language was spoken on the East Side.

JENNIE AND THE STORY OF GROSSINGER'S

Selig Grossinger led them up the steps of a shabby-looking red-brick building. They climbed up four flights before he threw a door open. This was where a cousin lived with his wife and two daughters. The two rooms were crowded with near and distant relatives assembled to make Malke and the children welcome. There were happy cries and tears and warm embraces, and Jennie and Lottie were hugged and kissed by everyone. If they were bewildered by the presence of all these relatives—none of whom they had ever seen—they still felt the warmth and the friendliness which filled the small flat. Selig led the children to a table heaped with food. Some of it, the pastry and bread, looked familiar, but their father smiled and pointed to a plateful of what he said was sausages. He put the long, slender objects, encased in skin-tight coverings, on slices of rye bread, spread them with a yellow sauce he called mustard, and handed one to each of his children. "Try it," he urged.

They bit into it hesitantly, and soon satisfied smiles appeared on their faces. It was most definitely a new kind of sausage. There was garlic in it, but it lacked the sharp taste of sausages they knew at home. It was bland and soft. Flavored with the mustard, it was delicious. "It is a large, American-style wurst, which the people here call 'frankfurter,' " Jennie repeated happily. Immigrants from Frankfurt had brought the German "sausage" to Coney Island where it had become immensely popular and where it was married to a roll. It wasn't long before a kosher version of the delicacy moved up to the East Side. Jennie, on that first day in America, knew only that it was the first American food she had ever tasted and that she liked the taste very much.

The grown-ups were busy hearing details of life at home, asking about relatives, and telling Malke what she could expect life to be like in New York. For the moment, the children were forgotten. Jennie led Lottie to an open window and, peering out anxiously, recoiled when her eyes met nothing but a dark, garbage-strewn alley. The back of the tenement opposite was defaced by dirty windows and laundry hanging from stretched ropes. The air was filled with the shrill yells of mothers trying to quiet crying children. Jennie thought of the lovely woods and rolling hills back home and grimaced as she compared them with the small flat and the ugly vistas of the East Side. And she wondered how many of these relatives would be living with her family in this tiny place?

Selig seemed to sense her dismay and puzzlement. When their eyes met, Jennie suddenly jumped up and whispered something to her father, who looked startled and then laughed uproariously. "We will not live here with anyone," he said. "We have our own home." Within the hour, they were in their new home at 158 Ridge Street. From outside, it looked just like the house they had just left, but when Selig proudly opened the door to the immaculately clean three-room flat, the family was overjoyed. This was their home. Dusk had crept into the canyons of the East Side, and now Selig, before the amazed eyes of the children, struck a match and held it over a gas jet. Miraculously, a bright yellow flame flooded the room. There were jets in each of the other two rooms. Selig showed his family a box containing several twenty-five-cent pieces that he kept in the top drawer of the bureau. He explained that when the light dimmed, they would have to insert a coin in a gas meter on the wall of the kitchen. Usually, he told them, one coin would keep the gas lights going for a week—if they were careful about using the light only when necessary.

There was a gas stove and an icebox brimming with ice chunks in the kitchen, but nothing else. Selig opened the back window. This, too, looked out on an alley where clotheslines were stretched from window to window of the tenement opposite. Jennie pointed to the small sticks attached to the lines and asked, "Poppa, are they little dolls?" Selig explained solemnly that they were clothespins and described how they were used. There was one thing Jennie did not mention—the dreadful odor. Some of it rose from the garbage that lay below in the alley and some of it came from a communal lavatory in the hallway used by the tenants who lived on the fourth floor. The little flat was clean, but flush toilets, shower stalls, or bathtubs were still very rare in most of the East Side slums. Yet Malke was not dismayed. Her family was together again; that was all that counted.

They had arrived in June. It did not take long for Malke and her children to adapt themselves to the customs of the East Side. With their cousins as guides and instructors in the ways of the New World, they soon discovered the neighborhood iceman who allowed children to gather handfuls of shavings that flew from the large blocks of ice when he hacked off a "five-cent piece." They would cool off by rubbing the icy flakes across their foreheads, arms, and legs and would then pop what was left into their mouths. They learned, too, the games the other children played with such gusto on the narrow asphalt pavements; and also discovered the most exciting "free show" on the East Side—the frequent visits of the organ-grinder and his dancing monkey. When the huge, mustachioed organ-grinder looked appealingly upward, a shower of pennies would fall from the more affluent neighbors. Jennie and Lottie would scramble for them and drop them into the red cap held out by the grinning monkey.

A few blocks away, on Pitt Street, a cousin introduced them to a park of sorts—a small plot where sparse strips of grass alternated with flagstone blocks. It compared sadly with the lush fields of Austria, but it did have slides and swings and a monkey bar which Jennie and Lottie learned to climb expertly. And there was always the color and excitement of the kaleidiscopic East Side streets. They were never quiet, but now the noise was part of their lives. The girls would watch and giggle while sharp-eyed women argued with the pushcart peddlers. It was a game, and both vendor and customers would have been disappointed were the ripeness of a tomato or the freshness of a piece of fish not questioned loudly, but always without rancor.

The children, shy at first, began to look forward to a weekly trip to the nearby public baths six or seven blocks from their home. It was here that Jennie saw—and took —her first shower, a ritual unknown back in Baligrod. She was also enrolled in a *cheder* (religious school) attached to one of the small synagogues that proliferated the East Side. Here, under the tutelage of a teacher of Hebrew education called a *Malamed*, she learned more of the traditions and laws of her faith. The East Side was, indeed, a ghetto. While most of the new settlers remained as Orthodox as they had been in Eastern Europe, certain compromises had to be made if Orthodoxy was to live side by side with American customs and habits.

There were newspapers printed in both Hebrew and Yiddish, but for a man to hold a decent job he had to know English. Moreover, he had to work the hours which American employers set, often conflicting with the strict observance of his faith. Many never compromised. It was not uncommon to see elderly men who had been renowned Hebrew scholars or religious leaders in the Old World slaving at the most menial tasks in this new, perplexing world where strong legs and strong arms were more in demand than brilliant scholarship or lofty spirituality. On the East Side of New York, Jewish immigrants found work as cigar-makers, pushcart peddlers, and garment workers. A dignified old man with a beard, who had sat over the Torah for long hours in his native town, might be seen hawking pretzels or pickles on Rivington or Orchid Street. Another worked 16 hours bent over a sewing machine in a dank loft. At best, men earned no more than $10 a week—often less. Women and girls could only hope for four or five dollars for 60 hours of labor. The Americanization process made the discarding of old values and the accepting of new ones a necessity. The culture of the *shtetl*, the traditional ways of the Eastern European Jewish life, were continually being submerged by the pressures—social, political, and economic—to adapt to the new environment. Tensions and conflict were inevitable as the straining toward ma-

terial success warred with a simultaneous yearning toward spiritual fulfillment. Moral intensity and worldly
ambition, forced to co-exist, did so uneasily.

The obsession to be American, to learn the language
and the customs, to throw off the label of "greenhorn"
and become fully integrated into the new society was
powerful and yet it was counterposed by an equal thrust
to hold on to the traditions of the past. And these
immigrant people did hold on as long as they could with
their Jewish newspapers; with their steadfast devotion to
the age-old traditions of piety, charity, and learning; with
their *landsman-schaft* groups, which were fraternal societies comprised of people who came from the same *shtetl*.
Nostalgia for the old country and a deep need to be with
one's own were the root of these clubs, but many also
had a practical purpose by serving as burial and insurance institutions whose members paid a small weekly
sum to guarantee a plot in a cemetery and the services of
a doctor.

Selig and Malke's deeply rooted piety was never compromised in the New World. It found expression in the
rigorous daily devotion to the six hundred and thirteen
commandments, the so-called *mitzvahs*, laid down by
God and given to Moses in the *Torah*. This body of law,
known as the *halakah*, contained the rules affecting every
aspect of a pious Jew's daily existence from the manner
of prayer to the finest points of ethical behavior. Whatever the pressures of life in America, any notion of
accommodation, compromise, or modification of the *halakah* was unthinkable.

Most parents insisted their children attend the traditional *cheder* and observe the dietary laws and religious

holidays. To Selig and Malke, the strict observance of their faith was not a question of geography—it was simply a way of life, the only one they knew or wished to know. Their children accepted this as a matter of course.

Jennie's first step toward integration into her adopted country came when she enrolled at Public School 174. During the early part of the 20th Century, public education was exclusively a mass-production affair. There were no such things as aptitude tests; little attention was paid to the individual pupil. Jennie, eight years old, promptly was placed in the third grade. During her two months in New York she managed to learn a few words of English. These Americanisms she shyly tried out on her parents. Selig laughed and said to her in Yiddish, "You're already becoming a little American. That is good." If someone asked, "What is your name?" she knew enough to say "Jennie Grossinger. I live at 158 Ridge Street." Her father had taught her and Lottie to say that in case they ever became lost in the maze of the East Side. This useful declaration was about the extent of her English. No matter—she was eight years of age, and, therefore, put in the third grade.

For two weeks she suffered in embarrased agony, unable to comprehend a word her teacher said. Finally, the teacher complained to the principal and Jennie was demoted to the first grade. It was humiliating enough to be the tallest girl in the class; it was even more so to discover that all her classmates spoke English. Her teacher, mistaking lack of understanding for stupidity, would apply the standard punishment of the day—a sharp slap on the face. Every time the teacher approached her, Jennie trembled. She never told her parents of these

37

almost daily punishments, but she often cried herself to sleep at night. Gradually, as she learned more and more English words, the slaps became fewer. The word "hygiene" was one she learned particularly well. Each week brought rigorous scalp and teeth inspections. The children were ordered to wash their scalps with warm water to which a few drops of kerosene were added. Jennie was also taught to brush her teeth daily with warm water and salt.

A year passed and Jennie was able to speak some halting English, but not enough to promote her to classes filled with girls her own age. She remained the clumsy giant nearly three years older and a head taller than her classmates. Still, she loved school, and, above all, she loved the communal life of the East Side. Even the most distant relatives greeted a child warmly if she came to borrow a half-cup of sugar. And when children came to a new three-room flat Selig soon found for his family on Houston Street, Malke greeted them with what was almost an East Side Jewish neighborhood ritual. "Come eat," she would say, beaming and throwing her arms around little Rachel or Esther or Benjamin. There was always a bowl of home-baked cookies on the table, as well as prune jam, a jar of borscht in the icebox, and pot cheese. When the youngster, having eaten his fill, started to leave, Mom Grossinger would say, "Now take this bag of *ruglach* [horn-shaped pastries] home to your mother." When adult relatives crowded into the apartment, Jennie and Lottie became Malke's apprentices. They would pass hazelnuts, homemade bread and apple strudel, and, inevitably, tall glasses of hot tea with lemon. Hot tea in tall glasses was a European tradition preserved on the East Side. The tea warmed the insides, and, if the glass was rotated in the hands, it warmed them as well. During the cold months, warmth was a valuable, often rare, commodity in the poorly heated tenements.

Had anyone told Jennie that her family was poor and that she was an "underprivileged" child, she would have been honestly puzzled. There was always enough food in her home, she always had warm clothing, and she loved the clean flat where she lived surrounded by love. If a child became sick, there were neighbors who hurried in to help care for it. Selig worked long hours pressing coats, but he never complained. Nearly everyone except the shopkeepers, the street peddlers, and a very few professional men, worked in the East Side factories. The more liberal newspapers such as the *New York World* were by now calling them sweatshops. A few daring spokesmen of the small, but articulate, Socialist Party were condemning the factories for making men, women, and children work inhuman hours, but this criticism did not reach men such as Selig Grossinger. To him, there was no alternative. Oh, he worked as he had never worked before, but now he had his family with him, and if he reached home completely exhausted after twelve hours in a sweatshop, he was met with the glowing warmth of his wife and the adoration of his two children.

It was, nonetheless, true, as one observer of the times wrote, that "life on the Lower East Side is a constantly changing panorama of hardship, greed, misery, ugliness, struggle, crowding, filth, uncertainty and alienation existing side-by-side with overflowing vitality, joy, love, aspiration, goodness, devotion, and, above all, hope for the future." However bleak one's immediate life may have been, there was always the certainty that things would be better before long. Everyone was aflame with the energy of ambition, thought, and hope—and this hope, particularly, Selig shared.

There came now an event that would forever shadow the settled pattern of the Grossinger family. Mrs. Selig Grossinger, without a word of warning to her two young daughters, gave birth to a baby boy. They named the infant *Hershele* (Harry), but Jennie always called him "my *Hershele*" which could be translated as "my baby brother." Jennie worshipped him. She could hardly wait to finish the school day and hurry home to care for the baby. She felt proud whenever she saw his eyes light up with recognition at her approach. She would chatter with him happily in her scanty English or her fluent Yiddish, and the baby would smile and hold her hand with his tiny fingers. Yet, Jennie was disturbed by intimations that all was not right. When playing with the baby, she could not help notice her parents anxiously watching the reactions of the infant. She was also puzzled by the frequent visits made by the doctor. To her, little Harry seemed a perfect child, even though he failed to respond when she spoke.

At eighteen months, he still did not speak any intelligible words; he hardly reacted to sound. But he had a sweet smile and was warm and cuddly. Jennie thought he was the most wonderful baby who ever lived. And then, for the first time, tragedy overtook the closely knit Grossinger family. Other doctors brought in for consultation gave Selig and Malke Grossinger the same dreaded verdict: little Harry was a deaf mute. As long as he lived, he would never hear or talk. Why? The doctors were not sure, but the baby had run a dangerously high fever only a couple of months after his birth. The doctors called it "brain fever," and felt that this might have caused the child's permanent infirmity.

For weeks, little Jennie refused to believe it. She clung protectively to her brother and he clung to her. But soon, even she had to acknowledge, for all the great affection between them, there was no other communication. And finally she had to admit to herself that this was something the family and its only son would have to live with always.

Chapter 4

In the Old World, the rabbinical sages were the source of all wisdom. If major or minor catastrophes visited a family, it was the custom to ask advice of a wise rabbi who, more often than not, was the only educated man in the community. When the East Side doctors shrugged their shoulders hopelessly, the sorrowing, deeply religious Malke Grossinger thought of the wise rabbis in Europe "who knew better of these matters." If anyone could help the baby, it would be one of them, not only with advice, but with prayers. She discussed this with Selig, and he agreed it was the right thing to do. His faith was so strong, that, like Malke, he believed the prayers of the good, wise rabbis might succeed where the efforts of the New York clinics and doctors had failed. And, she reasoned, too, they might recommend some of the great doctors in either Vienna or Berlin, then the twin capitals of world medicine.

Malke faltered. "But where will we get the money?"

"I will take care of that," Selig said simply.

He approached his uncles, Malke's uncles, their cousins and their neighbors. Not one refused to lend Selig what he or she could afford. This tragedy was felt by all the Grossinger relations; each was anxious to bear part of the responsibility. It did not take too long to collect enough for the steamship fare. Since Lottie was so young, it was decided that Malke would take her, too. One morning in June of 1904, Selig and Jennie stood on a pier and heard the doleful whistle of a ship sailing for Hamburg with Malke, Lottie and the afflicted infant. Malke was small and she appeared frail, but her faith gave her courage and physical strength. Selig's eyes welled up and Jennie sobbed. Her father tried to console her, but he could not salve her heartbreak.

A pile of overcoats awaited him back at his place of work. He put Jennie abroad a crosstown trolley headed for the East Side while he took one which would bring him to the factory. As Jennie's trolley lurched off, she suddenly felt totally desolate and forsaken and began to cry. Though the car was crowded, no one seemed to notice the weeping child. The indifference heightened her feeling of terror. After a few minutes, she fled from the trolley to go the rest of the way on foot. The vast, impersonal city ignored her. For the first time, she felt like an unwanted stranger in a foreign land.

When Jennie entered the apartment, she felt ill. The flat, stripped bare of furniture, was in complete disarray. Jennie knew her father had arranged for the two of them to board with Sarah Countryman, a maiden aunt who was also raising three nieces and a nephew, but she did not know that he had already sold their furniture. The barren apartment only mirrored her overpowering sense of loneliness. Still crying, convinced that her world was coming to an end, Jennie made her way to Sarah Countryman's door. She knocked weakly. There was no answer. She knocked again and again, but no one came to the door. She sat down on the stairs, huddling miserably against the bannister. After a time, she heard a friendly, comforting voice. "Why are you crying? Can I help you, child?" it asked. The voice belonged to one of the tenants. Between sobs, Jennie explained that she had been left alone and that she and her father were going to move in with Miss Countryman. The solicitous neighbor led the girl inside, gave her hot milk, and assured her that things would be made right when the lady returned.

In a little while, Sarah Countryman did arrive, laden with shopping bags and words of sympathy. She kept repeating to the red-eyed child that her mother and the children would be back soon, and that she would take care of her like a mother until they returned. On the East Side, the panacea for nearly all ills was food. Her aunt hurried to spread a large slice of pumpernickel with butter for Jennie. It helped, but the separation would leave a scar on Jennie for years to come. That night, for the first time in her life, she was not kissed good night by her mother.

But life went on, and gradually Jennie learned to adapt to her new circumstances. Sometimes, there were unexpected bright spots. In those days, Arbor Day was an important holiday in the New York schools. It was the harbinger of spring, and thousands of school children who lived near Central Park, Bronx Park, or Prospect Park would assemble and dance around a maypole. The parks were too far for the East Side children, but the youngsters at P.S. 174 danced around a maypole set up

in the school auditorium. There was always great specu-
lation among the children as to who would be selected as
the Queen of May Day. Usually it was the smartest and
prettiest girl in the school. Several teachers acted as a
committee to pick her. They visited Jennie's class twice
to appraise the girls and then, one afternoon, they entered the room again and the girls knew that they had
selected someone from their fourth-grade class. Compared to the younger girls in her class, Jennie was unu-
sually tall, and so was seated in the back row. The
teachers, smiling now, ignored the girls in the front row
to walk directly to where she sat.

"Jennie," one of them said gently, "we would like you
to be our May Queen."

"No!" Jennie gasped. "You don't really mean me!"

The overwhelmed girl could not restrain her tears. It
was the first formal honor she had ever received. Even
more important, it was an honor from Americans. For
the first time since she arrived in this country, she felt as
if she had been accepted. She was no longer the stranger
from Austria-Hungary; she belonged here now.

Jennie did not realize it, but her teachers recognized
how handicapped she was with so meager an English
vocabulary and often gave her special attention. The
influence these teachers had in Jennie's life was second
only to her parents. The woman who stood at the head
of the class was looked upon with awe and unquestion-
ing respect mingled with fear and mystery. A teacher was
regarded as infallible, omniscient, and superhuman—the
supreme authority figure, above parents and not much
below God.

At last, the special day arrived. The girls, with the help

of their mothers, made gowns for themselves of brightly colored crepe paper. Jennie wore a crown of real flowers. The audience—relatives filled the auditorium—cheered loudly for their lovely Queen of May. It was a joyous moment for Jennie.

But there were not many moments like that triumphant one. In the evenings when Selig came home, Jennie felt sad to see the tired lines that etched his face. He left for the factory at six each morning, working all day pushing a twenty-pound iron filled with burning charcoal across wrinkled coats. He did not return home until eight in the evening. Weary and spent, he still felt the need to fill the role of a comforting father, telling her of the events of the day and, occasionally, a little folk tale of the Old Country. He had one particular favorite.

"There was," he began after dinner one evening, "a well-to-do merchant who was traveling home by train, when a certain young man, not too well-dressed, entered the carriage. 'Could you tell me the time, please?' the newcomer asked politely. 'Don't bother me,' came the brusque reply. The young man, affronted, did not speak for the rest of the journey. However, when the train drew into the station, he would not control his curiosity. 'Just one thing I ask you. Why did you answer a civil question in such an uncivil manner?' 'I'll explain with pleasure,' replied the older man as he put on his overcoat. 'You look like such a nice young fellow. If I had spoken to you in a cordial way we would have fallen into conversation. After talking for half an hour, we would have become good friends. Naturally, I would invite you home to dinner. There you would meet my beautiful daughter. It would be just my luck that she would fall in love with

46

you and you would certainly fall in love with her. And before I knew where I was, you would be wanting to marry her. Well, who needs a son-in-law who can't even afford a watch!" Selig and Jennie both laughed heartily as he spoke the final word of the familiar little *geshichte* (story), but the lightness of their mood was forced.

Selig was a highly intelligent man who spoke Russian, Polish, Yiddish and Hebrew and he now had a working knowledge of English; yet this was the best job the New World could offer him. He had, after all, few skills that were useful in an urban, industrialized society. All day this man, who had been brought up in the clear air of mountainous Galicia, was forced to inhale the noxious fumes of charcoal. Selig worked directly under his uncle, Joseph Grumet, a kindly gentleman who managed the factory. Uncle Joe pleaded with him a dozen times to slow down. But Selig knew if he did, other workmen would think he was taking advantage of his relationship with the manager. He was proud that he worked as hard as any man in the small factory that made coats. Competition was fierce among the clothing factories; margins of profit small. If two or three men were out because of illness, Selig stayed on far into the night with his uncle, trying to get out the coats promised for delivery the next day.

More and more Jennie grew to know and respect her father. She heard a great deal about him from her landlady and her friends who often dropped in evenings for cookies and tea. Listening to them, she learned for the first time how much he had borrowed to send Malke, Harry and Lottie to Europe. She discovered that during the three years they had awaited transportation money from him in their clean, comfortable farm in Galicia, Selig, to save rent money, had often slept in the factory on piles of coats. She knew, too, (although he never mentioned it) that he was sending Malke money every month. But Selig had lost his customary cheerfulness. When he returned from work, he would sit for long hours staring at the floor, a blank expression masking his face as he puffed mechanically on his pipe. Often, Jennie cried herself to sleep because there was no way she could ease his burden. One night, lying in bed unable to sleep, she resolved to do something. If only she were able to work and bring him some money each week.

Classes at P.S. 174 extended merely through the fourth grade. Within a few weeks, in June, she would be "graduated" and, in the fall, automatically transfer to P.S. 4. She would be thirteen years and three months of age when the transfer came. The law forbade anyone under fourteen years of age to work. If, somehow, she would get lost in the swarming East Side so there would be no school record of where she lived, she might, possibly, get a job as a buttonhole-maker in the factory managed by her Great Uncle Joe. Sarah Countryman helped solve the problem. Because her flat was really too small for herself, her nieces and nephew, Selig and Jennie, she decided to move to a larger one on Pitt Street, near Grant.

This gave Jennie an idea. She just would not report to her new school. By judicious shopping at the pushcarts with a few dollars she had saved, she managed to buy an ankle-length, brown wool skirt and a pair of high-heeled shoes. Her plan was to wear these grown-up clothes, put her hair up in a bun, and look much older that her true age.

She practiced until she was able to master the high heels and the long skirt. She was now ready to face Poppa Grossinger. She knew he would be furious at the idea of her quitting school, and she was right. But she wore him down with the argument that she was doing this for her mother and little Harry. Besides, she would return to school as soon as Malke and the children came back.

A few days later, Jennie found herself sitting at a sewing bench. Needle and thread were no strangers to her; she had often helped her mother make clothes for the family. But this was different. The stitches had to be exactly in line and equally apart. If one stitch was out of place, the foreman would say just two words, "No good," and she had to do the same thing over again. The learning process was a painful one. This factory followed the custom long since established in similar factories—each worker was paid two cents for every buttonhole. During her first week, working over ten hours a day, Jennie made exactly a dollar and a half. Gradually she improved. The third week, she made $3, and eventually she began to earn between $10 and $12 a week.

It was tedious, monotonous labor. Jennie noticed most of the girls working any length of time had bent backs. They all worked from seven A.M. until six in the evening. But if Jennie looked rather fragile, she had the same inner strength her mother had and, somehow, she managed to ignore the pains in her back and the chronic stiffness of her neck. Upon arriving home each evening, the first thing she did was throw off her adult disguise and, within minutes, she would be running down to the street to play hop-scotch like any other thirteen-year-old. The sole redeeming aspect of the back-breaking job (in addition to a pay envelope she gave to her father each week without even opening it) was the warm camaraderie among the girls. Some were, in fact, her cousins; others were daughters of Italian immigrants to the East Side. All, of course, were older than she. They all knew her real age and were fiercely protective of her.

From time to time, the girls in the factory would get into a squabble. When they did, Jennie always assumed the role of peacemaker. Although she was the baby of the group, she seemed to have a natural talent for diplomacy—a gift that pre-figured the future.

Jennie's warm attachment to the Italian girls did not, alas, extend to the few males in the factory. A handsome Italian boy, much taken by her radiant good looks, flirted with her whenever he could catch her eye. She was pleased, but did not show it, and rebuffed him coldly. Her Orthodox Jewish upbringing would not permit her even to accept a casual date with an Italian youth for fear of a more serious romantic attachment.

One other fear lived constantly with Jennie—that a factory inspector would come and drag her back to school. Several months passed when, one day, the foreman, an affable Sicilian named Tony Costa, sent a co-worker over to whisper: "Inspector's here. Hide somewhere, Jennie." Jennie threw herself under a pile of unfinished coats and the girls threw still more coats on the pile. If she didn't move, she would be safe. She heard the heavy tread of footsteps stop abruptly at her bench.

"I could have sworn I saw a little girl in a long skirt here," the inspector growled.

"We got no kids here," Tony said. "The boss wouldn't allow it." The inspector was still suspicious.

"Maybe she ducked into the washroom."

"You go look for yourself," Tony said scornfully.

The inspector did, and returned disgruntled. He went up and down the line asking Jennie's friends where the little girl was.

"No spik English," each one of the loyal youngsters said.

"If you know where she is, tell me," he said angrily. "It's for her own good. She belongs in school."

He left, but the words, "she belongs in school," etched themselves into Jennie's mind. In her heart, she knew the man was right, but her family came first. Her weekly contribution was helping Selig. In order to earn more money, she even carried coats home with her, working on them late into the night. Sometimes she made an extra fifty cents, but the strain of working by the flickering light of a gas jet, or by candlelight, tired her eyes and strained her vision. Soon she was forced to stop.

Malke wrote every week, but the news was not good. The rabbinical sages were kind and sympathetic and prayed for the recovery of the baby—to no avail. She was now in Vienna visiting specialists in that city. So far, nothing had helped. Selig, working harder and harder to make a little extra money, grew more gaunt and tired looking each day. When Sarah Countryman persuaded him to get a medical examination, the doctor said there was nothing organically wrong with him.

One night, after he was asleep, Jennie heard her aunt talking with some friends.

"No, there is nothing wrong with Selig," she said sadly. "But he is like a bird who has spent all its life breathing the fresh air of the country. Bring that bird to the city, put him in a cage, and he will gradually fade away. Selig Grossinger is like that. He belongs in the country—not in a factory."

It was an accurate diagnosis. More and more, Selig talked of the Carpathian Mountains; of the brisk, cool air; of the brooks running with clean, fresh water. Jennie sensed that he was longing to get out of the asphalt jungle of the East Side and the sweatshops.

Emma Lazarus had written an inspirational poem which received so much acclaim it was engraved on a bronze plaque and attached to the Statue of Liberty. It read:

> Give me your tired, your poor,
> Your huddled masses yearning to breathe free,
> The wretched refuse of your teeming shore.
> Send these, the homeless, tempest-tossed, to me:
> I lift my lamp beside the golden door.

The first to applaud these noble sentiments were the cynical owners of the large East Side sweatshops. They welcomed any cheap labor, no matter where it came from.

At that time there were no such things as organized labor or collective bargaining or pension plans. These factory owners, not only on the East Side, but throughout New York, were interested only in profits and were happy to have young girls or old grandmothers working for them at starvation wages. When the employes were used up, they were fired. The immigrants working in the factories were almost exclusively Jews or Italians. New York was controlled politically by Tammany Hall, and most of the district leaders were Irish. They saw to it that their relatives or friends from the "Ould Sod" were given the comparatively pleasant and good-paying jobs on the police force, in the sanitation department, or with the trolley and elevated train lines. But even a relative had to make a "donation" to the party before being appointed. Since very few Jews or Italians had any friends in high political office, often their only alternative to working in a factory was starvation.

Jennie was fortunate during her factory-working days to have either distant relatives or other decent men as her bosses. If the salaries they paid were appallingly low, it wasn't entirely their fault. Wages were fixed by the big operators, just as the prices of garments were fixed. To make even a modest profit, owners of the small factories had to pay the prevailing wage scale or go out of business. Many of them on the East Side were open six days a week in order to observe the Sabbath. Others kept their doors open those six days plus a half a day on Sunday.

Jennie never worked on the Sabbath, but she did work Sunday mornings. The loft where she sewed buttonholes was on the twelfth floor, and on that day the elevator man was off. Each Sunday, she would trudge up the eleven flights to her work bench. She felt that the extra fifty cents she made was well worth the long climb. Then she heard of a factory on Lewis Street which was not only closer to home, but open all day on Sunday and paid half a cent more per buttonhole. She got a job at the Lewis Street plant. She still had to walk upstairs on Sunday, but the three flights were comparatively easy to negotiate.

Relief from the summer heat of the city came on weekends when one could walk to the East River docks

where an old wooden trawler with a make-shift swimming pool on the deck—"the swimming pool boat"—
was tied up. Many of Jennie's friends also went to Coney
Island on Sundays during the summer months. Coney
Island was a magic world that made them forget the
bleakness of the East Side tenements. A nickel was the
standard price for nearly everything. You could rent a
locker and change to your bathing suit for a nickel. For
another five cents, you could enjoy the breathtaking
thrill of the chute-the-chutes or the giant ferris wheel.
Food cost nothing: you always brought your own sandwiches from home. If you wished, you could buy a large
nickel bottle of sarsaparilla or celery tonic.

Jennie resisted the pleading of her friends for a long
time. One day, Sarah Countryman said anxiously, "You
work too hard, Jennie. You look very tired. Take a Sunday off and go to the beach." During a particularly hot
spell, she succumbed to the temptation. Coney Island
was everything Jennie expected. The water was cold and
clean. Once more, she was captivated by the sight of the
restless ocean. The breezes were cool and she became
infected by the air of excitement that prevailed. It was
not until she returned home happily exhausted that
doubts began to haunt her. She had spent fifty cents; it
sometimes took her half a day to earn that much. Worse,
she had taken the day off from the factory without
asking the foreman's permission.

Her fears were well-founded. For the first time, Jennie
was to know the fury of an irate boss. As he screamed at
the frightened child, she could only cower at her
bench. The other girls remained silent as the foreman
denounced Jennie angrily. Somehow, this was the final

humiliation—that everyone could hear what he was saying. If she ever became a boss, she vowed to herself, she
would never publicly reprimand anyone who worked for
her. (It was a promise she was not to forget—a fore-
runner of the strongly maternalistic attitudes she would
develop towards her employes in years to come. The
ruthlessness that often underscored the fanatical hard
work of many rising immigrant businessmen was always
unknown to her. In a different kind of enterprise, this
decency and "softness" might have been a blueprint for
failure. Paradoxically, in the relaxed atmosphere of the
resort business, these very qualities proved to be important assets.)

So Jennie's childhood years passed slowly, often painfully. She found there was such a thing as night school
and quickly enrolled. Because of her age, she was put in
the first year of high school. Lacking any idea about what
was going on in class, she simply pretended to be unpre-
pared. One night, she summoned up enough courage to
confess that she had never gone beyond the fourth grade.
There was no harm in disclosing it now; as soon as she
reached fourteen, she had applied for and received her
working papers. The sympathetic teacher soon had her
transferred to the fifth grade of a near-by elementary
night school. Her new teacher advised her to make one
purchase—a dictionary.

"Any time you hear a word that you don't understand," she told Jennie, "look it up in the dictionary and
you'll never forget it."

Jennie spent a dollar for a dictionary that soon became
her best friend. She studied it avidly, only dimly comprehending what she read. Gradually, her vocabulary did

increase. In time, she began to solve the mysteries of addition and subtraction. And, as she began to learn a little, her desire grew to learn a great deal. It was this hunger that gave her the strength to work ten and a half hours a day at the factory, hurry home for a quick meal, and then walk the half-mile to night school. An education became her strongest desire.

Chapter 5

Selig had one dream: escape from the prison of the factory. He was a humble man, but he desperately wanted Malke and his children to be happy and also proud of him. Selig wished to be dependent on nobody but himself. It would be wonderful, he thought, to surprise Malke on her return with some small business of his own where he would be his own master. One morning, on the way to work, he saw a "For Sale" sign in the window of a butcher shop. He talked to the owner, who admitted he was too old to deliver heavy packages of meat. Competition was intense on the East Side and customers refused to deal with a shop that didn't deliver.

Selig made a deal. He could make only a small down payment, but he would pay so much a month until the debt was discharged. Since Selig's reputation for honesty was a byword in the neighborhood, the owner of the butcher shop eagerly accepted his terms. He reminded Selig the shop's trade was small, but, he added, perhaps a younger man could instill new life into the moribund business.

"If hard work can do it," Selig said, "I'll make a success of this place."

But hard work wasn't enough. Every night, he wrapped meat in newspapers and often climbed five or six flights to deliver the purchases, but there never appeared to be enough customers. Furthermore, there were just too many well-established butcher shops in the crowded neighborhood. Within two months, Selig had to accept defeat and return to the bondage of the steam iron.

Three-and-a-half years after Malke, Lottie and the baby left for Europe, a letter arrived with news both sad and joyful. She had taken Harry to the most celebrated rabbinical sages and the best specialists in Europe; not one of them could help the child. He would never hear, never talk. There was nothing bitter about Malke's letter. Instead she wrote calmly, almost serenely, that this was God's will.

The part of the letter which made Selig and Jennie happy was the news that Malke and the children were leaving on the next ship and would be in New York within two weeks. Selig immediately found an apartment. Jennie spent hours scrubbing the floors, scouring the kitchen and making the little flat immaculate. The day before Malke was due to arrive, Selig bought some inexpensive furniture. On the next morning, he and Jennie moved in. Malke had a passion for order and cleanliness. Even she would be pleased at the way the three rooms shone.

Selig and Jennie made the trip to Ellis Island. The passengers were herded into cubicles, just as they had been when the family arrived in 1900, and names were called by immigration officials. One by one, families emerged to be greeted with joyous embraces from relatives. But the officials did not call the name Grossinger. Selig and Jennie waited. Soon the last of the families had been called; Selig and Jennie were alone. They asked an immigration officer if there was any possibility of a mistake. He looked at the long list of passengers; Grossinger was not there. Alarmed and distraught, the two returned silently to the gleaming apartment.

There they found a letter under the door addressed in Malke's familiar handwriting. Selig's hands trembled as he opened it and read it aloud. Malke said that as she was about to board the ship a doctor had noticed that her eyes were inflamed. She had what in those days was called "pinkeye," a highly contagious, but not very serious infection. Years later, it would be called conjunctivitis and modern drugs would cure it. In 1908, such drugs were unknown. Malke wrote that her eyes were slowly clearing up and she would be on the next ship.

Two weeks later, Selig and Jennie again journeyed to Ellis Island to welcome Malke and the two children. The returning woman clung to her husband, tears streaming down her face. Jennie threw her arms around six-year-old Harry. It was hardly likely he would remember her, but he could sense her warmth and her love; he smiled happily and his large, expressive eyes shone brilliantly. Lottie, too, had grown.

Once installed in their new home, they had to decide what would be best for Harry. Neighbors, who had faced the same problem, told Malke and Selig about the Fanwood School for the Deaf and Mute far uptown on 168th Street and Riverside Drive. They and their child had learned the language of "finger talking," and were now able to communicate. The very next day, Malke and Jennie took the child to the school. He went with them happily, unaware of the painful separation it would involve. The authorities at the institution said that they could give maximum help only if the boy was completely committed to their care.

When the arrangements had been made, Malke and Jennie hugged and kissed little Harry, trying hard to keep from crying. As they rose to go, Harry started to follow. One of the teachers put her arms around the child, and for the first time he sensed he was to be left alone with strangers. At first his face registered disbelief. He could not conceive that his devoted mother and adoring sister would desert him. Bewilderment and sorrow replaced disbelief on his face as they tried to explain this would be just for a short time. He could not understand. The tears came and frightful sobs wracked his frail body. They left after only a few minutes, both shaken. Jennie's reason told her that this would be best for Harry; her heart told her that they were doing a cruel thing to the boy. Malke tried to soothe her, but Jennie, for once, was helpless against the picture of her small brother alone with strangers. "Remember, Jennie," her mother said in Yiddish, "a heart never breaks, it only bleeds."

A sign on the gate of the institution said that patients could be visited on Tuesdays and Saturdays. Jennie returned eagerly the following Tuesday, only to be informed at the door that visitors were barred during the first three weeks of treatment. It seemed an unjust rule. She circled the building, hoping at least to get a glimpse of her brother. A playground was at the rear of the building enclosed by a wire fence. She stationed herself there outside the fence.

After a while, a group of children came tumbling out of the school, Harry among them. She waved frantically, hoping to catch his attention. He saw her and rushed to the fence, but instead of smiling with joy he became hysterical. Tears rolled down his face. Jennie shook her head ruefully to indicate that she could not join him. As a teacher led him away, she realized it would be wiser not to see her brother for a while, that the restrictions imposed by the school were necessary.

Once the three weeks had passed, Jennie visited the boy each Saturday while his mother came every Tuesday. Of the ten cents she received daily for lunch, five cents was put aside for Harry. By skimping on food, Jennie saved enough to bring him ice cream or fruit each week. The initial shock passed; Harry seemed content and proud of his progress with the sign language. Slowly, Jennie also learned this method of communication, and now for the first time she could "converse" at length with the boy. Malke never mastered the intricacies of this finger language. While still in Europe, she and the child devised their own private signs and gestures which they used as long as Malke lived.

The months passed slowly, but there was always the feeling that once Harry returned to his family everything would be fine again. One day when Jennie visited the school, the smiling principal took her aside and told her Harry no longer had any need of them.

"You must never confuse deafness and dumbness with stupidity," he told Jennie. "Harry is a bright boy and he has picked up the sign language remarkably well. He can read and write a little. Keep him at this and except for his disability he will grow up as a healthy child."

The resentment she once felt over what she thought to be callous rules vanished. When Harry said good-by, he threw his arms around the principal, his eyes mirroring his gratitude. But he wasn't happy until he walked into their home to find his father, mother and sister, Lottie, waiting for him. Harry was never to be a burden to his family. If anything, he was a catalyst, bringing them closer to one another, cementing their relationship by his open and sincere love.

The following autumn, he was enrolled at the highly regarded Lexington School for the Deaf on East 68th Street, where he received most of his early grade-school education and learned to lip-read. For the next few years, he would board at the school from Monday to Friday of each week and spent weekends at home with the family.

Harry's progress was gratifying, yet other problems clouded the family's happiness. Selig was obviously ill. Years behind a heavy stream iron had made him listless and weary, as though all strength had been drained from him. He realized he wasn't pulling his weight, that others were pressing many more coats a day than he. Though he appeared run-down, his doctor could still find nothing medically wrong with him. The shrewd doctor, knowing how fiercely competitive factory work was, counseled him to quit. Selig had reached that point of slow decline where it was only a matter of time before he would be discharged. Uncle Joe Grumet did his best to cover up for his lagging output, but the factory owner was not fooled. This was the law of the East Side jungle

—only the fittest could survive. Jennie was furious at a system that would work a man almost to death and then discard him when his usefulness was at an end. Selig's pride would not allow him to accept this destiny. He would leave before he was asked to go.

And so Selig did quit. With leisure and rest, his vitality slowly began to return. Unchained from the factory, his imagination took wing. He still fervently believed that the only way to make one's mark in the New World was to be your own boss. Excitedly, he discussed the idea of opening a small dairy shop. His butcher shop had failed, but that had been a lone venture. Here, he would have the help and advice of Malke. Selig's enthusiasm as he talked of the proposed little shop was contagious. If nothing else, it would keep him out of the factory.

With his small bank account he made a down payment on a little shop on East Fifth Street. The respect both he and Malke had for good food made them buy the very best freshly churned butter which came only in wooden casks. He also bought the highest quality cheese. The icebox that kept fresh the tiny snowballs of cream cheese was spotless. Selig and Malke worked long hours only to be defeated again by the law of supply and demand. The number of dairy shops in the Lower East Side far exceeded the need. They struggled on for four months, paid all their bills, and then reluctantly gave up the venture. A discouraged Selig, his pride hurt and his health still shaky, once more was sent to bed.

These were hard days for Jennie. In addition to working at the factory and going to school at night she helped care for little Harry and nurse her father. The walk to the factory seemed longer each morning as did the return trip each evening. Only by driving herself relentlessly was she able to maintain her normal quota of button-holes.

One night after examining Selig, the family doctor looked closely at Jennie.

"While I'm here," he said, "let me examine you."

"I'm all right, Doctor," she said, but the doctor insisted.

He asked a great many searching questions of her. How much sleep did she get? How many hours did she work? How was her appetite? When had she last had a day off?

When he finished, he shook his head. "You've been working too hard, Jennie. If you don't slow down, you'll have a complete collapse. Then you will be nothing but a burden to your family. With your father not well, they need you more than ever. Take a few weeks off and spend it in the country."

"We can't afford it, Doctor," she protested.

"You can't afford not to take a vacation," he said firmly.

Two days later, Jennie was living in a farmhouse in Mt. Freedom, New Jersey. She walked barefoot on the clean green grass and breathed deeply the same fresh air she had once known in Galicia.

For the first time since leaving Europe, she awoke to the sound of birds singing and chickens clucking. She discovered trees and flowers again and within two weeks had gained eight pounds. She also became aware of sunlight again. The East Side world of tenements and factories had always seemed dim and grey. It was not until she fled that bleak world that she realized how weak, sickly and dispirited she had become working so hard and living away from the nature she loved.

Back home, she bounded up the stairs which two weeks previously she had dragged herself up. She was pleased to learn that while she was away, Lottie had entered into an "understanding" with Louis Grau, a pleasant young man from the neighborhood. Best of all, he was a *landsman* whose family had also come from Austria-Hungary.

Courtship was not easy if you had parents like Selig and Malke. Selig, amenable to many New World customs, had never reconciled himself to the American custom of dating. He insisted that both his daughters be home by nine o'clock even on Saturday, the only free day they had. Jennie, the soul of responsibility, would invariably come home fifteen or thirty minutes before the curfew. One such evening, carefree and light-hearted, Lottie went to Coney Island with some friends and failed to come home at all. She had decided to sleep at a girl friend's house. Selig, Malke and Jennie, frantic with worry, remained awake through the night. When Lottie finally appeared early the next morning, a relieved but irate Selig scolded the girl fearfully and then proceeded to thrash her. Jennie had never seen her father so enraged.

"Please, Poppa, please don't hit her," Jennie begged.

Selig was unmoved. It was the only way, he said, to teach a child. Though Jennie pleaded in her behalf, Lottie brooded over the fact she was always punished while her sister seemed exempt from even a mild reproof. Open friction between the girls was rare, but a festering undercurrent of resentment began to cloud their relationship. It started some years before when the fifteen-year-old Jennie and her twelve-year-old sister engaged in a shouting, punching, and hair-pulling match over a trivial matter. The incident left the older girl troubled. It was the first time she had ever physically battled with her sister—or, for that matter, anyone. For weeks, thereafter, Jennie reproached herself. The girls did not speak for some time and Jennie felt desolate. She vowed, never again to resort to fighting to settle anything.

The Coney Island episode opened old wounds and fueled Lottie's ambivalent feelings toward Jennie. She loved her sister and also resented her deeply. In their tiny family orbit, it was always Jennie who was recognized as the one who did the right thing, the one who would achieve the most, the favored child.

For some time now, Jennie, too, had been conscious of a male world on the East Side—a world peopled with attractive young men. There was, for instance, Harry Grossinger, a first cousin, three years older than she. Because he was a cousin, therefore in the family and therefore solid and trustworthy, Selig relaxed his rigid rules and allowed his two daughters to attend the Yiddish theater on the Bowery with Harry and Louie. Often, another cousin, Esther Grossinger, and her beau, Max Schitzer, went with them, and occasionally on Sundays all six would go to Coney Island.

It wasn't very long before Harry became Jennie's only beau. One not insignificant reason why she liked this good-looking, reserved young man was the very circumstance that he *was* a cousin. The Jennie Grossinger who was to mature into a poised, gregarious resort operator was still many years away. This Jennie Grossinger was timid with strangers—particularly men. With Harry she felt at ease and comfortable from the start. An informal understanding soon sprang up between them although neither spoke the word "love." One night early in 1912, Harry took the twenty-year-old beauty for a walk to the Williamsburg Bridge and blurted out the news he was leaving New York to live and work in Chicago.

"Chicago?" Jennie repeated in astonishment.

"My brothers are out there working in a clothing factory," he said. "They have a very good job waiting for me. I can save money. I could be a foreman in no time. I'll have a future there."

"But, Harry, Chicago—"

"I want you to marry me, Jennie. Not yet, not until I've saved more money. It will be six months, a year at most, and then I'll send for you."

She could only nod. The idea of being married to Harry was like a dream come true. But the thought of leaving her parents and her young brother was disturbing. Still, being engaged was exciting and she reveled in it.

Jennie's new fiance left for Chicago a few days later. The courtly Harry said good-bye to Jennie with a gentle handclasp. When he left, she felt something was missing. She was engaged to him, wasn't she? He might have at least kissed her good-bye. After all, she was his cousin.

Harry wrote regularly, sending her a great many presents, very few of which she could use. But she treasured them nonetheless. What could she do with such an elaborate hair comb or all those startlingly large brooches he forwarded? But he wrote that he was doing well; had, in fact, been made a section head and further promotion seemed certain. He was saving his money and soon would have enough to send for her. Jennie knew that the moment of truth had arrived.

When a decision had to be made in the Grossinger family, it was never made by one person. She broke the news to her parents. Malke's eyes filled with tears at the thought of another separation.

"You're not going to leave us, my child," she whispered almost inaudibly, lowering her head over the ironing board where she was working.

Selig, too, looked stricken, not at the thought of her marriage to Harry, whom he liked and respected, but at the idea of his daughter living nearly a thousand miles away.

Jennie's response came unhesitatingly. "No, Momma, I won't leave. I can't. You and Poppa come first! If Harry really loves me enough, he'll come back to New York. He's been a success in Chicago—he can be the same success right here."

That night she wrote to Harry. It was a difficult letter to write and she felt sick when she finally dropped it in the corner mailbox. Three days later, his reply arrived. He understood. She was right. He would make good in New York. The experience he'd gained in Chicago would help him. He would return to New York within a few weeks.

It was not long before Harry returned from Chicago. Preparations for the wedding occupied the household almost exclusively for the next two months, from the rental of a bridal gown to Jennie's obligatory visit to the *mikveh*, the ritual purifying bath that all women of Orthodox Jewish faith had to take before marriage.

JENNIE AND THE STORY OF GROSSINGER'S

On May 25, 1912, Harry and his bride stood under the *chupah*, with its four posts representing the four corners of the happy home they hoped to have. To symbolize a life of sharing, each sipped wine from a silver cup. Next, Harry placed the wedding ring on the index finger of his bride's right hand, the finger the ancients believed contained a vein that led directly to the heart. Then the rabbi pronounced the beautiful Hebrew words which are part of the oldest marriage ceremony known to man. The traditional ending came when the rabbi placed a wine glass at Harry's feet. He raised his right foot and brought it down upon the thin goblet, a reminder that the destruction of the Temple in ancient days should never be forgotten. When the glass splintered, the guests applauded enthusiastically and now Harry and Jennie were man and wife.

The wedding reception was held in a hall on Sheriff Street. Selig invited all his relatives and a few friends, but soon the hall was jammed with the uninvited. Men who had worked with Selig at the factory came through the doors saying, "Ah, that Selig has been so busy he forgot to invite us. But we know he would want us to be here."

It was necessary to send out for more food, more wine, more celery tonic. Soon it seemed as if the whole East Side had crowded into the hall, but no one—least of all Selig—minded. The three musicians he hired for the occasion played the old songs of their homeland and some of the songs of their new land. Jennie, no longer a timid wallflower, danced with almost everyone. She was slim and shapely, and she had, as one of her cousins remarked, "the prettiest legs on the East Side."

JENNIE AND THE STORY OF GROSSINGER'S

In the year of Jennie's marriage, 1912, New York City was filled with poor people. Great waves of immigration continued to provide a flood of hopeful human beings. But most discovered only poverty and exploitation. Total Jewish immigration to the United States between 1899 and 1912, the overwhelming majority of whom settled or passed through the Lower East Side, reached 1,500,000. Tragic events like the Triangle Shirtwaist Company fire the year before, claiming 146 lives, spurred the beginning of legislative remedies. Workers began to organize. A great textile strike in Lawrence, Massachusetts, saw thousands leave their looms to protest a reduction in wages. The dispossessed also sought relief in direct political action. In the Presidential election of 1912, a new social awareness swept the country. Socialist candidate Eugene Debs, who promised to transform the society and end exploitation, received an unprecedented 900,672 votes. America was a nation in the throes of social ferment.

Harry had rented a flat (the word "apartment" was seldom used on the Lower East Side) not only in the same building, but right next door to where Selig, Malke, Lottie and young Harry lived. He sensed that Jennie would be happy only if she lived near her family. He now felt that he, too, belonged to that family.

Jennie's marriage seemed to be a harbinger of better things for the family. Before long, Selig and Malke found a small vacant shop on Columbia Street and decided to open "Grossinger's Dairy Restaurant." There were plenty of butcher shops and dairy stores in the neighborhood, but the astute Selig, still determined to be his own master, noticed there were not many restaurants. It seemed like a natural choice of business, too, for had not Malke's father been an innkeeper in the Old Country? Moreover, even on the East Side where every housewife took justifiable pride in her cooking, Malke Grossinger was acknowledged among the best. Well, if she was the best, Selig concluded, why wouldn't people pay to eat what she prepared? Borrowing money again, he plunged eagerly into his third business venture.

He was right about Malke's food. Although the restaurant could accommodate only a half-dozen tables, it was crowded from the opening day. At first, loyal relatives came. They quickly spread the word about the delicious food and generous portions. Soon, strangers appeared and reappeared. Selig acted as host and manager while Jennie waited on tables and helped Malke in the kitchen. Serene in her new marriage and delighted with the opportunity to help free her father from the factory, Jennie felt completely happy perhaps for the first time in her life. Learning how to deal with the patrons helped Jennie overcome still more of her shyness. She also learned how *not* to treat people.

A useful lesson for the future came from a gentleman who dined regularly at the restaurant. Here was a man whose hearty appetite paid tribute to Malke's cooking. One evening, Jennie hurried to greet him with the news that her mother had prepared a delicious new entree.

"You'll love it," she told him proudly. "Wait, I'll get some for you right now."

Without waiting for an answer, she ran into the kitchen, filled a plate and rushed back with a huge portion. Jennie sat down alongside him and chattered on about the care Malke had put into this dish. The man

71

said nothing. He proceeded to eat the soup he ordered, but totally ignored the plate Jennie forced upon him. Then, without a word, he stood up, placed some money on the table, turned and left the restaurant. It was weeks before he came back again. Jennie learned something invaluable from the episode. In years to come, she was to learn a great deal more from her customers.

Running the restaurant was hard work for everyone, but it was also a labor of love. Selig got up at dawn to go to the market. Malke often prepared dishes far into the night. Though profits were small, Selig refused to reduce the large portions of food he served his customers. They had come to expect not only good food, but plenty of it, and he and Malke felt that the customer was always right.

It wasn't too many weeks after Jennie started working in the restaurant that she learned she was to become a mother. Resolved not to pamper herself, she maintained an arduous schedule for almost seven-and-a-half months. When she was compelled to leave, Harry willingly lent a hand in the evenings after returning from his job in a men's clothing factory. Sometimes he would even rush over to help out during his lunch hour.

Jennie never doubted her firstborn would be a boy as, indeed, he was. But the child was born a month prematurely and was very tiny at birth. Twenty-four hours later, Jennie awoke to discover he felt cold to her touch. She was puzzled, for the infant was well covered. Then the awful, agonizing truth struck her. The baby had stopped breathing. Overwhelmed, she uttered a piercing shriek and wept uncontrollably. Why, she cried, had this terrible thing happened to her? What had she done to be so cruelly treated?

"God is good," the pious Malke repeated over and over. "We do not understand His ways, but there is a purpose in everything He does."

Jennie, although bitter at what she felt to be an unjust fate, tried desperately to accept this and somehow come to terms with the death of her baby. She recalled when doctors finally told the family that little Harry would never talk or hear how her mother refused to despair. Malke said it would be a blessing in disguise. Cheerful, gentle Harry had, indeed, brought the family much joy. But how could the death of her baby ever be a blessing?

Everyday she would see mothers wheeling their babies on the street and would try not to be resentful to their happiness. And then a sudden revelation seemed to bring everything into sharper focus and lighten her burden. Suppose her baby had lived to be eight or nine months old and then died? That would have been infinitely more painful than the loss of a newborn infant. Perhaps, she rationalized, it was better this way. It was this belief that ultimately sustained her during those dark days until gradually the agony of spirit left her. Paradoxically, the death of her firstborn served to strengthen her faith, a faith that was to be tested many times in the years to come.

Chapter 6

The prosperity of Grossinger's Dairy Restaurant was short-lived. Oversized portions of food kept profits small. Selig had also developed a persistent cough which kept him from working the long hours the restaurant demanded. Profits became losses and Selig was soon compelled to sell out to a young couple with capital enough to survive temporary slumps in the business. The new owners asked one member of the Grossinger family to stay on and introduce them to the regular customers. Jennie, knowing that hard work might dull the pain she still felt, volunteered. This third business failure in less than two years also took its toll on Selig's confidence and self-esteem. Psychologically drained and physically ill with chronic coughing, he was a picture of dejection.

The doctor told Selig that he had to go to the country for a rest. A few weeks of cool, fresh air might work wonders. Selig was reluctant to spend what little money he had for a vacation, but the entire family, including son-in-law Harry, insisted. Friends told him of a boarding house not far from Colchester, Connecticut. Still grumbling, he boarded a train and headed there. Three weeks later, a changed Selig returned to his family in New York. There was color in his cheeks; he stood erect; his cough had almost disappeared. (Today, doctors might diagnose that cough as psychosomatic—a protest his body was making at living in the cramped confines of New York's Lower East Side.) And he was wildly elated about a scheme which would eventually get the whole family out of the city and take them to the freshness and cleanliness of rural Connecticut.

"I have bought a farm," he said proudly. "Well, not exactly bought it, but I put down a deposit of $25. Next year, we'll be eating our own corn and our own potatoes and tomatoes."

The prospect seemed equally exciting to the family. That night, a neighbor, hearing Selig had returned, dropped in to see him. His face fell when he heard Selig's enthusiastic description of the little farm he now "owned."

"Connecticut?" He looked at his old friend as though he were crazy. "You will raise nothing but rocks in that part of the world. Terrible storms come in from the ocean and the winters are long and miserable. How did you ever get so *verblundjet* [mixed up]? Everything is expensive in Connecticut. Ask Uncle Joe! Better still, ask him about the Catskills. Things are much cheaper there, believe me. And the climate is just like Galicia. Spring comes early—and there is always a ready market for eggs and vegetables."

Selig listened without responding, but second thoughts began to assail him.

Uncle Joe Grumet was called in for a family confer-

75

ence. The one relative who had actually made good in the new land, he was a generous, kindly man. When one of his many nieces or nephews was married, his gift was always the largest. He was also renowned for dancing the traditional *kazotsky* at weddings. As he whirled around in the mad gyrations of the dance, he always plastered a five-dollar bill on his perspiring forehead. Then he would approach the orchestra leader and bend his head—an invitation to the leader to pluck the bill off as he swept by. Uncle Joe came for dinner the following evening along with other members of the family. While he and the others ate Momma's tasty cabbage soup and her pot roast with potato pancakes, Selig talked. He told of his ambition to own a farm and to get his family out of the crowded, airless East Side.

"My father and grandfather lived by the soil," he said earnestly. "The soil is in our blood. We can only be happy in the kind of country in which we grew up."

Uncle Joe didn't say much until he had finished the strong hot tea and apple strudel. "Of course, you are right, Selig. And your friend is right about the Catskills. Your family should have a farm. I don't know how much a farm costs in the Catskills, but—"

"Malke and I have $250 left in the bank," Selig interrupted.

"Jennie and I have saved $200," Harry Grossinger quickly added. "You know you can have that. Right, Jennie?" Jennie smiled happily and a bit proudly. Jennie's aunt, Sadie Roth, also volunteered $200.

"Well, I guess I will take care of the rest," Uncle Joe said. "But Selig, you are not a businessman. I am. I will go to the Catskills with you and help you find a farm at the right price."

That evening no one knew that in time Selig and his family would own an establishment that would dwarf the estate once owned by his father in far-off Austria. They only knew that the glow on Selig's face was wonderful to see and that when he stood up to bid Uncle Joe goodnight he seemed ten feet tall. The year was 1914.

A few days later Poppa Grossinger left for the Catskills to buy a farm and landed in a place called Sullivan County, which struck him at first as a very amusing place for an Orthodox Jew to come to. There were plenty of Sullivans around New York, he recalled, all big Irishmen. Founded in Revolutionary War days, the 986-square-mile block of the earth's land surface known as Sullivan County was named after a New Hampshire jurist-soldier, General John Sullivan, second-in-command to George Washington, who settled there at the end of the 18th Century. The principal residents he found were the Lenni-Lenape, Seneca and Mohawk Indians. One of the first industries was tanning, since the area was overrun with hemlock forests, a rich source of essential tannic acid.

Many fortunes were built on the thriving tanneries that appeared everywhere. By the 1890's, however, indiscriminate plundering of the forests virtually denuded the land of the hemlocks and tanning fell by the wayside. Farming was the obvious natural calling, but it never really flourished, for the top soil of Sullivan County was already too thin. The land was, at best, marginal when compared to the rich farmlands further upstate and on Long Island. Dairymen and poultry farmers prospered, but rarely the farmer who planted field crops. This, alas, Selig did not know. His mission was to buy a farm that would provide for the needs of his family and perhaps make a small profit, too. Within two days of his arrival in Sullivan County, Selig wrote back that he had found several farms for sale and was staying on to inspect them more closely. Uncle Joe next went up to confer with Selig, remained three days, and returned to report to the family.

"It is as if I saw a miracle happen before my eyes," he said. "Selig is a new person since he's been in the mountains. He tramps all over the countryside and when night comes he is as fresh as when he first got up that morning. Malke, he's like the young Selig you married."

Malke asked him about the land. Uncle Joe shrugged his shoulders. "I can't describe it, except to say it is like the country where we were born. The air is crisp and clear. The Catskill Mountains are just like the Carpathians—gentle rolling mountains with woods all around. And the water! It is like—well, it comes from springs and it is cold and bubbles like real champagne. They've just built something they call the Ashokan Dam, and soon they will be pumping this wonderful water to New York City."

"Is it good farming country?" Malke asked.

"I do not know," Uncle Joe said slowly. "Selig is a stubborn man. He says it is. He will have to find out for himself."

"Where is it?" Malke asked. Uncle Joe explained that the land was in Sullivan County, outside a small town called Ferndale. When Selig decided which farm offered the best opportunity, he would send for Malke and Jennie.

The summons came three days later, and Jennie and her mother prepared for the long trip to the Catskills. They had to cross the Hudson River to Weehawken on a ferry and then board an Ontario and Western train which left early in the evening. The train seemed to stop every few moments. Occasionally, they dozed off on the hard benches, but always the jerking of the railway car as it stopped and started woke them. It was eight in the morning when the train pulled into the tiny Ferndale station. As they stepped into the bright sunlight of a Catskill spring morning, all the discomforts of the endless trip were instantly forgotten. The calm quiet of the country was broken only by the chirping of the birds. Jennie breathed deeply of the cool air, and in that moment she knew this was where destiny intended her parents to live.

Selig, looking healthy and happy, stood on the station platform, beaming. With him was a real-estate agent, Max Fisch, with a snappy, horse-drawn carriage. Selig introduced them to the agent, who insisted that they go to his home for breakfast. It was an enormous breakfast, so delicious that Jennie and Malke could only marvel at the wonderful spread, saying over and over again that they hadn't tasted anything so good since arriving in America. Max Fisch explained that everything on the table had come from his own little farm. The eggs were laid that morning; the bread had been baked by his wife only a few hours before; the milk was cold and heavy with cream. Jennie's heart lifted. If a real-estate man could in his spare time take care of a farm which produced such riches, surely an experienced man of the soil like Poppa Grossinger would have no trouble raising crops for sale. She mentioned this to their host.

"Well," he said cautiously, "we raise only enough for our own table needs. Farming to make a living is something else again. There are some families who do this. A few very large farms seem to do fairly well, but whether or not a small farm can pay for itself—well, I'm just not sure."

"I am," Selig interrupted. "I can do it."

"I hope so, Mr. Grossinger," the agent said thoughtfully. "Now, let me show your wife and daughter some of the places you are considering."

The drive through the countryside was exhilarating, but as the carriage went farther and farther from the village questions began to trouble twenty-two-year-old Jennie. The country was sparsely settled. Would her parents be lonely so far from the nearest community? There was a synagogue in Ferndale, but now they were many miles from the village, too far for Selig and Malke to walk on the Sabbath. And suppose she and her husband were ever to join them—where would the children they hoped for attend school?

They looked at several farms up for sale. The prices seemed too high to the practical-minded Jennie, and always the distance from Ferndale seemed an almost insurmountable handicap. Weren't there any farms nearer to the village, she wondered? Max Fisch nodded, but said that the closer farms were to Ferndale, the more they would cost. But, he added, he would show them every farm for sale, even those which seemed too highly priced. For three days, they scoured the countryside, looking for something that would fit their needs and their pocketbooks. Jennie and her mother returned to New York, leaving Selig, still hopeful, to scout additional sites with the helpful real-estate man.

Back in New York, their apartment appeared more cramped than ever. The humid air of a warm spring seemed heavy and the incessant din of the busy streets seemed unbearably harsh to the ear. The thought of living in the country fired their imaginations despite the obvious problems that loomed. If Poppa did find a suitable farm, it wasn't likely that he and Malke could work it alone. He looked fine and his cough had gone, but Jennie knew that years of back-breaking labor had left their mark; that it would be some time before he completely regained his strength. She discussed the situation with her husband and her sister, Lottie. Harry, predictably, said that he would leave his job and go help his wife's parents whenever they wanted him, for as long as they wanted him. Lottie said she would get a leave of absence from the factory and spend at least a couple of months in the country.

There was another important consideration they said little about, but it remained very much in their minds. Young Harry was eleven now, sturdy and cheerful, but in many ways the little flat was a prison to him. His deafness and inability to speak prevented him from playing games on the street with the neighborhood boys. It wasn't that they didn't accept him; the peril lay in the possibility that a fire engine or one of the automobiles now beginning to appear on the East Side might whirl around a corner and the boy would not hear the clanging of the bells or the honking of the horns. On a farm, he would be in no such danger and he would have much to occupy his hands and his mind. The older Harry, who had grown very fond of his younger namesake, offered a temporary solution. Until the family got settled in the country, the youngster could spend his weekends away from school with Harry's aunt, Mrs. Joe Odza. The older Harry would give Mrs. Odza a few dollars each week. Once his schooling was completed and the family well settled, the boy could join them.

It was Selig who made the crucial decision. One morning a telegram arrived, saying simply: "Have bought a thirty-five-acre farm not far from station. Come at once." He had given the owner a down payment of $450 on the total price of $3,500. It was decided that Malke would go alone and that Jennie and Lottie would follow in two weeks. Actually Jennie, like her sister, did not intend to stay too long. She would help in every way she could to establish her parents and then return to her husband in New York. But a beneficent fate was to rule otherwise.

This time the train trip did not seem so long. Jennie and Lottie talked light-heartedly during the journey. Visions of a lovely farmhouse, a white picket fence around it, fat cows dozing contentedly in the sun, chickens clucking, and the lush ground bringing forth vegetables and fruit filled their minds.

"Jennie, I just thought of something," Lottie said suddenly. "We don't own one farm; we own two farms. Poppa never went to Connecticut to get back his $25!"

They laughed at the thought of the humble Grossinger family actually owning two farms.

The train crawled through Weehauken, Nyack, Goshen, Middletown, and then they were in the Catskills. The magic of the hills made them both silent. At Hurleyville, the conductor boomed loudly: "Next stop, Ferndale!" A number of smart-looking buggies, drawn by handsome horses, were at the station where a platoon of drivers called out the names of the small hotels and boarding houses that were already flourishing in the Catskills. Jennie and Lottie stood on the platform watching the carriages disappear one by one in a swirl of dust. As the last one left, they began to feel concerned and alone. Poppa had always been a stickler for punctuality. Where was he?

Just as nervousness was about to be replaced by anxiety, they saw his familiar figure trudging along. They hurried toward him. He enfolded them in a warm embrace. He explained he had hitched his horse and buggy to a tree a small distance from the station. They gathered the many bundles they had brought with them and ran to where the buggy was hitched. Both stopped short at the sight of the horse. In no way did he resemble the elegant, prancing steeds that had just left the station. This was a horse, to be sure, but it had skinny legs and a scrawny body. The emaciated nag, all skin and bones, dozed in the sunlight, taking no interest in what was going on. Poppa Grossinger seemed to sense their disappointment.

"Someday, my children, we'll have the nicest horse in the village," he assured them, "but this one is really not so bad." He added somewhat defensively, "His name is Brownie."

Once he loaded their bundles into the creaky buggy and helped them climb aboard, the ancient carriage seemed to sag under their weight. For a moment Jennie was sure it would collapse. And then Poppa flicked his whip and Brownie strained against his harness. Slowly the carriage started to move.

"How far is it, Poppa?" Jennie asked.

"Only five miles," he said brightly.

"Will Brownie be able to carry us that far?" she asked.

"Of course," her father said, adding, "He may need a little help going up some of the hills."

He did, indeed, need help. Poppa would climb down and lead the weary horse up each incline, and, because this was very hilly terrain, Poppa Grossinger did a great deal of walking. But it was easy going downhill and Selig chatted cheerfully, telling them a story he had heard as a boy in Austria: Two old friends had to make a trip to a village called Naplosh some ten miles away. When Jacob saw his neighbor Pincus about to set out on foot, he cried out, "Come on, Pincus, get up on my wagon and ride with me." Their road, too, was hilly. At the foot of each hill the two men would get off the wagon and half lead, half drag the horse up. So they continued for the ten miles to the village. As they topped the final hill, the sweating, tired Pincus said, "Jacob, my friend, you had to go to Naplosh. I had to go to Naplosh. But tell me, did the horse have to go to Naplosh?"

Poppa Grossinger roared with laughter as he finished the story, and Jennie's heart leaped. She hadn't heard her father laugh like this in years. It didn't matter what hardships lay ahead; to hear that open-throated laughter again was worth anything. They continued their slow trip on the main road for five miles and then turned left into a narrow dirt road. It was then that Selig pointed to a small square frame structure.

"Look," he said proudly, "that is our school. And we are just a short distance from here."

Soon they reached the farm where Malke was waiting outside for them. They rushed toward her as they had once done as children and threw their arms around her while she murmured soothing, happy Yiddish phrases. Their father said proudly, "Look, there is a barn—and here is the house."

Lottie and Jennie looked. Neither had imagined that their parents had bought a palace, but neither had they expected to see an old dilapidated barn which almost hid a shabby, ramshackle house. There were seven rooms in the house, all badly in need of repair. For drinking water there was a well in front of the house. For washing, there was a brook some thirty yards away. There was also a small chicken coop tenanted by a dozen or so scrawny chickens and six or seven chicks. The fields adjacent to the house were studded with rocks and boulders guaranteed to blunt any plowshare. The entire property looked worn, tired and dejected like the horse Brownie. Lottie and Jennie tried to hide their disappointment.

"Children," their father said with evident satisfaction, "you should have seen this place two weeks ago before we fixed it up."

Jennie laughed and hugged this amazing man who was her father. His eyes were shining and so were her mother's. Both were so obviously happy that she felt a pang of disloyalty at her disappointment with the run-down farm. Somehow—she had no idea how it could be done —this farm would have to be put in order and made to pay for itself. This was where her parents' happiness lay.

But the discouraging thought persisted: could this

rock-studded land support a large family? It didn't even look as though it could support the skinny chickens that cackled so loudly and laid very few eggs. Her discouragement increased when a day or two later Selig asked her to go down the road to buy some eggs from a neighbor, a man who had owned a farm here for many years. While making her purchase, she told him of her father's dream of operating a commercially successful farm. He shook his head.

"This land is too rocky to make a living from it. Believe me! Nobody around here makes a living out of farming alone. Sure, you can raise enough to feed your family, but when it comes time to paint your house or buy another cow or a horse to draw your buggy or to buy tools or lumber, you just won't have the money to spend." Then he added casually, "Lots of people take in summer boarders and make enough to carry them the rest of the year."

When she returned home she told her father what the friendly farmer had said. Poppa Grossinger smiled and pointed to the barren-looking soil: "Jennie, just wait till next year and you'll see what we are going to grow out there."

Each day, she and her mother and Lottie labored long hours, scrubbing the floors of the seven rooms and finally painting them. It was hard to feel discouraged in the morning when the sun came up and the country came to life. They all helped Poppa clear the land of rocks. With supreme confidence, only half shared by his daughters, he planted potatoes, cabbages, carrots, and cucumbers. He had bought three cows, one of which was pregnant. Even Lottie remembered Jhota, the yellow cow, and now they felt the same affection for this solemn-eyed cow.

Late one Friday afternoon, while Jennie and her mother were cleaning the kitchen before lighting the Sabbath candles, Selig burst into the room with tragic news. The expectant bovine had broken out of the barn and disappeared. Jennie and Lottie were all for hurrying into the deepening dusk to find the cow, but a reproachful look from their father stopped them. It was time to welcome the coming of the Sabbath with the traditional prayers. Only when the head of the family had recited the prayer of thanksgiving after the meal would he let them go searching for the cow. It was dark then, and he would not permit them to light a lantern. He did, however, allow them to run to the home of a Gentile neighbor and ask him to light a kerosene lantern for them. For two hours, they searched the hills and pastures, but could not find a trace of the animal. They returned, exhausted and sick at heart, convinced she had fallen into a ravine and broken a leg or drowned in one of the small lakes that dotted the area. Selig heard the news calmly, then went to the barn to check on the other cows. They heard his joyous cry and rushed out to the barn.

"Momma, Jennie, Lottie! Look, our cow has returned. And she has had her calf. The first calf born on our farm!" It was a joyous Sabbath for the little family that May evening in 1914.

During the days that followed, they went to work painting, papering and scrubbing. Slowly, the farmhouse assumed the look and warmth of a home. But as one problem was solved another presented itself. A twenty-four-hour rain brought running water to every newly painted room. The previous owner had left a number of buckets in the barn. Now they knew why. As the rain poured from the leaky roof, they formed a bucket brigade to empty the pails. At last the rains stopped and Selig had to spend more of his dwindling capital for new shingles, nails and additional paint. It was becoming increasingly obvious that any income from the land's produce was more than a year away. Selig worried constantly about the $1,000 he had borrowed from Uncle Joe Grumet. How could this ever be repaid? There was an answer staring at them. They saw it on the porches of their neighbors—city folk rocking comfortably in the cool of the Catskill evenings. Jennie remembered hearing the answer from the neighbor down the road.

When Harry came up on weekends, he saw it in the crowded train and in the carriages that met the summer boarders at the station. A shopkeeper in Ferndale had said to Selig: "Mr. Grossinger, the sooner you find out the most important crop in these parts is boarders, the better off you're going to be."

The following weekend, the arrival of Harry Grossinger galvanized the family's thinking into a critical decision. They discussed it through the evening. What were their assets for such an undertaking? They now had fifty chickens, enough to start a boarding house on a small scale. The three cows would provide all the butter and cheese that guests could eat. When the cream was removed from the top of the milk, there was sour milk and buttermilk needed for either cooking or drinking. There were empty rooms just waiting to be lived in and, above all, there was Malke's cooking.

Neighbors were getting $12 a week for room and

board. It was also true, as their neighbor had told Jennie some weeks before, many made enough money in the summer months to provide security for the rest of the year. The discussion that evening was spirited. If one of them raised an objection, another had an answer for it.

That the Grossinger family should become inn-keepers in this verdant Catskill country was perhaps inevitable. Sullivan County had been enjoying renown as a vacation mecca since the 1880's. At first, it prospered as a summer playground for well-born, upper-class New Yorkers, almost always Protestant, who patronized a number of elegant, Victorian hotels that filled the countryside. In Liberty alone, a few miles from the Grossinger property, such popular inns as the Lenape, the Mecca, and the Lancashire—all imposing wooden structures— boasted considerable reputations. These posh hotels reached their pinnacle during the first decade of the century. By the end of World War I, most of them had closed up or burned down.

A radical change in the ethnic composition of the area had begun to take hold at the turn of the century—a change that was a by-product of the activities of the Jewish Agricultural Society organized by philanthropist Baron de Hirsch to help re-settle Jewish refugees from the ghettos of *Mittel Europa,* and those fleeing pogroms in Russia and Poland. The Society set them up on small farms removed from the alien concrete vastness of the big cities where they first landed. The Catskills—notably Sullivan and Ulster Counties—caught the attention of the organization. Like the Grossingers, other immigrant families were eager to escape from the oppressive warrens of Manhattan's crowded East Side. They sought liberation from the ghettoes they discovered in America, yearning instead to tend flocks and plow fields. And like the Grossingers, these farmers, too, soon found the land unprofitable and quickly discovered an infinitely more viable crop: boarders from the city. Thus began the influx of New York Jewry to the Sullivan-Ulster region.

As early as 1898, two families named Morgenstern and Fleischer opened a little boarding house in the town of Fallsburgh which was to become the Flagler Hotel, the showplace of the Catskills in the days before Grossinger's achieved ascendancy. Many others followed in the first decade of the new century before the Grossinger family's arrival: Abraham Brickman in South Fallsburgh; Charles Slutsky, who started what was to become the Nevele Hotel in Ellenville; Louis and Max Kutsher in Monticello; "Pop" Weiner in Livingston Manor; Louis Nemerson, also in South Fallsburgh; Isaac Sussman in Woodridge; and Emanuel Paul in Swan Lake. By the mid-Twenties, with the old hotels all but vanished, the region assumed an almost exclusive Jewish ethnic orientation, not to be altered significantly for the next three decades.

In 1914, however, Selig Grossinger did not wish to be the head of a boarding house—he wanted to be a farmer. Well, he figured, if they took in paying guests, the farming could be more important than ever. If they had to buy all their meat, eggs, and vegetables in Ferndale, there wouldn't be any margin of profit. Unless he could coax vegetables and fruit from the land, the entire operation might as well be abandoned. Then Harry brought a key problem into the discussion.

"Now that we've decided to take in boarders," he said

quietly, "how are we going to get them? Many of the places here have been established for years. Their customers come back summer after summer. They advertise in the New York newspapers and new customers come. But we can't afford advertising."

There was an uncomfortable silence. Harry was right. How could they attract customers? Not many of their East Side neighbors could afford to spend $12 a week for a vacation, and those who could usually went to Far Rockaway or Long Beach in New York or the established boarding houses in the Catskills.

Louis Grau, Lottie's fiance, might have been right after all when he had refused to invest any money in the farm. It would take more than willingness and enthusiasm to get customers, they now realized.

"Jennie and I have saved some money," Harry finally said. "You know you can have that. Perhaps I could just work part time in New York and use the rest of the time to look for customers. I always liked the idea of selling, anyway."

Selig responded with quiet confidence, "Yes, Harry, we will be partners, you and I." He reached across the table to shake hands with his son-in-law. To Selig, a handshake meant more than any contract ever devised by the cleverest lawyers. On that night, a partnership was formed that would last as long as either of them lived; one that would eventually make not only the two partners, but distant, as yet unborn, relatives wealthy beyond their dreams.

Malke said, "This will be good, I know. It is meant to be. We must have faith. God will help us."

The next morning, Jennie, unable to sleep any longer,

arose early, still pondering the question: how to attract boarders? She went to scatter grain to the cackling chickens who ate from her hands. She inspected the vegetable garden her father had planted only a few weeks before and was happy to see tiny green sprouts beginning to show their heads above the soil. Then she heard her mother call. She turned and saw Malke standing in front of the house with a pleasant-faced woman. Jennie walked toward them.

"Jennie," her mother said, "this is Mrs. Carolyn Brown. She is staying down the road. But she isn't happy there and she wondered whether we would take in boarders."

"I hope you'll let me stay at your place," the woman said earnestly. "It is too active for me where I'm living. And everything here seems so quiet and peaceful."

"It's up to my mother, Mrs. Brown," Jennie said.

Momma Grossinger drew a breath. "We'll be glad to have you. And we'll try to make you comfortable."

"Mrs. Brown," Jennie asked curiously, "we have never taken in boarders before, so I know nobody recommended us. What made you stop and ask my mother if you could stay with us?"

"My husband and I have passed your farm several times," she answered. "And I've always noticed that your mother wore a *sheitel*. I knew then that she was as religious as my husband and I are. Often we wonder if the food served at the boarding house where we stay is strictly kosher. When I saw the *sheitel*, I knew yours must be a truly kosher household."

"I once promised my father that I would always wear

92

a *sheitel*," Malke said simply. "And my home is strictly kosher."

Jennie remembered how often neighbors and relatives on the East Side had tried to persuade her mother to discard the old-fashioned symbol of Orthodoxy. Malke always told them the story of her last meeting with her father before she and her two daughters had left for Hamburg to take the boat for America. He asked of his daughter just one promise—never to discard the *sheitel*. And so, over the years, she had periodically cut off her lovely hair to make the wig fit snugly. Now, fifteen years later and four thousand miles from the village where she gave that vow, the *sheitel* had brought them their first boarder. Mrs. Brown and her husband moved in the following day, and the empire which would one day flourish in the Catskills was born. Forty years later, Mrs. Brown would say proudly, "I discovered Grossinger's!" It was hardly an earth-shaking discovery in 1914.

Chapter 7

Two boarders did not offer any guarantee that the farm would make enough money to give the family security. But it was a beginning. Jennie and her husband suggested that they use the name the previous owner had used for the farm—Longbrook House. The family agreed. It had a nice "American" sound and the clear running brook, so important for washing and bathing, had been known as Longbrook for decades. They had a name now, but they still needed boarders.

Harry returned to New York City to sell the merits of Longbrook House. He knew it would be difficult to wean people away from the established boarding houses, most of which offered far more attractive facilities. Their little farmhouse didn't have inside plumbing or a telephone or electricity and so it was agreed that Longbrook House would charge only $9 a week instead of the prevailing $12 rate. Harry had three other selling points to work with: the quiet, secluded location of the farm; the beauty of the country; and his mother-in-law's cooking. When he finished work each afternoon, he would canvass the neighborhood, ringing doorbells to extol the wonders of Longbrook House. Few of the neighbors appeared interested. He went to the West Side, took the subway to the Bronx, the elevated to Brooklyn's Eastern Parkway. It was July now and most families had long since made their vacation plans. Unfailingly cheerful, Harry even began stopping mothers with baby carriages on the street to sell them on Longbrook House, but with little success.

One day in desperation he made a novel plea to a housewife. "Come up to our place with your family," he urged. "If you aren't satisfied, there will be no charge. Not only that, but we'll find another place for you and my father-in-law will move you in his buggy."

The housewife asked him to tell her more about the farm and the country around it. He indicated this was no luxury boarding house; that was why they could charge so little. And he told her of Malke's cooking.

The subject of cooking was something the woman knew well and her eyes were bright with interest as he elaborated on the food served at the farm.

"All right," she said suddenly, "I accept your offer. Can we go to the mountains next Tuesday?"

"Of course," Harry said, very pleased. "By the way, how many will there be?"

"There are ten of us," the woman replied.

Harry gulped, but nodded. He hurried to send a telegram to the family. Although all admired Harry for his resourcefulness, they clearly recognized the risk in taking in ten boarders. They might stay three days and then leave. Three days of feeding ten people would exhaust their food reserve; it might even plunge them into further debt and put them out of business. Only Malke remained unworried. The family put a crash program into operation. Selig hurried to Ferndale to buy cots, sheets and additional pots and pans. When the delegation arrived, Longbrook House was as ready as its limited accommodations permitted.

Back in New York City, Harry Grossinger was filled with doubt. Had he been over-confident in his offer?

It was a nervous young man who stepped off the train on Friday. As soon as he saw the smile on Selig's face, he knew everything had turned out all right. When they reached Longbrook House, the woman rushed over and announced that everything, "especially the food," was even better than he had described it.

When he left on Sunday night, she gave him a list of her friends and suggested he use her name as a reference. She even wrote to several of them personally and for the first time the Grossinger family understood the expression "word-of-mouth" advertising. It would have to do until they were solvent enough to put advertisements in the newspapers.

After the big family of vacationers left with promises to return the next year, the Grossingers paused to catch their breath. But they were soon faced with a new crisis: scrawny old Brownie at last yielded up his ghost. They must get a new horse.

Selig sought advice from a neighbor named Adolph Tripps. He immediately hitched up his own fine team of horses and drove Selig to a harness shop in Ferndale run by Elias Grant. Selig Grossinger did not yet realize that even after such a short time he had earned the respect of Ferndale merchants. He paid his bills forty-eight hours after he received them. They respected his integrity.

Besides, Mr. Tripps was a solid man. When he walked into the harness shop with Selig Grossinger it was, in effect, his way of saying: "Grossinger is a good man. I vouch for him." It didn't take Selig long to buy a fine, robust horse and the necessary harness. Elias Grant was happy to arrange for Selig to pay his bill in installments.

Other reliable standbys in those days were Dave and Gussie Maltz, Jennie's cousins, who could be counted on for a loan whenever the family needed additional funds to put into the business. Dave Maltz, employed in the garment industry, became an unpaid agent for Grossinger's in the district, spreading the word of the obscure Catskill farmhouse-hotel to co-workers in the needle trades and often bringing up groups of his own friends.

Harry continued his selling campaign in the city. Toward the end of July, the little house was bulging with guests. Soon, Jennie sent a telegram telling him they had no room for anyone else. When the long summer ended, everyone in the Grossinger family was exhausted. After all accounts in Ferndale had been settled and Selig counted the bills in the family cash register (an old cigar box), he announced joyfully they had earned a profit of $400. But much more important than the profit was the confidence it gave the family. Longbrook House was now established as a going concern. The legend of Momma Grossinger's cooking had been born.

While the Grossinger family was launching a new life in a remote rural community, the summer of 1914 brought darkly turbulent times to the rest of the world. In late June, a Serbian national assassinated Archduke Francis Ferdinand of Austro-Hungary in Sarajevo. At the news, all of the Lower East Side, as well as the Grossingers, were plunged into sorrow, for the Jews loved the Archduke's father, Emperor Franz Joseph. Selig and Malke recalled thankfully that pogroms which decimated Eastern Europe's Jewish population were spared Austro-Hungary under the Emperor whom they regarded as a benefactor. Now the booming guns of August signalled the start of a great and savage war that would endure for four terrible years.

In Ferndale, however, life went on virtually untouched. By trial and error, the Grossingers learned a great deal that first summer about how to run a boarding house. They found, above all, guests wanted good food and plenty of it. At first they served meals in what was called "family style." Jennie or Lottie would carry in a huge food-laden platter, put it in the center of the table and from then on it was every guest for himself. One evening, Jennie placed a heaping dish of chicken in front of a newly arrived guest. The face of the woman brightened with anticipation as she reached for the platter and said earnestly: "My goodness, I may need some help to finish all of this!"

After that, Jennie and Lottie made sure to pass the platter around the table from guest to guest. The word "calorie" was not part of the American language in 1914. In those days, the more weight one gained, the more satisfactory the vacation. Hills of butter disappeared at every dairy meal as guests spread it half an inch high on thick chunks of fresh-baked black bread. Selig's modest garden fared better than anyone had expected, especially the potatoes. Malke served potatoes in every conceivable form. There were potato and cheese *kreplachs*, potato pancakes, potato puddings, potato knishes, and huge platters of mashed potatoes swimming in butter. Chicken soup was a standard dish in most Jewish homes, but it increased in value if golden drops of chicken fat floated around in it.

The Grossinger chickens had been fattened up, but plump as they were there was never enough chicken fat. Malke solved the problem by buying chicken fat in Ferndale, melting it down, and adding it to the broth. No matter how much guests ate and no matter their age, Malke would invariably come from her kitchen, look reproachful, and say, *"Ess Mein Kinderlach"* (Eat, my children). Not once, but many, many times during that first summer (and to the day she died), she would counsel her daughters: "You must never let a guest go away hungry."

Momma Grossinger was not only a good cook who specialized in the food of Austria, she was also anxious to learn about new dishes from her boarders. Carolyn Brown, for instance, was fond of dishes she had known in her native Rumania. She taught Malke how to prepare stuffed cabbage in the Rumanian style. She introduced Malke to *mama liga*, a tasty pudding made with yellow corn meal. Guests, who came from varied national backgrounds, brought a variety of recipes with them. A woman born in Vienna showed Malke how the sophisticated cooks of that city, famed for its food, prepared *wienerschnitzel*. Another, brought up in Russia, introduced her to the peasant dish, "potato pirogen." Malke had cooked goulash as a bride, but a guest from Budapest taught her how the Hungarians did it.

That first summer, the family learned that boarders

could be made happy only if all the unpleasant tasks were done quickly and quietly by Malke, Lottie and Jennie. There were two out-houses, but there were also chamber pots in each room. The two girls emptied these each morning and cleaned them out with chloride. Beside scouring pots and pans, they also had to clean lamp wicks. Malke had a passion for cleanliness. Each day the girls would wash the used tablecloths and napkins in the brook and dry them in the sun. There was also the constant battle against a leaky roof. A carpenter had been called in to help Selig stop the leaks, but as soon as old leaks were stopped new ones appeared.

That first summer the ingenuity of the new boarding house operators was tested repeatedly. For one thing, evenings in the Catskills were often chilly and there was no heat, except for the stoves in the kitchen. But resourceful Malke soon hit on a solution adapted from Old Country ways. She searched the farm land for large flat rocks, which she heated in the oven on cold nights. After they were hot, Malke would wrap the rocks in towels before placing them at the feet of her guests' beds. Icy toes found a happy refuge on the warm spots directly above the improvised "heaters."

Malke was the first to begin work each day. She was usually in the kitchen while the stars were still in the sky, putting up box lunches for guests who faced the long seven-hour trip back to the city. Before they left for the early train, they had to be fortified with breakfast. Breakfast over, Malke would summon Jennie and Lottie to perform one of the day's more unpleasant tasks—the plucking of chickens. The girls preferred working on the white-feathered chickens because any unplucked feathers would not show up as sharply as would those on brown pullets. But Malke had an Old World notion that dark-feathered birds had better taste and flavor. It was seldom that the girls had the easier job of plucking white ones.

Then Malke set about getting lunch ready. That finished and the dishes done, she began to prepare supper. Because she rose so early, her daughters persuaded her to go to bed once supper was over. Washing and drying the dishes usually fell to Jennie. Finding the long job less onerous if it was accompanied by music, she would move the Victrola into the kitchen and wash dishes to the accompaniment of Galli-Curci warbling "Lo, Hear the Gentle Lark" or Caruso singing an aria from "Pagliacci."

Often, the boarders would eat better than the family, for there never was any stinting when it came to guests. That, and paying bills on time, were articles of faith with Selig. If money was short, you could always save a little from your own table. Although meat or chicken was served every night to the guests, many an evening meal served by Malke to the family had something modest like tomato herring for the main course.

Selig's day began at five when he rang a cowbell, a signal that he was about to milk the cows. No one objected to this early call; everyone wanted to watch the proceedings and be rewarded with a cup of foaming milk. No one in the mountains had ever heard of Louis Pasteur and his theories.

Before Carolyn Brown left, she said to Malke: "Mrs. Grossinger, from now on don't worry about where you're going to get boarders—just worry about where you're going to put them. I'll tell everyone in the Bronx about the delicious food you serve and they will come like an army."

Malke and Selig took this advice seriously. Selig bought lumber in Ferndale and with the help of a carpenter built a six-room bungalow addition. They also enlarged the kitchen and gave it a new ceiling so that Malke would not get wet when cooking on rainy days. The cooking was done with coal and wood which Selig chopped. Completely well now, he handled an axe as powerfully as he had once done in his homeland. His carriage was erect and his arms incredibly strong. When the improvements were made, Jennie and Lottie returned to New York. Right after *Yom Kippur*, Lottie and Louis Grau were married—a wedding that brought as much joy to Malke and Selig as had the union of Jennie and Harry.

This was to be the last time Jennie would return to the city to live. In the spring of 1915, she and Harry gave up their Lower East Side apartment. They agreed that Jennie should live permanently with her parents in Longbrook House. Harry, meanwhile, would move in with his aunt, Mrs. Odza, continue working in New York and spend weekends with the family in Ferndale.

In early May, Jennie and Lottie hurried to the mountains to help their parents prepare for the anticipated rush of guests. For the Memorial Day weekend, which marked the formal start of the "season," Harry and word-of-mouth advertising combined to attract a full house. So many guests came that Jennie and Lottie had to give up their room and move to the attic. A week later, another crowd arrived, and now Selig and Malke also had to give up their room. The attic was divided into two sections, separated by a sheet hung from the ceiling. Still more guests arrived and this time the family moved from the attic to the barn. They spread clean bedding over the hay and found it comfortable, with the added blessing that the barn seemed impervious to the hardest rains.

By the middle of June, the farmhouse was overrun with guests, while more requests for rooms kept pouring in. It was too late to build additional rooms, but Selig remembered having seen tents for sale at Manion's General Store in Ferndale. He purchased six of them and twelve cots. Longbrook House was now ready for any invasion. The "invading forces," as it turned out, were bell-wethered by two families named Kriendler and Mandelbaum whose lives and fortunes were to be intimately intertwined with those of the Grossingers during the next few decades.

During her girlhood on the Lower East Side, Jennie had been too shy and later too busy working to make many friends. On a summer evening in 1905, Jennie attended an open-air dance on the rooftop of P.S. 188. As she stood alone amidst hundreds of laughing young boys and girls, her searching eyes suddenly fixed on a radiant, sweet-faced girl about her own age also standing by herself. Jennie sensed a response in the girl's open wholesome face. Though painfully shy, she could not resist the impulse to approach the girl and ask her name.

"Anna Kriendler," the girl replied.

In this simple and direct fashion a friendship was born that was to play a key role in the Grossinger saga and to endure to this day, more than three score years later.

Living as a boarder with no real home of her own, Jennie was taken into the large Kriendler household, three boys and three girls, as one of its own. In time, it was perfectly natural that everyone began to consider her the "seventh Kriendler child."

The same year that Jennie married Harry, Anna became engaged to a young man named Sol Mandelbaum. But it was not until the July Fourth weekend of 1915 that Jennie's best friend, Anna, and her husband, Sol, came to the farm for the first time along with Anna's brother, Steve.

When they found they would have to sleep in tents, they were far from annoyed. On the contrary, they seemed pleased. The Grossingers were amazed to discover that city folk actually enjoyed roughing it. The experience of camping out was a genuine adventure to heat-plagued urban refugees escaping from the steaming asphalt of the Lower East Side.

That first July weekend of Longbrook House's second year was to be a fateful one. Hours after arriving, Anna Mandelbaum met Carolyn Brown's oldest daughter, Clara. A born matchmaker, Anna instantly decided that Clara Brown would be "just right" for her older brother, Harry. She phoned Harry and persuaded him to come up without delay. As anticipated, and with a little nudge from Anna and husband, Sol, the liaison blossomed. The marriage of Clara Brown and Harry Kriendler proved to be only the first of thousands of "Grossinger romances" during the next five decades.

From that day on, the Kriendlers were indissolubly bound to the Grossingers. Anna, with sisters, Estelle and

Evelyn, and brothers, Harry, Dave and Steve, would one day become important cogs in the machinery of the resort as would their cousins, Jack and Mack, who, years later, would parlay a small speakeasy into the famous New York restaurant known as "21."

Not all vacationers, of course, were interested in romance. But having worked so hard during the long winter months when they had little or no time for relaxation, they hated to be bored. They wanted some kind of entertainment, even if they had to provide it themselves. Big Harry organized a strawberry festival and a masquerade ball. Often Jennie would listen unhappily to the orchestra playing at Bigger's Hotel only a half-mile away and wish that Longbrook House could afford even a two-piece band.

Harry, on his selling campaigns, helped solve that difficulty. After he persuaded a family to try a vacation at the farm, he would casually add, "If anyone in your family plays a musical instrument, have him bring it along." And so, there was always a guest with an accordion, a violin, or a harmonica who seldom had to be coaxed to perform. This was a lesson not lost on either Jennie or Harry. It was obvious that people liked entertainment in which they could participate. It broke down the reserve between guests who had just met; it helped conquer shyness; and it kept people entertained.

The time came when even Selig's strength and Malke's willingness to work from sun-up until midnight felt the strain. Jennie and Lottie, too, were beginning to wilt—understandably, for both were pregnant. Only Little Harry, perhaps truly happy for the first time in his life, seemed to thrive on constant hard work. Selig and Malke disliked the idea of getting outside help, but they had to admit that the guests were entitled to better service than the family alone could provide. Before long, a chambermaid, an assistant cook, a waiter, and a farmhand were hired, and the hotel had its first official staff. All were reliable and efficient with the occasional exception of the chambermaid. A fondness for tippling caused her work habits to be unpredictable. Whenever the bibulous maid failed to show up, uncomplaining guests thought nothing of making their own beds. This was the kind of affection everyone seemed to have for the Grossingers.

During those early years, it also seemed as if the weather had become an implacable enemy, always trying to catch the farmhouse unawares. Actually there was no such thing as a rainy season in the Catskills, but when the rain did fall, it invariably managed to find some porous spot in the oft-repaired roof.

Usually lightning in the mountains is only a brief flash in the distance and thunder merely a muted rumble. One afternoon, however, these manifestations of a storm invaded the kitchen of Longbrook House with frightening and almost tragic consequences. It was a hot, grayish day in August. Malke was at the kitchen sink pumping water into a bucket. Jennie and Lottie were drying dishes. They had left the door open to let any breeze drift in. Suddenly there was a sharp clap of thunder as a flash of light flared outside the kitchen window. Then a second sharp thunderclap filled the room. At the same instant, lightning flared again and an orange ball, the size of a small watermelon, flashed out of the ceiling ventilator. It leaped toward the bucket of water Momma Grossinger held in her hand and knocked it from her grasp; it rolled to the floor and toward Jennie.

Jennie was standing with legs apart to ease the strain caused by her unborn child. The ball of fire streaked between her feet, flashed out the open door and disappeared into the fields. For a moment the three of them stood frozen. Lottie and Jennie stared at their mother in terror, wondering if she had been hurt, but Malke only looked back at them calmly. The bolt of lightning which should have electrocuted her had merely knocked the bucket from her hand.

Jennie gasped, "It's a miracle, Momma!"

"Yes, it is," Malke said gravely, but without surprise. "God is good. He has saved us."

The following year more help had to be hired, since Jennie was busy taking care of young Paul, who arrived September 17, 1915. With lingering memories of her dead first child still painful, the arrival of a radiantly healthy boy brought Jennie much happiness. The infant, weighing nine pounds, was sturdy and grew rapidly in the salubrious environment of the country. Yet, Jennie's new role as mother—as well as wife and jack-of-all-boarding house trades—soon created a disturbing problem for her. Preoccupied with the never-ending chores at Longbrook House, she often berated herself for being away from the infant. It was a conflict that was to beset her for years to come.

An incident that took place when Paul was barely three years old brought the matter to a head. Late one

Friday afternoon, after she had put in an extremely tiring day helping her parents prepare for the Sabbath, a woman came running toward her in a rage. Paul had been playing with his cousin, Seymour Grau, on the steps of the Main House. When the woman's daughter tried to join them, Paul bit the girl's hand. The child was not really hurt, but the mother was livid as she recounted the incident and snapped: "Why don't you take care of your boy like a mother should, instead of letting him run around?"

Stung by the criticism, Jennie's first instinct was to lash back at the woman, to remind her that she had not been exactly unoccupied. Indeed, she had been up before dawn after working very late Thursday night. But the maxim the "guest is always right" was by now too deeply ingrained. She said nothing. Instead, she sought out Paul. Without telling him why she was angry, she gave the boy a painful beating. Afterwards, Jennie was deeply disquieted. She reproached herself for taking out her anger and frustrations on a three-year-old child. Thereafter, she never struck the boy again. Even when Harry administered some well-deserved punishment, feelings of remorse made her drag the irate father away. Paul was often to be wildly indulged by the guilt-plagued Jennie.

Meanwhile, business was booming—so much so that additions to the original framework of the old farmhouse were impractical. At capacity, little more than thirty-five guests could be accommodated. Some of the newer guests were beginning to complain about the lack of indoor bathrooms, electric light, steam heat and sinks in the room. It was Sol Mandelbaum who made the obvious suggestion.

"When your shoes get too tight," he told Selig, "you have to buy bigger ones."

"I suppose we could keep stretching the shoes, but in the end we would have to buy new ones," Selig agreed.

Once Selig Grossinger made up his mind, he moved quickly. The following morning he drove to the real-estate office of Fisch and Weiner in Ferndale. He had recently purchased a new Ford on payments. Selig discussed the problem of expansion with the two partners. They had several attractive properties listed for sale. Both felt the Brooks Spring House on a hill overlooking Route 17, not far from the Ferndale station, seemed just right. It was listed at $18,000. Selig knew the place well and felt the asking price was a fair one. The real-estate men got in touch with the owner and told him that Selig Grossinger was very much interested. Owner Steve Brooks seemed delighted and agreed to terms.

Selig asked Sol Mandelbaum to go with him on the inspection trip to Brooks Spring House. When they knocked at the door, Brooks opened it and said cheerfully, "I'm on the phone, but come right in. I won't be long." They heard the owner speaking loudly into the phone. "Yes, I'd like to sell my place . . . I've received several attractive offers. One man offered me $24,000, but I think I can do better . . . $22,000? Oh, no, I wouldn't even consider that." He hung up and turned to Selig and Sol.

"*Nu*," Selig said, "are you ready to go to the lawyer's office?"

"For what?" Brooks asked.

"To close our deal."

"Close our deal?" Brooks said in a surprised voice.

"Didn't you just hear me turn down $22,000 on the phone? Am I out of my mind? Should I accept $18,000 from you?"

Selig and Sol looked at each other in disbelief and left. As they drove back to the farm Sol said comfortingly, "Pop, it just isn't *beshert*. No, it isn't meant to be. You will find a better place."

Brooks had apparently been playing the ancient game of businessman's bluff, but in the end it was the Grossinger family that won the game. A short time later, the real-estate firm told Selig that they had an even better buy for him.

"There's a place just outside Liberty," Sam Weiner said. "It has about a hundred acres and there are six or seven buildings on the land. The man who owned it made a tragic mistake. The health authorities told him that the water of Lake Ophelia, which is on the property, was polluted, but he didn't believe it. He laid pipe and used the lake water for all purposes, including drinking. He died of typhoid a few weeks later. Because of the scare, the place has been on the market for four years. Now the widow is willing to split up the property. She will sell the three largest buildings and six acres of land with an option to buy the rest. She is asking $27,500 for it, and believe me, at that price, it's well worth it. It's part of the Nichols estate; they call it the Terrace Hill House.

"I could never afford that," Selig shook his head sadly. He had often passed the Nichols estate and admired it.

"Why not take a look at it, anyway? You never can tell," Weiner suggested. "Mrs. Nichols lives in Brooklyn.

I'll call her and ask her to send me the key to the main building."

That evening, Selig told the family and Sol Mandelbaum about his conversation and the Nichols place. They all knew it well. In many ways the property was the showplace of the community. But they knew that the family could hardly afford anything like the asking price.

The next day after lunch, Sol Mandelbaum said, "Let's take a drive."

"Where to?" Selig asked.

"The Nichols place. Just for the fun of it, let's look it over."

Seven of them, including old friends Max Epstein and Harry Bobker, crowded into Selig's Ford and headed for the estate. They stopped in front of the Main Building and walked around it, looking at it with unconcealed admiration.

"It's well built," Big Harry said. Harry had done so much repair work on the farm that he was becoming something of an expert on construction.

"Pop," said Sol Mandelbaum, "let's take a look inside."

They moved on to the back of the house. It was Sol who spotted an unlocked window. He opened it and climbed inside. Within a minute, he had opened the front door. Although Selig was still frowning, he followed the others into the big house.

They walked through the spacious rooms, exclaiming with delight as one amazing feature after another presented itself. There were several bathrooms with showers; electric lights; a magnificent kitchen; and there was even a party-line telephone. Immediately, Jennie began to envision the building filled with guests. In the four years at Longbrook she had never even allowed herself to hope they might some day own such a place. As they left and stood on the front porch for a moment, her father's calm but authoritative voice broke the spell.

"It's a palace," he said. "But it isn't for us. We better just forget it."

When they reached Longbrook House, it seemed more primitive and crowded than ever.

The following weekend, both Sol Mandelbaum and Harry Bobker came back to the farm. It seemed they hadn't forgotten the Nichols estate, either. After dinner on Saturday, Sol handed Selig a piece of paper and said casually, "Pop, here's $1,000 toward buying the estate. Pay me back when you can. And if you try to add interest, I'll never talk to you again."

Harry Bobker, not to be outdone, said, "Selig, I've been thinking about this all week. You'll need linens, blankets, silverware, dishes. I'll get you all you need. After all, I'm in the business. When you get started in the Nichols place, my family and I will be steady guests. Everytime we come up you can deduct something from our bill and that can go towards the money you owe me. Also I'll make sure that a lot of my friends come up and the cost of their vacations can be charged off against what you owe me. You'll be paid up in no time!"

The tides of friendship were pulling Selig toward an affirmative decision. Jennie, too, put pressure on her father to move ahead. She was particularly taken with the Nichols place because there was an elementary and high school nearby for Paul.

"Poppa," she pleaded, "please say yes! I know we'll make a go of it."

Selig Grossinger knitted his brows and puffed slowly on his pipe. He wanted to gamble, but he had to remember he would be gambling not only his future but the money of friends. Still, the friends were so eager, so confident. . . .

Finally, he turned toward them and said, "Sol . . . Harry . . . Jennie, you are all right. This time it is *beshert!*"

Chapter 8

The firm of Max Fisch and Sam Weiner was kept busy during the following month. Before Selig could even think of actually buying the estate, he had to sell Longbrook House and the neighboring Tripps house which he had also purchased in 1916. The real-estate agents succeeded in getting an offer of $10,000 for a property which only four years before had been bought by Selig for $3,500 with a $450 down payment.

But now the roof was no longer porous; additions had been built; there was the sturdy barn; and, above all, there was the intangible asset known as "good will." Longbrook House enjoyed an enviable reputation in the community. Yet, few of the local burghers knew of a macabre event during their last season at Longbrook that nearly destroyed the market value of the boarding house as well as the Grossinger family's future as resort owners.

When a middle-aged spinster checked in early during the summer of 1918 with a persistent cough, an apprehensive chambermaid cautioned Jennie that it might be tuberculosis. This was the time of a deadly world-wide

"Spanish influenza" epidemic that scourged humanity from 1918–19. In that year alone, it left more than 20,000,000 dead in its wake, including half a million in this country. Everyone was jittery.

The new arrival assured everyone it was only a bad cold. She left at the end of a week. Several weeks later, she wrote asking to return. Fearful the woman might actually have the dread contagious disease, Jennie replied there was no room available. The unbidden guest came up anyway. Still suffering from a wracking cough, she insisted the country air would cure her "cold." A worried Jennie decided to put her up in a tent some distance from the Main House.

A few nights later when Jennie was bathing Paul, she heard choking sounds coming from the tent. Wrapping Paul in a blanket, she ran to the tent and was horrified to see blood pouring from the woman's mouth. Panic-stricken, she called Pop. He hitched up his horses and went off to find help. By the time the doctor arrived, the poor tormented body had breathed its last. Several guests were sitting less than fifty feet from the tent while the desperately ill woman was going through her death throes. But they heard nothing, for all were lustily singing patriotic war songs of the day.

With the cooperation of the doctor, Selig managed to remove the body to the village hospital without being observed. Meanwhile, next of kin were notified. To prevent any possibility of contagion, Selig and a handyman took the bed the woman had slept in, along with all of her clothing, and buried them in the deepest part of the woods. Secrecy was absolutely essential. In those days before antibiotics, morbid fear of contagious diseases was commonplace. Even a rumor that someone had died of tuberculosis would have sent panicky guests fleeing en masse back to the city. Luck was with the Grossingers again.

Everyone was eager to help the family get started at the new location, including the Messrs. Wiener and Fisch who volunteered to defer payment of their regular brokerage fee until the Terrace Hill House was a going concern.

The small but quite evident success Selig and Malke had achieved at Longbrook House had not gone unnoticed in Ferndale, or nearby Liberty. Selig knew it would cost several thousand dollars to transform Terrace Hill House into a place able to accommodate 150 or more guests. The only solution would be a bank mortgage, but would any bank risk its money on such a hazardous undertaking as the establishment of yet another boarding house? When he confided his doubts to the two real-estate men, they laughed at what they knew to be his genuine naiveté. They told him he would have no trouble raising money, not only on the tangible assets of the new acquisition, but on his reputation. And, of course, they were right.

By February 12, 1919, everything had been signed, sealed and delivered for the move to the Nichols estate. The furniture, linens, kitchen utensils, tools, chickens and cows had all been moved to the new property, which the family renamed Grossinger's Terrace Hill House. As the Ford drove away with Selig at the wheel, Jennie looked back silently at the farm which had brought them to the country and restored her father's health. For a moment, she experienced a pang of nostalgia, but it was only a fleeting sensation. It vanished at almost the precise moment Longbrook House disappeared from view. In its place came a surge of anticipation over what the future would hold for the family in their new home.

She thought of being able to press a switch to get light; of having hot and cold running water by simply turning on a faucet; of showers and steam heat. Her mood brightened with each passing mile, as she realized there would be no more foul-smelling chamber pots to empty, no more washing in the brook, no more outhouses, and, best of all, no more grimy kerosene lamps to scrub clean every morning. During the years at Longbrook, she had never quite been able to wash the odor of kerosene from her hands.

Finally, the chugging Ford reached the estate which would be their home for the rest of their lives. Health authorities had drained Lake Ophelia and pure water now came from an artesian well. Not even the drifts of snow could hide the magnificent landscaping the Nichols family had tended for so many years. And, most importantly, the property stood on top of a hill. The view from the porch of Longbrook House had always been obstructed by an ugly barn. No such barrier existed here. There were, to be sure, some old-time residents who did not take kindly to the idea that "foreigners" from New York City were taking over a landmark as well known as the Nichols estate. They didn't mind boarding houses ten or twelve miles away, but the Nichols property was right on the outskirts of Liberty, a conservative community of third- and fourth-generation Protestants. The Terrace Hill House had been in the Nichols family for a hundred years; it seemed almost sacrilegious to some of them that it now be turned into an alien boarding house run by a family out of the East Side ghetto. Why, not one of those "foreigners" could even speak proper English! Jennie was blissfully unaware of the sullen resentment of so many of the neighbors. If Selig knew, he never mentioned it.

The family, including Harry who would soon give up his job in New York entirely, moved into two large rooms on the top floor. Jennie was delighted by the breathtaking view of the countryside from her bedroom window. Only one problem disturbed them: the cost of heating the family rooms, as well as the rest of the house, turned out to be far more than anticipated. This was not a house that could be heated by wood. Not even Selig's expert wielding of an ax could feed a hungry furnace designed to operate on coal. And coal was expensive.

Somehow they managed and by the time spring arrived, everything was ready to receive guests. Grossinger's Terrace Hill House was a real hotel, if only a small one. Although many onerous boarding house tasks had been eliminated, running a hotel presented new and often unfamiliar problems. Guests expected more from a hotel. The guest rate was raised to $18 a week, largely because wartime inflation caused all prices to spiral. This rate still made the new resort one of the least expensive in the Catskills. Withal, it was a good deal higher than the Grossingers' boarding house rate and guests wanted commensurate service. For one thing, they weren't satisfied with hot water for showers during certain specified hours; they expected to get it any time they turned on the faucet.

Selig could hardly keep up with all he had to do. He

attended to his livestock (six cows and five hundred chickens), ordered food from local merchants, and met guests at the railroad station. Jennie, in addition to waiting on table and washing dishes, took charge of reservations and complaints, but her knowledge of hotel administration was just about equal to her knowledge of Sanskrit. When people would phone or write for reservations, Jennie wouldn't bother to make written notations. She would remember them. At least, she would remember most of them. Often, on a Friday afternoon, there were more arrivals than accommodations. Then she would have to plead with single girls to double up or ask married couples with children to let her put cots in their room for the youngsters. What's more, Jennie could never say "no" to anyone who wanted to stay beyond the term of his reservation. If a family decided to spend an additional week at the hotel, Jennie was thrilled; it meant they were pleased. An old friend once said to Jennie: "My dear, you stuff your rooms the way your mother stuffs a chicken." Beds placed on the porch for overflow male guests were not an uncommon sight in those early days at Grossinger's Terrace Hill House.

Jennie was beginning to develop the personality that many years later would become the symbol of the hotel. At Longbrook House the atmosphere had been one of *gemutlich* or, in Yiddish, *haimish* (congenial). Guests were treated as welcome relatives or friends. Selig and Malke were Pop and Mom now to many of the guests, and only the aged vacationers were addressed as Mr. or Mrs. Guests who arrived as strangers on a Friday would by Saturday morning be on a first-name basis, not only with the Grossinger family but with each other. Malke still performed her magic in the kitchen. Her weekly triumph was the Sabbath dinner. Most of her guests preferred the traditional dishes—golden egg-crusted *challahs,* rich-gravied pot roast, light, moist slices of *gefullte* fish, and plump chickens simmering in a fragrant, savory soup.

One Saturday afternoon, Jennie was horrified to see a number of bowls of chicken soup sent back to the kitchen barely touched. She was too busy to worry much about it, but when other orders of the usually savory soup came back she knew that something was wrong. She tasted the soup and let out a cry. It was spoiled! This had never happened before. Tears of mortification filled her eyes. Where dining was the major event of the day, this had all the impact of a small catastrophe.

Just then Mrs. Anna Neugeborn, a good friend, walked into the kitchen. "Don't worry, Jennie," she said comfortingly. "We all understand."

Why had the chicken spoiled and the pot roast not been affected? She discussed the puzzling question with Selig, Malke and Harry and together they came up with an answer.

On Friday night, a kitchen man had mistakenly placed the big pots of chicken and soup in the ice box while they were still steaming hot. Before the soup had cooled, the chicken had spoiled. From that time on, Momma Grossinger stationed herself permanently in the kitchen watching everything that went into or came out of the ice box.

Harry, who was now working full time at the hotel, also spent much of his time in the kitchen. He did everything but actually cook. He became Malke's chief taster when she was uncertain as to whether a dish had been properly seasoned.

He made salads, carved the meat and waited on tables. He was also bellboy, porter, bed-maker, plumber and general handy man. It was in this latter capacity that the bundle of bespectacled energy named Harry Grossinger excelled particularly. During the first season at the new location, the Grossingers discovered that modern conveniences could break down as inconveniently as the old-fashioned facilities at Longbrook House. The fine water heater, excellent for ordinary purposes, had vexing limitations, most apparent before the dinner hour when thirty or more guests might simultaneously decide it was time for a bath or shower. Inevitably, a bathrobed guest shouted from the head of the stairs: "Jennie, the water is finished!"

She cried for Harry, who uttered soothing words to half-showered or half-bathed guests, and then made a tour of inspection. Every tap from roof to cellar was dry. He phoned a plumber in Liberty, who told him calmly that there was nothing he could do to help. This happened to be one of the driest seasons in years. Harry told everyone that for a day or two they would have to walk a quarter of a mile to a lake on the Nichols property to take their baths. Then he and Pete, the hired man, began hauling water by horse and wagon from near-by natural springs not yet dried up. The guests took the indignity in stride. Not one asked for a refund or left.

Harry, still traveling to New York City to drum up new trade, was never afraid to try the unorthodox in his selling campaigns. Having worked briefly for a clothing manufacturers' trade association, he went to see his former boss.

"Mr. Silverman," Harry said, "once you said if I ever needed help to come to you. I know that you and your family are used to staying at the best hotels in this part of the country. So this is the favor I ask. Please come to our place some weekend and when you are ready to leave —criticize us."

Simon Silverman, flattered that this bright young man had asked his advice, said he would come to the hotel the following weekend with one or two members of the association.

No doubt about it, Harry had taken a gamble. If Silverman and his friends thought the place inadequate, the word would spread in the garment industry and Grossinger's Terrace Hill House might suffer a damaging blow. All weekend he worried. After lunch on Sunday Harry, trying to conceal his anxiety with a bluff heartiness, approached Silverman. "Mr. Silverman, what can you tell us? What are we doing wrong?"

The executive hesitated for a moment and then replied: "Harry, it's not exactly perfect. The food? Wonderful! The service? No, it does not compare with other places where we have been. And Harry, you need more room—more space for guests to roam around. Too much experience in running a hotel you and your family do not have. But enthusiasm and friendliness and eagerness to please I see everywhere. Yes, Harry, my friends and I like it here. Many of them want to make reservations for next weekend. One even wants to make reservations for the rest of the summer."

Harry stammered, "Th-thank you, Mr. Silverman," and hurried to the front desk to tell Jennie.

That evening the family had a conference. Although many Catskill hotels and boarding houses were family affairs, one member of the family was invariably the boss. With the Grossingers, there was no single boss. Every time a decision had to be made, it was a family matter. Technically, the Terrace Hill House was in Selig's name (with Harry as his partner), and, of course, the kitchen was Malke's private domain. But increasingly, they listened to Jennie. Her constant contact with guests nurtured a quality she never suspected she possessed.

Gone was the self-consciousness that had always assailed her. Life in the country had made her healthy. She carried herself erect and proudly. Because the years of peering closely at button-holes had impaired her vision, she sometimes wore glasses, but her complexion was smooth and her hair golden. Many a single male visitor was disappointed to learn she was married. As a child in Europe she had been gay, vivacious, gregarious; now, these traits, hidden for so many years, bubbled to the surface again. Her exuberant good nature and uncanny ability to meet people and make immediate, warm contact were tangible assets to the hotel, even though Jennie was not conscious of it. She and Harry looked up to her parents as the two who were responsible for the small miracle that was taking place in a hotel only a few months old. They, on the other hand, knew their daughter and her husband were the ones who so easily managed to communicate with the guests, especially the younger ones.

The reservations made by the members of Silverman's organization virtually guaranteed a successful first season at the Terrace Hill House. A neighbor named Siegel then suggested raising a second mortgage on the property to enable the family to buy the remaining ninety acres of the Nichols estate. This would include not only the land itself, but two small cottages and a large barn. The decision to act was triggered by Mr. Silverman's opinion that "you people need more room." Harry and Jennie enthusiastically supported the proposal for expansion.

Invaluable counsel and guidance at this juncture also came from Harry and Jack Beck, one a young Liberty lawyer, the other a banker, who had become good friends and could always be relied upon for advice. The Beck brothers approved. Selig heard them out, all the while puffing thoughtfully on his pipe. At the end of the family conference, all agreed Selig should take out the second mortgage and purchase the rest of the land.

The Grossinger family was beginning to think big even if the embryo empire was heavily mortgaged and brought in only small profits. They still did not have enough money to advertise, but one afternoon Harry and Jennie, while walking along Main Street in Liberty, stopped to admire some snapshots in the window of Otto Hillig's photography shop. They went inside and asked him to take pictures of the grounds, the Main Building, the dining room, and—almost an afterthought—the cows. When Mr. Hillig showed them the results, they were delighted. The pictures could be made into postcards and mailed to prospective guests. It was the publicity-conscious Harry who suggested the trademark of the hotel be the picture of the cows. "We'll just print three words on the card," he said. "Our Bovine Beauties."

During the next few years, the word spread about Malke's cooking made Grossinger's much more widely known and the visual appeal of three contented cows grazing on a hillside did its part, too.

There were some things they did not have to advertise. New Jersey, traditionally, had been the vacationland for refugees from the hot, crowded cities of New York and Philadelphia. But the Catskills had two natural advantages. There were no mosquitoes, and the terrain of New Jersey could not compare with the gently rolling mountains of Sullivan County. Guests from New York, or a few who came from Philadelphia, had never seen such sunrises and sunsets as in the Catskills. At night when a white moon, riding high in the heavens, bathed the mountains in soft light, it seemed to melt the hearts of the most confirmed city dwellers.

Always in close contact with her guests, Jennie noticed that older couples were content to eat, sleep, doze comfortably on the porch, rock in hammocks, take long walks on the country roads, or discuss their successful sons—especially if they were doctors or lawyers. But she also noted that many of the younger guests were often restless. More than once she heard one of them grumble, "That place we went to last year had a tennis court. Why isn't there one here?" When Jennie discussed this with Harry and Selig, they agreed to build a tennis court. Her father had seen one at a nearby boys' camp and thought it would be a simple matter. In no time, he had laid out a playing area as he remembered it. Now on the reservation letters that Harry sent out was the proud boast: "Tennis court on premises."

When the 1921 season opened, two girls arrived with tennis rackets. Jennie beamed happily and insisted upon personally taking them to the court, some hundred yards away from the Main House. The girls looked at one another in astonishment and then broke into gales of laughter.

"This is a tennis court?" one asked mockingly. "Jennie, do you think four posts enclosed by chicken wire with a net in the middle makes a tennis court? You've laid this out on bumpy, uneven ground. Why, Jennie, you don't even have any white lines to show us where to hit the ball."

Jennie looked embarrassed. That evening, she confided her troubles to Herman Phillips, who was earning his way through medical school by working behind the desk as the hotel's first night manager. He promised to help out. He had a good friend, Iby Corwin, a first-rate tennis player, working as a tennis pro at another hotel. Corwin complied with Jennie's request and designed a proper layout—not one, but four regulation courts. And then he consented to remain at the hotel as a tennis instructor.

The episode made Jennie conscious of how little she really knew about the resort business. What she did know, she had learned from her guests. Fortunately, it didn't take her too long to shed some of the naiveté that clung to anybody raised in the protected environment of an Orthodox Jewish home. There was the day a dignified-looking man came up to the desk accompanied by an attractive young girl, who looked thirty years his junior. After reading the man's name in the registration book, she asked cheerily: "Will you and your daughter share the same room, Mr. Shapiro?"

The man scowled and replied: "This is Mrs. Shapiro and, yes, we will share the same room!"

Neither Jennie nor any member of her family had ever spent a night in a first-class resort hotel. Often having heard guests talk about the Laurel-in-the-Pines in Lakewood, New Jersey, then considered one of the East's finest Jewish resorts, Jennie made a reservation and checked into the magnificent hotel. Mr. and Mrs. Frank Seiden, owners of the establishment, were gracious and cooperative. They showed her everything that made their hotel a distinguished one.

Jennie was amazed at what she felt to be regal luxury. There were, she noticed, shining crystal goblets on the dining room tables. Back in Ferndale, guests drank from a mongrel collection of thick glassware. At home, waiters rolled up their shirt sleeves and tied aprons around their waists; here, the waiters wore immaculately clean white starched jackets. There were linen napkins at every plate. The food was no better than what her mother cooked (if as good), but it looked better. The portions weren't as large, but they were beautifully served. Olives, radishes and celery were put on every table and beds of crushed ice kept them cold and crisp.

"We feed the eye as well as the stomach," Mr. Seiden said proudly. Moreover, there was much for guests to do at Laurel-in-the-Pines: handball courts, horses to ride, boats, and a small orchestra playing at night. When men walked into the dining room in the evening, they wore ties and coats and women wore their best. Yet this did not lessen the *haimish* spirit so important to a resort hotel.

Jennie brought the knowledge she had gained at the Laurel-in-the-Pines back to the Catskills. The changes she had in mind, which her family approved, could not be made at once. There were mortgages to be paid off. But she resolved that eventually these changes would be made.

The economic upswing that swept the country when World War I ended was a great boon to the Grossingers. In addition to enjoying a full house during the summer months, they began to attract a few people in November, December, January and February. There were no winter sports facilities as such, but there was plenty of snow for sledding and ice on a nearby lake. The family decided the only sensible thing to do was to keep open all year. After all, since they lived at the hotel, they could easily take care of the few guests who might come up during the off-season months.

But a growing hotel required a growing staff. A young girl named Pauline Karp was hired to help Dave Kriendler with finances and bookkeeping, while Jennie's friend, Fannie Mayerson, became her right hand in the reservations department. Evelyn Brown, the youngest daughter of Grossinger's very first guest, Mrs. Caroline Brown, also came up to help out as did two of Harry's sisters, Regina and Rose.

Slowly some of the improvements Jennie wanted so badly were introduced. During the peak season, a three-piece band made up of college students played dance

music, and now the younger guests grew more enthusiastic. The hotel was thriving far beyond the little family's
modest expectations when they began nearly a decade
before. Things were going well.

Then Jennie fell sick. For the rest of her life, she
would be forced to fight an unrelenting battle against
illness, a struggle that was to see her in and out of many
hospitals. At first she dismissed her abdominal pains and
backaches as nothing more than the symptoms of over-
work. She tried to do less, but slowing down was foreign
to her. Eventually the pains became more acute. Harry
insisted she visit Dr. Emanuel Singer, a highly regarded
young physician whose parents, Mr. and Mrs. Morris
Singer, had come to America on the same ship as the
Grossingers in 1900, and now owned a thriving little
restaurant in the town of Liberty. The doctor's medical
diagnosis was a shock. Dr. Singer explained that Jennie
must have returned to work too soon after Paul's birth.
In any case, an operation was imperative, the sooner the
better.

"It's Thanksgiving now, Doctor," Jennie said. "Christmas is almost here. That has become a good week for us.
As soon as the holidays are over, I'll have the operation."

Dr. Singer picked up his phone to call a New York
number. "Jennie," he said, "you must have surgery as
soon as possible. Tomorrow, you must go to New York
to see a specialist, Dr. Abraham Rongy. If he agrees with
my diagnosis, he'll want to operate within a day or two."

Jennie nodded. "All right. Harry is in New York; I will
join him."

The following day in New York, Dr. Rongy confirmed

Dr. Singer's findings. He told Jennie to check in at Lebanon Hospital immediately. He would operate in the morning.

"But Harry and I have tickets to see a show tonight," Jennie said. "Can't I check in after the show?"

Reluctantly, the doctor agreed. After the theater, Jennie decided to get something to read. She wanted a copy of Edna Ferber's new novel, *Fanny Herself.* For some time, Jennie had been troubled by her meager education. Knowing that she had had only a little more than four years of formal schooling and that she still spoke with a noticeable accent left her intimidated in the presence of her intellectual betters. Sometimes when guests left books behind Jennie would take these to bed with her and try to read them, often without fully comprehending all the words. Lacking a teacher or any guidance, she felt that reading would be her passport to a whole new world —and novels seemed to her the most interesting of all the books she came upon.

In her free moments, she began to absorb everything like a sponge, indiscriminately. It was this compulsion that made the idea of spending a few days in the hospital almost attractive. And so she took the Edna Ferber book with her. Thinking about the operation, she had absolutely no fear, but hers was the courage of ignorance. She was facing major surgery.

It turned out that she didn't read much that night at Lebanon Hospital after all, because a nurse gave her a sleeping pill. It was the first one she had ever taken and had immediate effect. But at seven the next morning, when two operating-room attendants arrived to take her to surgery, they were amazed to see their patient sitting up in bed absorbed in a book.

A few hours after the surgery, she woke to sharp pain. To complicate matters, she developed a serious abcess and a bad cold. Constant coughing disturbed her sutures and added to the stabbing pain. When Dr. Singer came down from Liberty to see her, his eyes mirrored grave concern. He was afraid that she might develop pneumonia. Jennie was kept in the hospital three weeks. Even then, the cautious physician refused to let her go back to Liberty.

"But I'm needed, Doctor," she said. "This is not only *Chanukah*, it's also Christmas and people have vacations. Our place will be very busy."

"That's why Dr. Rongy and I aren't letting you go back to the hotel," he said grimly. "You've got to rest for at least another month. I've been talking to Sol and Anna Mandelbaum. They want you to stay at their apartment here in New York until you're strong again."

Jennie spent three weeks with her old friends, relishing the unique experience of having others serve and take care of her. When Dr. Singer and Harry drove her back to the Catskills, the Christmas rush was over. Worried that many things might have gone wrong in her absence, she was pleased to discover that her fears were unfounded.

"It's a good lesson," she told Harry sadly, "to know that no one is indispensable. I haven't been missed at all."

This was not precisely the case. For her family, Jennie's home-coming was in the nature of a celebration.

Selig and Malke tried to persuade her to take it easy for a few weeks. She agreed, if reluctantly. The post-operative pain soon disappeared and her body felt stronger than it had ever been. It was, she told Harry, almost as if she had been reborn.

"After all," he said, "it's the first real rest you've ever had in your life—and it's not going to be the last. From now on, you are going to take a few weeks off every year."

She laughed. "We'll see, Harry."

Chapter 9

It was in the heady post-World War I years that Grossinger's (by now, very few called it the Terrace Hill House) began its slow, but steady, climb. A dining room, seating four hundred guests, was added to the Main House at a cost of $7,000. The money came principally through a loan from Lottie's husband, Louis Grau, who asked a full 6 per cent interest from Selig. When the structure was completed, Jennie prophesized inaccurately: "We will never have the problem of an overcrowded dining room again!"

The Grossingers also purchased an eleven-room cottage on the adjacent Girod estate. It had formerly been rented to a man who, everyone said in awe, was worth millions. He must have been worth millions, guests said, because he rode in a chauffeur-driven Pierce-Arrow. Accordingly, the cottage was named "The Millionaire." Jennie and Harry were learning more about this strange hotel business every day. They knew, for instance, that there was such a thing as snob appeal. To prove her point, Jennie had only to cite the many reservations from

guests who asked specifically for rooms in "The Millionaire Cottage."

During that summer of 1924 there came to the Catskills an ambitious, good-natured twenty-two-year-old
from the Lower East Side whom destiny was to cast for a
major role in the Grossinger chronicle. Abe Friedman
applied for a job as a busboy at the suggestion of a girl
friend working as a chambermaid. After nine years of
menial labor in New York's garment industry and with
little to show for it, he was eager to get out of the city
"and try something new." Totally without experience in
a dining room, Abe fumbled through his first weekend.
On Sunday, he overturned a cart of dishes and was fired.
Fortunately for Abe—and Grossinger's—Regina Grossinger had taken a liking to the youth and pleaded that
he be given another chance. Re-hired the next day, he
began a career that would see him become one of Jennie's closest and most devoted associates during the next
four decades.

In the mid-Twenties, with demand for rooms always
greater than the available space, an imposing, new forty-
five room building was opened. Every bedroom had a
bath, something revolutionary among Catskill resort hotels. Jennie proposed that the guests themselves name
this newest Grossinger addition. A contest was held and
a honeymooning couple, Mr. and Mrs. Herman Gaba,
came up with the winning name which re-inforced Jennie's belief in snob appeal. By an overwhelming majority, the guests voted for the name suggested by the
Gabas—"The Ritz," symbol in the Twenties of everything that was elegant and luxurious.

Three other small cottages were bought and, when

furnished, gave the hotel an additional eighteen rooms. With forty-five rooms in the Main House and fourteen in the Winter Cottage, now Grossinger's could boast proudly that it had one-hundred-and-six rooms for the accommodation of guests. Most of the rooms could house two guests, and cots could always be added for children. On peak weekends these beds weren't enough to take care of the many vacationers who arrived without reservations. When that happened the family would sleep in the "winter kitchen" unused during the summer months. Harry sometimes even slept on a sofa in the lobby. More than once cots were placed in the lobby of the Main House to accommodate the overflow. Beds were also placed on the porch for rugged single men who didn't mind sleeping *al fresco* on warm nights. With rare exceptions, guests never complained.

"Don't worry, Jennie," one said, "we didn't come here to sleep—we can always sleep at home."

Selig still insisted on meeting the trains. This was a duty he would never delegate to anyone else, except, of course, on Friday nights when the Talmudic injunctions forbad any kind of vehicular travel.

To all Catskill voyagers, the trip northward in those days was an exhausting adventure—usually aboard the New York, Ontario, and Western Railroad that first brought Jennie and her family to the new "Promised Land." Thousands of passengers each year swayed to and fro in the ancient green, gas-lit, wooden coaches headed for Grossinger's and hundreds of other hotels, boarding houses and camps. The trip invariably left the resort-bound travelers fatigued and dirty, for the O & W (nick-named the "Old and Weary") was already beginning to run down badly, its rolling stock antiquated and rickety. Inside the cars, few passengers were able to escape the omnipresent coal grains and soot that entered the windows to lodge in the eyes, dirty clothes, and make a clean seat a rarity. The sight of Selig's smiling face at the Ferndale station was like a welcome beacon to arriving Grossinger guests, for it meant the uncomfortable journey was at last over.

Usually, there were a few arrivals who had never bothered to make reservations. They were good-natured about the crowded conditions. One Friday night, two young men arrived and Jennie had to tell them that there was only one cot left. They tossed for it. The loser grinned and said, "Sleep fast, my friend. I'll need your pillow in about eight hours." It was an unusual way to run a hotel, but, then, it was an unusual hotel.

Before long, Jennie instituted a custom she found particularly intriguing at the Laurel-in-the-Pines, something she felt would give more class to the hotel. Male guests were requested to wear coats and ties when they came to dinner. A few protested, but most complied willingly. Grossinger's was, indeed, moving up the social ladder.

Romance was not exactly a commodity served à la carte by the management, but it was beginning to flourish with a little assist from the staff. Often, three or four single young ladies would save all year for a two-week vacation at the hotel. They would arrive together, and, although no girl ever said that she had come in search of a husband, no girl ever objected if Jennie, Harry, Regina or Dave Kriendler introduced her to a nice young man. And out of these casual introductions many temporary and some permanent attachments evolved. Jennie was never happier than when two young people, who met at the hotel, phoned to say they were getting married and wished to spend their honeymoon at Grossinger's. Newly-weds always received the red-carpet treatment and the best room available.

One evening, a radiant bride, still wearing a sprig of white orchids, and her brand-new husband arrived. Evelyn Brown had a bellboy usher them to the finest room in the house. Ten minutes later, the bride came back to the front desk on the brink of tears.

"Evelyn," she said, "we're on our honeymoon. The room you gave us has two double beds. I know you. If you get crowded you'll put another couple in with us!"

Jennie and Harry were elated by the steady growth of the hotel, but one "land problem" continued to harass them. A public road bisecting their entire property divided the Main House from the newly erected and recently purchased cottages. All day long farmers' carts and trucks creaked by laden with vegetables, cows, geese, and chickens en route to market in Liberty or to other hotels and boarding houses. The noise was a nuisance, while the road presented an obvious hazard to guests' children constantly running across it. Still, it was a public road and there didn't seem much that could be done about it. At a family meeting, Selig came up with an idea which everyone approved. The next morning, he went off to see the town officials in charge of building and maintaining the public roads of the community. His proposition was as startling as it was unorthodox.

If they would close the dirt road that ran through his grounds, he would pay for the construction of a fine paved road that would serve the same area, but just skirt his property. Getting a new paved road in exchange for one which often mired trucks in its mud or snow was attractive, but they told Selig they would have to consult with other town officials first. Several days later, Selig received the reasonable answer that if he could get permission from neighbors affected by the change, he could go ahead.

Selig called on every neighbor and was welcomed with friendly interest—and their permission.

Mrs. Nichols, a visitor only a few weeks before, told Jennie something she had not known. "When I sold your father this property five years ago, some of the neighbors resented it," she disclosed. "They didn't like the idea of a hotel run by New Yorkers right in their own backyards. They were concerned about the class of boarders you would have. They felt that if you let the property run down it would decrease the value of their holdings. But it wasn't so. They saw that your father was developing and improving the property. They saw that your guests were decent family people who minded their own business."

Those neighbors, fourth- and fifth-generation Americans of Christian heritage who resisted the very idea of Jews with a ghetto background coming into their backyard, had completely reversed their attitudes. Once they got to know the Grossinger family and were able to appraise them first-hand, prejudices handed down through ignorance no longer made sense.

Late in 1924, the dirt road that ran through the Grossinger grounds was closed and the new paved one constructed. Selig and Harry built terraces and walks over the old road and Jennie hired her first landscape gardener who installed a rock garden and fountain.

Other improvements followed. The lake that adjoined the Grossinger property had always been a tantalizing sight to the family and guests. At first Selig wouldn't even discuss buying it; the new buildings had multiplied maintenance expenses and the paved road had been costly. Every penny left over at the end of the season was either put back into the hotel in the form of equipment or used to pay interest on the mortgages. Selig said that it was out of the question; the owners were asking $10,000 for the lake and the land around it.

It was, however, not out of the question. Again banks and old friends helped out. A great deal of work was necessary, including leveling of a small forest of underwater tree stumps, before the lake was ready for swimmers and oarsmen using the tiny fleet of rowboats Selig also purchased. The lake not only delighted the guests; it delighted Jack Kriendler. Steve Kriendler asked his cousin, Jack, and Jack's partner, Charlie Berns, another cousin, to visit the hotel. Jack and Charlie operated one of New York's better-known Prohibition speakeasies, The Club Fronton. But trade was slow in the summer months and they accepted cousin Steve's invitation. Suave Jack Kriendler had a built-in cash register in his alert mind. He took one look at the lovely lake and asked Jennie if she would give him the row-boat concession. He might also accept a canteen concession in the Main House. When the enterprising Mr. Kriendler turned on the charm no one was safe. Since Jennie greatly admired Jack Kriendler, it was with complete confidence that she turned both concessions over to him. Jack's younger brother, Maxwell, then a college student, took charge of the two concessions.

One day, passing the canteen, Jennie was startled to hear the clinking of a slot machine and an occasional roar from a happy customer as a stream of nickels tumbled into eager hands. In time, the partners installed three more. Jennie, torn between her affection for the Kriendlers and an uneasy feeling that they were breaking some kind of law, wanted to remove the slot machines. It was, after all, gambling.

She tried to be stern with Jack. "People should earn their money," she said. "And, anyway, most of the time, they lose. I don't think it's right."

She was persuaded to relent, not by Jack's self-serving arguments, but by many of her guests whom, she was surprised to discover, were very enthusiastic about the machines.

(Gambling and resort hotels seem to have a natural affinity and, especially during the Forties, some of the biggest card and floating crap games around were being played in certain Catskill hotels favored by the "Mob." Jennie never lost her innate distaste for games of chance. Even today, when she sees a few players huddling over a table in the Card Room, she shakes her head regretfully and sighs: "Here, they have all this beautiful country to enjoy. Cards, they can always play at home. Such a waste."

A few years after Jack Kriendler began his sideline operations in Ferndale, he and Charlie Berns opened a new speakeasy at 21 West 52nd Street in New York which enjoyed immediate success. The two bonifaces first called their somewhat illicit club, "Jack and Charlie's." It was later to become simply "21," where Jennie is still one of the few V.I.P.'s who never needs a reservation when she's in New York.)

The purchase of the lake gave Harry a chance to put his bridle path project into action. Six saddle horses were acquired and a British ex-cavalry officer hired to supervise the stables and teach riding. Jennie was one of his most avid pupils. When he left, a young man named Bernie Sper, an experienced horseman, took over the job. Bernie's pre-breakfast rides were a popular activity even though they were one of the few things available to guests at the hotel for which a charge was made. He would sell tickets for the ride during dinner. The next morning, he would knock on the door of each of his customers to be sure that all were awake and ready for the morning canter. (Today, only golfers at Grossinger's seem able to face the world so early in the day, but during the Twenties no liquor was sold at the hotel, hangovers were unknown, and most guests, asleep by midnight, were glad to rise early.)

Occasionally, Jennie rode with the group, but her day still began at six-thirty in the morning and more often than not, she would embark on a pre-breakfast ride with Bernie at five A.M. This became the happiest hour of her long day. The misty air was cool then, and there was always a brisk morning breeze. At that hour, she had the mountains to herself—not even the birds were awake.

The East Side of New York seemed so far away as to be almost forgotten. She would breathe deeply of the fresh air and thank God that she was alive and healthy enough to enjoy the mountains just as she had enjoyed the foothills of the Carpathians as a child.

One morning, while riding the paths around the lake she stopped short when she heard laughter. She turned her horse toward the lake, to be greeted by Evelyn Brown and several staff members who were swimming. Jennie had always urged the busboys, waiters, bellhops, kitchen help and clerks to make use of the hotel facilities. She was happy to see this group had heeded her advice even if it was only five-thirty in the morning.

"I'm glad you all got up so early," she said, beaming. "Having a dip in the lake is a good way to start the day."

"It sure is, Jennie," Evelyn answered, and plunged back into the water.

A day or two later Evelyn said, "Jennie, I have a confession to make. When you saw us swimming, we hadn't just gotten up. We were celebrating Jack Kriendler's birthday and stayed up all night."

Rainy days have always been the bane of resort hotels in the Catskills. The card game called gin rummy had not as yet become part of our national life, and time hung heavy on the hands of guests who felt cheated if they had to spend even one idle hour during their vacation.

Some of the Catskill resorts hired a *toomler*—literally, a noise creator; in fact, a boisterous clown majoring in versatility. He was the chap who would stand on his head, wear funny hats, sing comic songs, lead the guests in games, or do anything else he could think of to make them forget the cold, dank rain falling outside.

As field marshall of fun, man of all talents and dispenser of total distraction on inclement days to keep guests from checking out, he was, as one writer put it, "the closest thing to a Renaissance man that Jewish-American popular culture has produced."

A *toomler* was a luxury Grossinger's could not quite afford as yet, but Benny Kolodny, an uninhibited waiter with a comic gift and a few magic tricks, did his best. At breakfast one morning, Jennie couldn't believe her eyes and ears when she saw Benny emerge from the kitchen carrying a struggling, squawking chicken under his arm.

"Benny," she said with a gasp, "where are you going with that hen?"

"You'll see, Jennie," he answered gaily, and continued on to one of the tables he was serving. His five customers looked up in alarm. With a deft motion he produced two eggs, apparently from beneath the hen.

"You ordered strictly fresh eggs, ma'am?" he asked. "Here, they are, right from the hen."

The stunt was received with such applause it became a weekly feature. When new guests from the city arrived eager to enjoy real fresh country food, one would invariably admonish him, "Benny, the eggs should be strictly fresh—right from the chicken."

The victim enjoyed the temporary opportunity to bask in the limelight, and regular guests, who had seen Benny's act before, seemed to enjoy it more each time he performed it.

About this time another Benny joined the staff and also began to double as an amateur *toomler*. Benny Rheingold's regular daytime job was head of the bellboys. After dinner, the guests usually took a long stroll, almost a necessity in view of the huge amount of food they ate. Benny presided over a little room where they stopped in for tea and cookies before retiring. It was a nightly ritual. If a guest asked for "dark tea" Benny would pour a glass, pull the light cord, and yell, "So there it is—dark tea!"

One of the busboys became Benny Rheingold's straight man. When there was a lull in the room his stooge would ask, "Benny, give me a sentence with the word 'envy' in it."

"That's easy," Benny would say, assuming a heavy Yiddish accent. "I vent to a vedding last night, envy had fish, envy had *kreplech*, envy had chicken, envy had *strudel*."

"How about a sentence using the word tennis?"

"Sure," Benny would say. "At school I learned that tennis two times five."

"Tell me, Benny, what is a *schlemiel*?"

"A *schlemiel* is a *nudnik* who, when he is hungry, dreams about a big bowl of hot soup—only he ain't got a spoon."

Corny entertainment was a standard Catskill commodity in the Twenties. The well-fed older guests would laugh at any humor as long as it was broad and clean. Younger visitors were not quite so appreciative. Jennie often heard them compare the entertainment facilities at such adult camps as Tamiment or Totem or Napanoch to that provided by Grossinger's, and the hotel suffered by comparison.

"Jennie," they would tell her, "those camps have social directors and singers and dancers. There is something going on every afternoon and every night."

"But this isn't an adult camp, it's a hotel," Jennie would protest weakly.

They would shrug expressive shoulders. "So?"

She talked it over with Harry and her helpers behind the desk. They sympathized with the young guests who wanted more action. They realized, too, that in the resort business to stand still was to slip back.

"Progress is an alarm clock," Jennie said. "Just when you're falling asleep, it wakes you up. Maybe if we added a full program of camp activities to what we already have, it would keep our younger guests from deserting us."

This decision charted the direction of Grossinger's for all time. The first bona fide professional entertainer to be presented was David Lubritsky, a member of a well-known Yiddish theatrical family.

He had come to the hotel to recuperate from an illness, but remained to sing, dance and tell stories. He was greeted with such enthusiasm, Jennie felt it was time to move the entertainment from the dining room table to the stage. It was clear that this was what the guests wanted, and Jennie was still learning her trade from them. The next thing to do was hire a social director who would coordinate professional talent with the do-it-yourself type of entertainment so many of the guests liked.

Fortuitously, not one but two social directors applied for jobs. They said they were a team and that they had been employed at the respected Camp Napanoch. Their names were Mannie Mislanski and Eddie Citron and both were working their way through dental school. Jennie hired the two energetic extroverts, who, within twenty-four hours, were on a first-name basis with every guest in the hotel. They sang, danced, told stories and, in general, spread good humor all over the hotel. Jennie was a bit dubious when she first heard them telling Yiddish stories, as often as not making someone in the audience the butt of their humor. But these clever boys knew their audiences would react favorably to stories told on themselves. They had seen this again and again in the Yiddish theater and at parties in their own neighborhoods.

Mannie and Eddie were a great success that year. When the season ended and Jennie gave them a bonus, they admitted sheepishly that they came to the hotel under false pretenses. Yes, they had been employed at Camp Napanoch, but as waiters—not social directors. Still, they had felt they could make good if given a chance. Their harmless deception, as it turned out, worked out well for everyone.

Jennie decided then and there that if two amateurs could make her guests happy, two professionals could make them twice as happy. Friends recommended a talented young stage designer and director named Frank Buchanan, an amiable Scotsman. Jennie gave him an assistant, Freddie Weitzner, who was working his way through law school by acting as a social director at various Catskill camps. He had just graduated and this would be his last summer in the mountains. He and Buchanan made a fine team from the start.

To begin with, they felt that the makeshift stage thrown together hurriedly for Mannie and Eddie the previous year wasn't big enough for the kind of productions they had in mind. The team approached Jennie and Harry with an idea for building a real theater with professional lighting, stage curtains and a revolving center.

"Who would design it?" Harry wanted to know.

"I can design it myself and build it myself, too, if you'll let me have some carpenters to work with," Frank Buchanan said confidently.

Jennie and Harry decided to take them up on the offer. When the new casino, as it was called, was finished, he and Freddie Weitzner presented revues every Wednesday night.

By this time, it was obvious that a social director at a resort hotel was as necessary as a menu. Among the early directors, Ben Silver was one of the most successful. Irreverent, resourceful and talented, he was actor, director, producer, dancing teacher, and, of course, *toomler*. On the stage that Frank Buchanan built, he produced everything from Broadway melodramas to full-dress grand operas such as "Carmen."

He had a staff of twelve young men and women who often doubled as waiters, bellboys, maids and busboys. If a guest could sing or act, he was immediately recruited by Silver and would spend most of his vacation rehearsing and appearing in musicals or skits. Talented guests were also tapped for weekly amateur nights.

One June, Ben auditioned some college musicians from several schools. Jennie liked them enormously. She asked each of them to play alone, and each, even Ben admitted, was fine. But he warned Jennie the group had no experience playing as a unit.

Though they looked good on the bandstand and usually started a musical number together, they didn't always finish that way. Unfortunately, they made the dancers feel as if each had two left feet. But Ben Silver knew he could never persuade Jennie to fire them. (Once she tried to fire a waiter who was a model worker most of the time, with certain lunar exceptions. "If the moon is full, I got to have my drink," he would declare after a three-or-four day unexplained absence during the height of the season. When Jennie told him that he would have to go, because the hotel was just as busy when the moon was full, he said indignantly, "You can't fire me, Mrs. Grossinger—I live here!" He stayed.)

Exasperated, Ben Silver told Jennie, somewhat dolefully, that the amateur band had to go.

"People are dancing more and more, Jennie," Ben said earnestly. "I know business isn't too good and it will cost more than we can afford, but we must have a professional band."

"All right, Ben," she agreed. "Go to New York and hire one."

It was equally apparent that a permanent athletic director had to be a part of the staff also. One of the first was Abe Sharkey, a New York high-school teacher. He had been on the job only a week when he was confronted with a crisis. A man with a passion for handball went from table to table signing up fellow guests for a tournament. When he had twenty-six applicants, he announced the tournament would begin the next morning. Then he asked Abe Sharkey where the handball courts were located.

"What handball courts?" Abe asked.

The amateur organizer was dismayed. "You mean you have no handball courts?"

"No," replied Sharkey, "but let's get your twenty-six players to help and we'll build one."

"When?"

"Well, why not right now?" Sharkey said hopefully.

Sharkey requisitioned lumber from Pop Grossinger and with the help of the would-be players hurriedly erected a wall. It was easy enough to flatten a dirt plot. A week later, the handball tournament was held. It was a success not only for the players, but for the spectators. Sharkey had often heard Jennie say, "I learn from my guests." Well, he had learned something that day: younger guests enjoyed competitive sports, older guests enjoyed being spectators. He went into a huddle with Harry and in quick order, a baseball diamond was laid out, additional handball courts constructed, and a basketball court added.

In the Twenties, as today, many of the summer employes were college students trying to make enough money to help them through the next college year. Some of these were athletes. It wasn't long before they formed baseball and basketball teams.

Abe Sharkey got in touch with other camps and hotels which had teams and worked out a schedule pitting the Grossinger stalwarts against theirs. Because the Grossinger players easily defeated the other resort establishments, Sharkey invited a quintet from the City College of New York to visit the hotel and play his boys. CCNY was just beginning to be a real power in the world of basketball, but to everyone's amazement (including Sharkey's) the hotel team defeated the invaders from the big city.

Sharkey was too smart to concentrate exclusively on competitive sports for husky young college athletes. His main concern was the average guest whose most strenuous physical exercise was the three-times-a-day round trip from lobby to dining room. So he inaugurated his early-bird club. Members hiked to the recently acquired lake at seven-thirty each morning for a pre-breakfast swim. When they returned to the hotel, Sharkey put them through fifteen minutes of brisk calisthenics. By nine, they were ravenous and breakfast tasted better. Before lunch, Sharkey organized hikes through the woods. Once you marched two hundred yards from the hotel grounds, you were in cool woodland with many varieties of birds to be identified and where, occasionally, a startled deer would flash across your vision. Campfires, community sings, and "game nights" were other Sharkey specialties.

By now, the hotel stationery bore the legend, "The Grossinger—Kingdom of Outdoor Happiness." It was a proud boast, but the lake, athletic contests, hikes, and other outdoor activities justified it.

While the great outdoors was Abe Sharkey's domain, Jennie herself was constantly concerned about shy or lonely female guests. She confided her anxiety to Freddie Weitzner who usually had an answer for everything.

"I have a positively foolproof system," he declared. "Would you like to know how I can tell if a girl is shy or lonely or unhappy?"

"Maybe you just look at them," Jennie responded, "and you can tell."

"No, no. They've got pride. They wouldn't show it on their faces and they wouldn't tell you. Do girls sometimes complain about their rooms or the food?"

"Sometimes," Jennie admitted.

"So," Freddie said triumphantly. "Beneath these complaints is really disappointment, because they aren't getting enough male attention. You just give me the names of girls who have complained about anything these past few days and I'll take care of matters."

Jennie and Evelyn gave him a list of the girls who had made complaints. Freddie went into a huddle with the headwaiter. He found where each girl sat in the dining room and which guests shared her table. Often, there wasn't an unattached male at the table. That night there was. Freddie arranged for the most attractive male staff members to sit next to the girls he diagnosed as shy and lonely. He gave the young men their orders and they rose to the occasion nobly.

Each of the men asked the girl to whom he was assigned for the first dance after dinner. When the music began the girls were first on the dance floor. Then the staff members, according to plan, would switch to other girls, rotating from one to another.

The regular male guests couldn't help noticing that these girls were being enthusiastically rushed by the college boys on the staff. They began to think they may have underrated the girls—or perhaps the college kids "knew something." Now it was they who asked the girls to dance and the girls, more confident, chatted easily with their new partners and friends.

This brand of involuntary staff gallantry was the inevitable result of the unfailing over-abundance of female guests—many of whom were not especially favored by the Almighty when it came to handing out good looks. The social and athletic lads also recruited allies among the waiters, bellhops and busboys who were often hired as much for their social and terpsichorean capabilities as for their service skills. "Dance only with the ugly girls," was the rigidly enforced rule.

Freddie's system was, indeed, foolproof. After starting the practice of law he returned to the hotel for a vacation. Jennie told him two attractive girls who had reservations for two weeks were going to check out the next day.

"Leave it to Dr. Weitzner," he said with confidence.

That night he briefed three staff members on the way his operation worked. He would even join them, he said, entertaining the girls. The system worked perfectly. It worked so well that both girls stopped at the desk to say that they had changed their minds and would stay for the full two weeks. The system worked on its creator, too. Freddie was smitten with one of the girls. Three months later, they were married. That same season, prematurely bald Abe Sharkey met a pretty young guest named Rhoda. He, too, soon walked down the aisle.

Chapter 10

In the Twenties, doctors in New York City were regularly prescribing fresh air and quiet for convalescent patients. If you had minor respiratory ailments or were run down after an operation, they often suggested the Catskills, and Grossinger's welcomed its share of health seekers. Many were attracted by the altitude of the hotel, the absence of mosquitoes and the moderate rates.

One visitor who came to recuperate from an operation and who remained to become one of the most imaginative cogs in the wheels that made Grossinger's run was Milton Blackstone. An athletic youngster from Jersey City, he was a student at Lehigh University when an acute infection made it imperative that he have extensive dental surgery. His doctor told him that he would have to stay out of college for a semester and suggested he go to the mountains. This was a hard blow to young Blackstone who thought of college mostly in terms of football and basketball. The year before he had scored twenty-one points in Lehigh's victory over the Naval Academy, but his doctor said that walking would be the most vigorous form of exercise he could undertake for some months.

On the recommendation of a friend, Blackstone went to Grossinger's. He did go on hikes every day, but, more significantly, he discovered the basketball court. He wasn't strong enough to play, but he could stand on the foul line and shoot baskets. One day, while dropping in fifteen consecutive baskets, he noticed a pale-looking, shy youngster watching in awe. The boy was Paul Grossinger, recovering from a siege of pneumonia.

This was the beginning of a long-enduring friendship. For a nineteen-year-old, Milton Blackstone was a fairly sophisticated youth. He had worked his way to Europe and had seen Paris and Antwerp and Berlin. Paul was a willing audience for his tales of travel in Europe. It was Regina Grossinger who noticed the camaraderie between them and it was she who suggested that Milton tutor Paul until he was able to return to school. Harry and Jennie liked the idea, and so the college boy became a combination counselor-teacher to the youngest Grossinger.

Still racked by guilt feelings over her failure to spend more time with her son, Jennie felt that the attention he would get from Milton might compensate for what she was unable to give the boy. Paul didn't mind studying history, English and arithmetic, knowing that there would be a session of basketball when school was out. Then Milton bought a football and taught his young charge how to toss spiral passes. Paul soon became adept at this. His enthusiasm was such that he often practiced alone. One morning, he threw one a little too long; it

managed to find a window. Hearing the crash, Pop Grossinger came running.

"Who broke the window?" he demanded angrily.

"Milton and I broke it," Paul answered sturdily, feeling perhaps that if he could share his teacher's knowledge, his teacher could share his blame.

By January, both pupil and teacher were well enough
to return to school. The climate of Bethlehem, Pennsylvania, where Lehigh is located, apparently was not right
for someone recovering from a bad infection. After a
month, Milton had to submit to a second operation.
When his doctor told him he could not go back to
college until the fall, Milton returned to Grossinger's,
this time as an employe. He worked at the front desk.
Using a gift for words, he wrote thirty letters a night to
Grossinger guests who hadn't yet made reservations for
the coming season.

By trial and error, he was learning the fundamentals of
the promotion and advertising business. So naturally did
he adapt himself to the hotel, Jennie and Harry begged
him to remain on a permanent basis. The idea appealed
to Milton, but his family raised strenuous objections.
"We didn't send you to college so you could go to work
in a little country hotel," they remonstrated.

Milton listened, but he was convinced his future lay
with "this little country hotel." He decided to stay on.
His first step was to take a course at the Lewis Hotel
Training School in Washington, D. C. It was an inten-
sive course that took up every phase of staffing, maintaining and advertising a hotel.

As the hotel grew, the number of employes grew, too.

Milton was only one of countless new faces that appeared on the Grossinger landscape. Inadvertently, Selig's strict Orthodoxy caused a minor ruckus when he asked Jennie to advertise for some non-Jewish personnel who could work on the Sabbath. His motives were entirely benevolent.

He was understandably bewildered when a few neighboring hotel owners accused him of anti-Semitism. He explained he wished only to spare Jewish employes from working on the Sabbath. Some of the workers asked Jennie to tell her father that it really didn't matter to them. If they worked at any other Catskill hotel, they would have to work on the Sabbath, anyway, and they would much rather work at Grossinger's. Besides, some of them confessed, they really weren't that Orthodox.

"Don't let Pop advertise for non-Jewish help, Jennie," they pleaded, "or we may all find ourselves out of work."

Jennie re-assured them: "You are all like members of the family, so please, don't worry. You will work here as long as you wish."

In April of 1927, the entire family journeyed to New York for an especially joyous event—the marriage of Little Harry to Flo Goldwasser whom he had met while both were attending the Lexington School for the Deaf.

To mark the occasion, Jennie decided to surprise her mother with a fur coat for the wedding trip. Tingling with excitement, she carried the coat, encased in a huge box, into the kitchen. A broad grin crossed Jennie's face as she opened the elegantly wrapped container. Malke stared at the coat in bewilderment and then began to inspect the rich-looking fur hesitantly. After a few minutes, she turned to Jennie and asked reproachfully,

"Why did you buy this? My winter coat from last year is like new."

"But, Mom," Jennie protested, "that's only a cloth coat with a tiny fur collar. This is a genuine fur coat. It cost four hundred dollars."

Mention of the price brought another dismayed look to the older woman's countenance. She shook her head a few times and said wistfully, "Four hundred dollars. It would have been better to give the money to charity."

Not long after the wedding, Jennie had a long talk with Selig about the future of the newlyweds. Little Harry had returned to the country with his bride and resumed working in the kitchen at a variety of jobs. Smiling and gentle, he was a favorite with both guests and staff who found his unfailing good nature irresistible. By this time, he was able to shape certain sounds and form words with his underdeveloped vocal chords. If one took the time, it was not too difficult to understand what he was saying. For others, he would thoughtfully pull out a little pad he always carried for writing out what he, or they, wished to convey.

Jennie convinced her father that some special provisions should be made for Harry now that he was married and might become a parent. She suggested an endowment insurance policy. Whatever might happen to the Grossingers in the future, he and his new family would be protected. Selig arranged to purchase a $40,000 policy in his son's name which would give Harry $2,400 annually upon maturity. Happily, the sunny financial fates that were to shine on the Grossinger family in succeeding years would make this sum seem trifling, to say the least.

The summer season of 1927 was another highly successful one, particularly in the entertainment department. According to a copy of the July 4, 1927 issue of the *Grossinger Gossip*, social activities for the season "are expertly master-minded by Frank Buchanan and Social Director Ben Silver assisted by Bert Gilbert, formerly of the Hofbrau Restaurant in New York City."

A typical evening schedule for the week as reported in the paper reads: "Monday: Dance Contest; Tuesday: Movies or Guest Amateur Night; Wednesday: Camp Fire; Thursday: Musicale; Friday: Stage Comedy: 'Mr Tittle Drums Along'; Saturday: Original Revue: 'Silhouettes of 1927.' Highlight next week: 'Good News' (straight from Broadway) starring Phil Reed." Listed among the social staff members are dancer Lou Brecher (who later founded the famous Roseland Ballroom) and one Aaron Schachne with the title, "Motion Picture Director."

An article in the same paper reveals that Grossinger's —and Mr. Schachne—were offering a very unique form of guest divertissement in 1927: "At last we have our own D. W. Griffith watching for scenes to shoot with his trusty motion picture camera. Outdoor-lovers take heed! A film is as good as a letter in a breach of promise suit. Aaron has seen service with several prominent film producing firms. He will show the product of his brilliant shooting talents on the screen every Saturday afternoon. Don't miss 'The Grossinger Newsreel' starring YOU the guests."

Later that year, on December 9, 1927, a permanent new guest arrived at Grossinger's, courtesy of Jennie and

Harry. Her name was Elaine Joy Grossinger, and no one cared a bit that she made her debut nearly a month before she was due. Early in December, weeks before her baby was scheduled to arrive, Jennie was troubled by a severe backache. When she phoned Dr. Rongy he counseled her to come to New York the next day. She next called Harry who was in New York and told him what the doctor had said. Alarmed, he said he would meet the train.

It was a bitter cold day when her mother bundled her up in her squirrel coat and put her on the train accompanied by Gertrude, a waitress who had become a close friend. By the time the train reached Middletown, its second stop, a pain-wracked Jennie was tempted to get off and check into the hospital there. But she stayed on and finally reached New York where Harry was waiting. He hurried her to the warmth and comfort of the house jointly occupied by the Mandelbaums and Clara and Harry Kriendler. It was not a comfortable night. At five A.M., Jennie knew that sleep was out of the question. She phoned the doctor, who told her to go immediately to the hospital. Not long afterwards, Dr. Rongy arrived.

"We're going to deliver your baby now, Mrs. Grossinger," he said. "I'll have to give you some anesthetic."

When Jennie came out of the cloudy mists of ether she asked feebly, "Is my baby going to live?"

"Of course," he said. "She is a normal baby and she is beautiful."

When Jennie left the hospital, she was still quite weak. Her dearest friends, Anna and Sol Mandelbaum and Harry and Clara Kriendler, would not permit her to rush back to the country. They insisted she recuperate in the large home the two couples now shared on Madison Avenue in New York City.

Jennie originally consented to stay a single week, but the devoted foursome kept her for twelve, caring for her lavishly. She used to say jokingly: "They almost spoiled me for the hotel business for good. All that fussing. I'm the one used to doing the fussing."

Back in the mountains, a surprise awaited her. For some time she and Harry had spoken of a house of their own. Construction began before she left for New York. During her absence, Harry and his helpers worked feverishly to finish and furnish it. Now it was ready, complete with nursery. Jennie immediately named it the Joy Cottage after her baby's middle name.

While in New York, Jennie had solicited an employment agency for a nurse who would like to live in the country. When a large, matronly woman with excellent references arrived, she hired her instantly. Two days later, a charming, gentle-faced French woman named Martha also applied for the job. She mentioned casually that, in addition to nursing the baby, she would also teach her German and French as she grew older. Jennie liked this quiet woman enormously. She couldn't resist hiring her, too. She found herself with two nurses.

But what would she do with the first nurse? Constitutionally, she was still incapable of discharging anyone. The sticky situation came near resolution a few days later when Jennie heard the child crying hysterically. Hurrying to her crib, she saw Elaine being fed from a bottle too hot to hold. For one of the few times in her life, Jennie lost her temper. Yet, she could not bring herself to hurt the woman, let alone discharge her. Jennie did nothing for a few more days and finally fell back on a white lie. She told nurse No. 1 the family wished Jennie to look after the child personally, so both women would have to leave. To ease matters, and her conscience, she gave the woman a month's additional wages before sending her back to New York.

Mademoiselle Martha now took sole charge of the child and Jennie again immersed herself in the world of the hotel. As the baby grew older, Mlle. Martha taught her knitting, cooking, sewing, German and French. One morning, Jennie slipped into the nursery as Mlle. Martha was putting a stocking on the child's chubby leg.

"*C'est le bas,*" she said, pointing to the stocking. "*C'est le bas.* Stocking."

"*Le bas,*" Elaine repeated, and so did the listening Jennie. She resolved that some day she, too, would learn French.

Still disturbed by her unavoidable neglect of the growing Paul, Jennie vowed to spend more time with her young daughter. Yet the insistent demands of a prospering resort continued to restrict her maternal role. When Jennie began to have sieges of serious illness, her free time for Elaine was reduced even more. Mlle. Martha filled the breach, becoming much more than a governess to the girl. Jennie felt her daughter had come to regard the French woman as her real mother. This thought plunged her into acute fits of depression.

When Elaine was about to enter her teens, a troubled Jennie reluctantly decided she had to discharge the devoted lady. Each time she began to discuss the subject with the governess, however, she was unable to follow through. In her innermost heart, Jennie knew the conflict between career and motherhood should not be blamed on a governess. She kept delaying the unpleasant task. Finally, recognizing that a break would be extremely painful to Elaine, Jennie abandoned the idea. Instead, she resolved more firmly than ever to find more time for her daughter.

With the resolve went a hope that as Elaine matured she would understand that though her mother was busier than most mothers, she had as much concern and love for her children as they did.

As for Mlle. Martha, she was not immune to the aura of romance that seemed to hang over the hotel. One day she and a violinist named Paul Helgesen, playing in the hotel orchestra, slipped away to the local Catholic Church and took their vows. Thenceforth, she was known to the family as Madame Paul. She was to remain part of the Grossinger household for eighteen years, until the day Elaine left home to enter Russel Sage College.

Jennie's thirst for knowledge did not abate during these years. She had a few informal private teachers, but it was not until she became a pupil of her cousin, Jesse Grumette (he spelled his name the French way), that she really entered into the mind-expanding world of literature and poetry. Jesse, who taught English and speech in one of the New York high schools, spent long hours each summer and on weekends teaching her English composition and making her read aloud. Being a bit of an actor, he also enjoyed reading to her, mostly from the classics.

He introduced her to Shakespeare and the glorious realm of English poetry, to the French novelists (Balzac was an early favorite of hers) and to the finer points of grammar and also to the art of what was then called elocution. Slowly, she began to absorb the magnificent language that at first was so alien to her.

About the same time, another kind of drama was taking place on Wall Street. The second half of the third decade of the 20th Century were the heady days when bellhops and busboys were getting rich (on paper, anyway) through the painless device of something called "buying on margin."

Many guests, making large profits from a stock market which seemed unable to go anywhere but up, urged Selig and Harry to plow some of the hotel profits into the market, but neither appeared interested. Brother-in-law Louie Grau, whose children's clothing business had been booming, repeatedly told Jennie to get her father and husband to invest in the market.

"You'll become millionaires," he promised. "Everybody is getting rich. Don't be crazy and bury your money in the bank."

"It's too much like gambling, Louie," Jennie said. "I wouldn't feel comfortable making money we didn't work for. Poppa and Momma feel the same. We would all rather put whatever money we can make back into the hotel."

Yet the pressures to invest in the stock market were unrelenting. As one slogan of those surrealistic days put it: "Buy, buy, buy. Selling stock is selling America short." Jennie, herself, was sorely tempted one crowded weekend when a haughty-looking woman came to check in without a reservation. Jennie knew she would not be able to please this fine lady. When the imperious woman insisted she be shown "something," Jennie asked a bell-boy to take her to a small, unpretentious room—the only one available—in the Main House.

In a few minutes, the woman came storming back to the desk and in a loud, angry voice, audible throughout the lobby, proceeded to berate Jennie: "How dare you send me to such a place? I wouldn't put one of my servants in that hole you have the nerve to call a room!"

Jennie attempted to reason with her for a second or two—and then rushed away from the desk in tears and embarrassment.

Louie Grau, who witnessed the entire episode, seemed to take it as a cue to renew his stock market campaign. "See, what did I tell you? If you listened to me, you wouldn't have to listen to anyone like that. You'd be making so much money you could afford to build a palace with the profits and tell someone like her to go to hell."

For a moment, Jennie was almost moved to agree with Louie, but she held firm. In her heart she knew no matter what he said that gambling was never a sure thing. The money they made should be used for new facilities and improvements, things that would endure and add prestige to the hotel.

Louis shrugged his shoulders. The hotel did exceptionally good business during the opening weeks of the 1929 summer season. In late July of that year, Selig and Harry found they actually had $10,000 in cash on hand.

"Let's put it in the bank, Harry," Selig said, and Harry nodded agreement.

They made the long trip from Ferndale to the Bank of America on Delancy Street in the East Side to deposit the money. Less than three months later, Jennie ran to her father with a copy of *The New York Times*. The big black headlines told the bleak story of the Wall Street collapse. It was October 29, 1929, "Black Tuesday." The greatest selling wave in history touched off a panic that would, almost overnight, destroy $30 billion dollars in paper wealth.

"You see, Jennie, you were right all the time," he said.

"You know, Poppa, I never liked gambling," she answered.

Though the beauty of the snow-covered countryside during the winter months had always delighted Jennie and proved a magnet for moderate-sized crowds during the Christmas and *Chanukah* holidays, the idea of the hotel as a winter resort was still remote. During the holidays some guests brought skates with them, cleaned snow from a small pond on the grounds or the larger lake and slid and slipped over the smooth surface. Others bought sleds in Liberty and coasted down the hills in back of the hotel. The term "winter sports" was virtually unknown in the Catskills, but the obvious enjoyment shared by these daring adventurers started Jennie thinking.

"You know," she said to Abe Sharkey, "we have to stay open all winter. Suppose we advertised that we could give our guests skating and sleighing. Do you think we could attract people?"

"We might" Abe said. "Lake Placid does well as a winter resort. So does Lakewood."

"If you could only take a year off to supervise our winter activities," Jennie said hopefully.

"Maybe I could," Abe Sharkey said.

The following year he was granted a sabbatical leave by the New York City public school system and helped launch Grossinger's as a winter resort.

Jennie had a hand in everything that went on at Grossinger's—and that everything ranged from planning menus to acting as personnel manager. She did most of the hiring. She also took care of what more sophisticated employers know as "labor relations," which Jennie simply called "keeping peace in the family." With her talent for soothing ruffled feelings, peacemaker Jennie was the mediator in uncounted disputes between members of the staff. ("Call Jennie—and let her decide!")

Jennie had never forgotten her visit to Laurel-in-the-Pines in Lakewood. In 1929, she hired a well-recommended professional head waiter, Leon Hirsch, obtained through an employment agency. She was delighted to discover he was the same gentleman who had catered her wedding on the Lower East Side back in 1912. When Jennie saw Mr. Hirsch make his first appearance dressed in a splendid tuxedo, she said, half in jest: "Leon, you're too grand looking to be an ordinary head waiter. We'll call you the maitre d'hotel."

Urbane in manner, he took Jennie's words seriously. Within a week, he had a list of suggestions. Guests should be offered menus with a choice of entrées. Until now, they all took the same appetizer, the same entrée, and the same dessert—family-style service it was called. Jennie liked the idea, and now, each day, menus were mimeographed by one of the office girls.

"They still order the same things you've always given them," Hirsh said, "but they take the menus home for souvenirs. That's good advertising and it's much classier."

The new headwaiter had two great enthusiasms: the dining room and his four-year-old granddaughter. He would talk for hours about the youngster's gift for singing. He was very proud.

"How can you tell if a four-year-old girl can sing well?" Jennie asked.

"Some day you'll see her name up in lights, Jennie," he said defensively.

(He proved to be a wise prophet. If you pass the Metropolitan Opera House today, you'll often see her name prominently displayed, a name any opera buff will instantly recognize—Roberta Peters.)

Leon Hirsch had a tireless aide-de-camp in Abe Friedman. From the time he was first hired as an inexperienced busboy, Abe had been a special favorite of Jennie's. She took an immediate liking to the earnest young man who thought nothing of working twelve and fourteen hours a day. He was usually the first to arrive in the dining room each morning and the last to leave at night. When Abe began courting Harry's youngest sister, Rose, a pretty, fresh-faced girl who frequently helped out with the housekeeping, Jennie and Harry were pleased. When it came to his many sisters, the protective Harry took to the role of matchmaker with zest and determination. A few years earlier, he had given a boost to the marriage of Regina, his eldest sister, to a rising young lawyer from Jersey City named Meyer Pesin.

It wasn't long before Harry arranged to take Abe on a trip to Chicago, ostensibly for sight-seeing, but in truth to meet his (and Rose's) parents, Leah and Isa. Events moved swiftly after that. On a sunless day in January of 1930, Abe and Rose were united under the *chupah*, with the entire Grossinger family from both New York and Chicago on hand. The newlyweds were to leave that evening for their honeymoon at the Laurel-in-the-Pines, when a heavy snowfall late in the afternoon made all roads impassable.

"We can't go tonight," the nervous bridegroom announced apologetically to his wife. "We'll remain overnight and start in the morning."

Without another word, Abe escorted Rose to the Winter Cottage where she had been staying with her parents. When Isa Grossinger saw his new son-in-law and realized he was leaving his daughter behind, the pious gentleman shook his head disapprovingly and looked very dour. He took Abe aside and said sternly, in Yiddish: *"Mir tur nicht!"* ("It is not allowed!") For, indeed, it was a rigid precept of Orthodox Judaism that the newly married had to consummate their union on the very first night.

"I know," Abe stammered, his voice barely audible. "We wanted to leave tonight, but the roads are terrible and there are no empty rooms left. The wedding guests took everything!" Embarrassed and confused, the bridegroom raced back through the snow to the tiny room above the laundry he shared with a room clerk. His still-innocent bride, alas, spent her wedding night with no husband and two very distraught parents!

With an elegant maitre d' like Leon Hirsch in command of the dining room, other departments at the hotel had to keep step with the new Grossinger image. Uniformed bellmen were formally introduced around the end of the decade. Bossing the crew of eight college boys was Benny Reingold who was immediately given the grandiose title of "Superintendent of Service." Until then, the bellhops had worked in tee shirts and shorts. With official uniforms, Benny insisted upon a little spit-and-polish in manner and appearance. Seeing one of the newly caparisoned baggage-toters, a slightly startled older guest commented brightly: "Fancy-schmancy! Jennie, you're beginning to look like a real classy hotel."

Grossinger's had now reached the stage in its development when certain facilities began to loom as absolute necessities. A man named Michael Chernow and an unknown girl were to become the godparents of the first eighteen-hole golf course ever laid out in the Catskills resort.

Chernow checked into the hotel one afternoon complete with a rifle and a set of golf clubs. Soon he and Milton Blackstone were discussing college sports in general and hunting and golf in particular. Like Milton, he had been an athlete at college, but now that he was out in the business world, he found the only sports that were practical were those in which he could indulge alone.

"Even if I can't find a foursome or even another player," he said, "I can always enjoy a round of golf."

"Our guests are welcome at a country club in Liberty, you know," Milton countered.

Chernow nodded. "I know. But it's still a nuisance to get there and you always feel like an outsider. You should have a course here at Grossinger's."

A day or so later, Jennie returned from a trip to New York with upsetting news. She had seen a former guest on the train. The girl had a golf bag tied to her luggage and left the train at Fallsburgh—the station before Ferndale. Jennie watched from the train as she climbed into a station wagon owned by the Flagler Hotel which had a nine-hole golf course.

"That nice girl has been coming here for eight years," Jennie said unhappily. "How many more will leave us because we have no golf course?"

"So, let's build one," Milton said.

The inevitable family council was called. Although Selig and Malke were a bit puzzled over people who wanted to walk around the country hitting a little white ball, they agreed if Harry and Jennie really wanted a golf course, they should have it. The problem of additional land was easily solved. Because the adjacent Lakeside Hotel was not doing well, the owners were glad to sell some of their property to Selig. Selig ordered heavy machinery from Pennsylvania and he and Harry began to clear the site. With the help of a local golf pro, who said he was also an amateur golf course architect, the beginnings of a fairway were laid out.

As the work progressed, it became apparent to Milton and Harry that this was not shaping up like any course they had ever seen. Before they could make a formal protest, the self-styled "architect" mysteriously departed.

Milton decided to write to the United States Golf Association to ask it to recommend a man who could build a golf course. Within days, a short, sturdy young man named Andy Salerno appeared. He announced he could certainly build a golf course, but he could not design one. This was a job for a specially trained professional. He added there were no more than a dozen really good golf architects in the world.

"Who is the best?" Jennie asked.

"A. W. Tillinghast," Andy said. "He designed Fresh Meadows, Winged Foot, the beautiful Baltusrol course, and a number of others."

"See, if you can get him for us, Milton," Jennie urged.

Not many golf courses were being built in 1930. Even the construction of a miniature layout would have taxed the financial resources of most resort hotels. Demands for the specialized talents of Mr. Tillinghast were at an absolute minimum. The architect wasted no time getting to the Catskills, surveyed the completed nine-hole layout with a pained expression, and then quickly toured the rest of the property.

By a happy coincidence, the terrain was perfect for the construction of a course. Mr. Tillinghast tested the soil —it would grow the kind of seed that would produce crisp fairways and velvety greens—and went to his drawing board. It wasn't long before Andy Salerno's men were exploding dynamite charges, building sand traps, and finding wells to irrigate what would be thirsty fairways. Within a few weeks, the outline of a links began to appear.

The eighteen-hole course was opened in 1931. There were those who thought that Selig was just a bit *meshugah* (crazy) sinking so much money into a golf course in the midst of the Depression. But, as yet, the hotel hadn't felt its full impact. Providentially, the $10,000 Selig and Harry had the foresight not to invest in the stock market provided the initial capital needed to construct the course. Their wisdom and vision in building the links soon became apparent. Many who had formerly enjoyed expensive European vacations couldn't afford that luxury now, but they could afford a Catskill holiday.

The golf course was, in a very real sense, a milestone in the hotel's development, for it marked the transition from a successful medium-sized family enterprise into the realm of a luxury hotel. The effect the wondrous new facility had on everyone was overwhelming.

An elated Jennie said to Selig as she traipsed around the course: "Poppa, I'm so happy, I'm walking on air. Who would ever believe the Grossingers from the Lower East Side would ever own their own golf course? It's another miracle!"

"An American miracle," the old gentleman added softly.

Work continued to be a mania with Selig Grossinger. Rain or shine, he met the trains from New York. Sometimes, there were more hotel representatives at the station than there were passengers on the train, and they all fought for the prospective customers. They shouted the special virtues of the hotel or boarding house they represented, often engaging in sleeve-tugging contests. But not Pop Grossinger. He stood quietly at the side of his Hupmobile (which had replaced the Ford) waiting for guests who had reservations at Grossinger's. He knew nearly all of them by sight and would take their heavy bags (and golf clubs now) and strap them to the top of the car. No matter how old these guests were, he always called them "my boys and girls."

Jennie pleaded with him to let someone else meet the trains, but he was adamant. "Jennie, how would my boys and girls feel if they stepped off the train and Pop wasn't there to greet them?"

"At least take someone else to handle the heavy baggage," she begged.

"So, I carry their bags." He shrugged his broad shoulders. "It's nothing, really."

His refusal to solicit guests, even when the family was struggling at Longbrook House, had not gone unnoticed by his fellow hotel-owners. Jack Feldman, the highly respected owner of the neighboring Queen Mountain House, who was to become the first Jewish deputy sheriff of Sullivan County, suggested that an association of hotel owners be formed. The association could draw up a code of conduct designed to eliminate the marketplace hassles and unseemly jockeying for uncommitted guests at the Ferndale station. Other hotelmen agreed. The association was duly organized with Feldman as its first president and Selig Grossinger as vice-president. Markers were placed along the railroad platform with the names of the various hotels and drivers parked their cars or horse-drawn carriages beside them. The days of bickering and sleeve-tugging were over.

Pop did not like to delegate authority. If there was a job to be done on the grounds or the golf course he preferred to do it himself. Rain or sleet storms meant nothing to a man who had known the fierce winters of the Carpathians. Late one December afternoon when a chill rain was slanting down, Jennie noticed him working with a construction gang.

"Come home, Poppa," she said uneasily. "You're wet and chilled. "Go to bed and I'll fix you some hot tea."

"I'm all right, Jennie," he said, but his voice was

hoarse. She persuaded him to drive back to the hotel. In bed, he swallowed some hot tea. Then Jennie told Sam Mendel, the hotel butcher and expert in the ancient art of *bankes*, to apply his skill to her father. Mendel applied several heated glass cups to Selig's back to draw and circulate the blood. Selig soon felt a little better. Jennie waited until he fell asleep and then tip-toed out of his room.

The next morning was bleak and cold, but, unknown to both Jennie and Malke, Selig arose as usual and went to meet the early train. It was Friday and many of his "boys and girls" were expected. Later that day, he confided to Jennie (not wishing to alarm his wife) that he had actually been embarrassed at the station.

"My back hurt so," he said, as though ashamed of the weakness of his strong body, "some friends had to help me back into the car."

"Please go to bed now, Poppa," Jennie pleaded. She was shocked, because she had never heard him confess a weakness or admit pain.

"My child," he said pleadingly, "this is the Sabbath. A family should be together for the Sabbath meal."

At dinner, the waiter set a platter of potted meatballs before her father. Jennie suggested they might be too heavy for a person who wasn't feeling well. "Why not have a piece of chicken—some white meat—instead?"

"My child," he said with a smile, "you know how I love Momma's meatballs. You worry too much about me and aren't eating enough yourself."

The next morning from behind the desk, Jennie saw her father pass on his way to Sabbath services in Liberty. His face was flushed, but when she asked him to go back to bed he merely smiled and continued on. Later she went to the kitchen where Anna, her mother's assistant, remarked that Selig had been in early inspecting every corner of the kitchen, something he seldom did. That morning, he inspected areas of the hotel he had not visited in years, as if taking a careful inventory.

Meeting Evelyn Brown in the lobby, he said to her pensively, "You know, Evelyn, I believe that God doesn't want me to be here any more." Before she could answer, he walked on.

Deeply disquieted, Jennie went directly to the cottage where her parents lived. Dr. Dworetsky, a Liberty physician, was just leaving the house. He said that he had been called by Malke.

"It's nothing to worry about," he said. "Your father has the grippe. We'll take good care of him." Jennie was relieved. The grippe was something everyone contracted soon or later; it was no worse than a heavy cold.

The following morning, he seemed weaker. Without saying anything to anybody, Jennie sent for a nurse. About noon, the nurse told her his fever had gone down.

Jennie's spirits soared. "Momma," she said, hugging her mother "the crisis must be over. Poppa will get well now." A relieved Jennie went back to the front desk and was soon absorbed in the hectic Sunday routine of checking guests out and greeting new arrivals. That same evening, Lottie, now living in Brooklyn with her family, arrived. She had learned of Pop's illness in a phone call from Jennie the previous night.

"I know he'll be all right," she told Jennie, "but I'll feel better being here."

As they entered their parents' cottage, they saw two

men wheeling a tank of oxygen into their father's room. Jennie realized at once something was terribly wrong. Her heart pounded as she ran to find the nurse. "Tell me the truth," she demanded. "How is my father?"

"If he were my father," the nurse said, "I would get the best doctor in the world."

To Jennie, there was only one doctor—Dr. Emanuel Singer. Rushing to a telephone, she was informed the doctor was spending the weekend in New York with friends.

That evening, Jennie stood fixed at the window late into the night praying that the doctor would arrive. But not until the next morning did he return from the city.

Without a word, he went into Selig's room. A half-hour later he emerged, shaking his head gravely.

"It isn't good, Jennie," he whispered. "Pop is very sick."

"You've got to make him better," she said imploringly.

The old man heard her voice and called to Dr. Singer. "Make Jennie go to bed. She needs her rest."

Only after Dr. Singer gave Jennie a sedative was she able to slip into a troubled sleep. The doctor himself stayed in the room next to Selig's that night.

It was still dark when a hand on her arm awoke Jennie from her drugged sleep. Abe Friedman whispered, "Come, Jennie. Pop is asking for you." She frantically put on a robe and ran to her father's room. Dr. Singer was standing inside, deep in thought.

"Is there any hope for my father?" she asked in a trembling voice.

"Yes," he said quietly.

She went into the room. Selig opened his eyes and smiled. The doctor's one word and the smile on her father's tired face gave her the reassurance she so desperately needed. Dr. Singer then gently said, "I think it would be best for you to go now. Pop must conserve every bit of energy."

She pressed her lips against her father's hand and said in a desperate voice, "Fight, Poppa, fight." The dying man framed an answer on his lips, but no words came. Yet, Jennie would not admit to herself that her father might die. She clung fiercely to any straw of hope. As long as he was breathing, she told herself, somehow, this gallant man would survive.

Pop Grossinger lingered on through the night and into the next morning. At noon, faintly hearing the familiar cow bell summoning the staff to lunch, he beckoned the faithful Abe Friedman to come closer and whispered feebly, "Abie, make sure everybody eats." At one o'clock on the afternoon of December 8, 1931, the old gentleman breathed his last.

Seconds later, Lottie's shrieking voice pierced the silent room. Jennie did not utter a sound, did not cry, did not open her mouth. All her emotions seemed frozen.

"You said there was hope for Poppa," she said accusingly to Dr. Singer.

He nodded. "Always, when there is life, there is hope," he said quietly.

Mom Grossinger was dry-eyed through the hours that followed. As always, she accepted the will of God.

Selig was buried in the family plot at Long Island's Mount Hebron Cemetery. Just before his casket was lowered into the grave, Malke tipped the contents of a bulging pillowcase she had brought from the mountains into the open grave. Sod from Israel and a cloud of crumpled slips of paper—receipts from individuals and organizations who had sought and been given Selig's charity—fluttered into the grave. She wanted her husband to have these signs of his goodness when he went to his final rest. As Jennie's father's casket was lowered into place, she suddenly turned away. She could not bear to watch.

There were many who wanted to testify to the unobtrusive goodness of Pop Grossinger. One man, a stranger to the family, raised his voice and intoned in Yiddish, "The Depression hurt us badly for we were new in Ferndale and no one would give me a job. Just when things were at their worst, we found a large box of food on our porch. The same thing happened the next week and the next and every week. From whom? We didn't know. It seemed that the food came from a messenger of God. We got up early one morning hoping to see our unknown benefactor. We heard a car stop in front of our house. We saw a tall man with a thin beard carry a big box from the car to our porch. We had never met him, but we knew who he was. He didn't want us to know lest we feel ashamed. But now the whole world should know what kind of a man was Selig Grossinger."

One mourner recalled that Selig loved to tell the story of Rabbi Hillel, a celebrated sage of pre-Christian days, who was challenged by an idolator to explain the meaning of Judaism in the brief time the questioner could stand on one foot. The learned rabbi is said to have replied: "What is hateful to thee, do not do unto thy fellowman. This is the whole law. The rest is mere commentary." No one lived closer to that precept than the man who was laid to rest that chill December day in 1931.

The family returned to the hotel for the traditional week of mourning. As they sat *shiva* (seven days of mourning), they heard many stories of the anonymous acts of charity Selig had performed. Andy Salerno told how Pop Grossinger would stack five or six large cartons with canned goods, meat, milk, butter, cheese, bread and vegetables each Friday morning at seven A.M. With Andy's help, these would be stowed in the Hupmobile and off the two would go. Andy said that usually Pop would drive down unfamiliar rocky back roads and stop at rundown farms. He would merely say, "Please, Andy, put a box on the porch." And then they would go on to the next port of call. Andy never knew how Selig found out who in the neighborhood was in need, but he did.

Selig had one faithful visitor each spring, a huge Negro hobo he and the dining room staff knew only as Sam. Sam rode the freight to Ferndale and then would walk to the hotel. The ritual never varied.

"You eat today, Sam?" Pop would ask.

Sam would grin. "No, sir."

"Come on in, I will feed you."

He would lead this giant of a man to a table and tell a waiter to bring plenty of meat, potatoes, gravy and bread. When Sam had about finished, he would ask Abe Friedman to fill a box with food for Sam to carry away with him. When the man, his appetite sated, was about to leave, Pop would give him a five-dollar bill, shake his hand, and say cheerfully, "Good luck, I'll see you next year."

Men of all faiths in the town of Liberty mourned the old gentleman. Those who had done business with Selig over the years came to join the family in its time of bereavement. And, finally, the tears that Jennie had been unable to shed flowed. But they assuaged her grief only slightly.

Good friends urged her to accept the traditional Orthodox Hebrew philosophy, *Baruch dayan emes* (Blessed by Thy judgment). Jennie's mind accepted this, but her heart for a long time refused the comforting philosophy. Her relationship with Selig had been rare. First, she had adored him as a father. Then, during the long years when her mother was in Europe with Lottie and young Harry, she had cared for and nursed him in his illness. Because he was so dependent upon her, she regarded him with the protective feeling of a parent. They had never been separated since the day she arrived in America.

When Jennie's blood pressure rose to an alarming degree, she was confined in Mount Sinai Hospital. Dr. Phineas Bernstein, employed at the hotel as a riding instructor while attending medical school and now a young gynecologist on the hospital staff, sought her out at the suggestion of the family.

He admonished her: "The nurses say that you cry almost continuously. If you go on like this, your condition will only worsen. Uncontrolled grief can be a disease. It is the last thing your father would wish for you."

"But I was never prepared. I was never warned he would die," Jennie argued.

"There is only one great physician—God," the doctor told her solemnly. "We doctors are merely human.

While Pop breathed, there was always a chance that a miracle might happen. Unfortunately, it did not."

Jennie left Mt. Sinai, but her depression persisted. Dr. Bernstein continued to see her.

Whenever he found her crying or depressed, he would speak to her sympathetically, but firmly. He tried to make her see the damage she was doing to her health— both physical and mental—and the futility of her protracted grief. He employed logic, sternness, cajolery, empathy, tenderness, and every other device at his command. Ultimately, he was able to reach her where so many others had failed until one day her tears stopped completely.

It was a little over three years since her father had died.

Chapter 11

When the Eighteenth Amendment was repealed, many hotels in the mountains applied for liquor licenses. The Grossinger family hesitated. Neither Jennie nor Malke had ever tasted anything alcoholic beyond the sweet wine they sipped during Passover and a Sabbath meal or at a *bar mitzvah* or wedding party. They knew that most of their older guests had the same temperate habits. Harry Grossinger, too, was a confirmed teetotaler. After much deliberation, they agreed that since the sons and daughters of their original guests were now coming in increasing numbers, they were obliged to put in a bar. Steve Kriendler, who had held a variety of jobs at the hotel since 1919, was selected to run the new watering spot in the Main House. He was promptly dispatched to New York for a three-week crash course to learn the business from his cousins, Jack and Mack, at the flourishing restaurant they ran at 21 West 52nd Street.

On the evening the bar first opened, many of the older guests, whose imbibing habits were like those of the

Grossinger family, cautiously tried such drinks as martinis, whiskey sours, and Manhattans. After one or two of these concoctions, they blinked a few times and made their shaky way to bed. They would never be drinkers; it was not in the Old World tradition to down fancy mixed drinks.

Despite the new bar and other modern facilities, as the Depression intensified, guests began to curtail the length of their stays. Rates were adjusted downward to meet the deflationary trends. Many families, long-time guests wiped out by Wall Street reverses, were told by Jennie they would not have to pay until "things got better." Nobody at Grossinger's was panicky though the business was barely breaking even. It was a period of retrenchment everywhere.

Not all of the hotels in the mountains managed to stay afloat. Mortgage foreclosures and bankruptcies were commonplace. One of the ways that some desperate owners elected to cope with economic strangulation did not exactly delight the hard-pressed insurance firms that protected many of the resort properties. Fires of suspicious or "unknown" origin became a regular occurrence in the post-1929 era. Even when a fire was legitimate— and many of the structures in those days were tinder boxes—everyone assumed automatically that it was a way out for a failing establishment—especially so since these fires always seemed to ignite immediately after the season when buildings were empty and bills were pressing. A popular joke of the time involved two mournful-looking hotel owners who meet accidently in town. The first one says with some concern: "Hello, Max. I hear you had a bad fire." Max quickly raises his finger to his lips, shakes his head, and whispers furtively. "Shhh. It's not till next week."

Grossinger's was just managing to get by when Jennie received a letter which at first amused, but later alarmed, her. It came from a restaurant equipment dealer with whom the family had done business for years. It read, "Dear Mrs. Grossinger: We have had numerous letters asking us what we know about the Grossinger family having gone into bankruptcy. We are replying with the following note: 'The Grossingers have always paid their bills on time. But this year they have paid their bills ahead of time.' May we continue to be of service?"

Harry, Jennie and Dave Kriendler laughed at the letter and Jennie wrote to the man thanking him for his thoughtfulness. A week later one of the staff paid a visit to a nearby adult camp and returned considerably agitated. "Jennie," he said in worried tones, "Someone has deliberately started a rumor that we are going bankrupt and it's spread like fire all through the mountains. By now it's being heard in New York and Philadelphia and New Jersey. I met several old guests of ours at the camp who told me frankly, they didn't come back because they had heard the news and were convinced Grossinger's was going out of business."

Each day's mail brought additional evidence that the rumor had been so widely circulated that in the minds of hundreds of former guests it was an established fact. One friend wrote that someone told her he actually saw a sign reading "Closed" across the front door. Another wrote saying that a friend of hers had been at the hotel the day the sheriff had moved in to foreclose the property. A third wrote that he met someone from the mountains who had seen the Grossinger name signed to a bank-ruptcy petition in federal court. Chasing these rumors and pinning them down was like chasing a butterfly. They seemed to come from all directions. The decline in reservations showed they were having a serious effect on business. Veteran guest Harry Goldblatt, sitting in the dining room, heard someone at the same table say. "Why, the food is as good as ever. But what a shame the hotel had to go into bankruptcy!"

Goldblatt looked up and said wryly, "Madam, I can tell you for sure that there is no truth in that at all. And if it were true, I'd be the first to know. I happen to be the Grossinger accountant."

At first, everyone hoped the canard would quietly go away, since the hotel was operating normally. They soon found that an ostrich-like defense was useless against the insistent sniping of gossips. Jennie and Harry decided to face it openly. The hotel had a list of nearly ten thousand names of regular and prospective guests. Cards were printed and mailed saying: "There is a rumor about that Grossinger's has gone bankrupt. Please pay no attention to it. There is absolutely no truth to it. We are open as always and look forward to welcoming you on your next visit."

Old guests, knowing the reputation for truthfulness enjoyed by the Grossingers, were convinced, but there were still hundreds of skeptics. Often one would come to the hotel and some time during his stay would say confidentially to Jennie, "Come on, you can tell me the truth. There's no disgrace about going into bankruptcy these days."

Jennie would reply wearily, "Phone Dun and Bradstreet and ask for our credit rating."

For a long time, it never occurred to anyone on the staff that the rumors had been mischievously planted. Finally, incontrovertible evidence came from friends indignant enough to trace the rumors to their source. They had been instigated by a small rival establishment, badly hit by the Depression, that was trying to woo regular Grossinger visitors. "Mr. Gordon," the owner, was the only hotel-keeper in the mountains who had always been hostile toward the Grossinger enterprise. Now Harry and Jennie recalled the many times their patience had been tried by "Mr. Gordon."

There was, for instance, the matter of the casino, now called the Playhouse, where all evening entertainment took place. Guests often complained that even on slow weeks the Playhouse was overcrowded. There were never enough seats to go around. Jennie couldn't understand this until one evening she stood near the entrance watching the parade of vacationers enter the theater. She recognized all her regular guests, but there were also many unfamiliar faces. Where did all the strangers come from?

"We're staying at Gordon's," they said. "He told us that he had made an arrangement with Mrs. Grossinger for us to use her facilities anytime, including the Playhouse."

"Let's not make a big *tzimmes* [to-do] about it," Harry said unhappily. But when the devious gentleman's guests showed up to rent the horses and use the golf course, tennis courts, and lake, even Harry lost his patience. "Next thing you know, he said, "he'll put up a sign on Route 17 saying "Come to Gordon's—use Grossinger's facilities." Harry came close to the truth. A large sign did appear: "GORDON'S HOTEL—ENJOY GOLF, TENNIS, LAKE SWIMMING, RIDING, and BROADWAY SHOWS."

This, then, was the man who had so industriously planted the rumors of bankruptcy. His invidious tactics were no longer to be taken lightly. Upon investigation, it developed that "Mr. Gordon" was in serious financial straits and wanted to sell. He would consider almost any buyer except the Grossingers. An old friend and regular guest finally entered the picture as a middleman and arranged for the sale. It took a week for the friend to acquire the property and then re-sell to Harry. The little war of Sullivan County was over. It was the only time that a neighboring hotel-owner ever carried on a mean-spirited feud with the Grossinger family.

Some two decades later, in the early 1950's, the bankruptcy episode was to have a curious reprise with the widespread circulation of a rumor that Grossinger's had been sold to the Barton's Candy Company, a large chain of Eastern retail candy shops. The story, fueled by seemingly authoritative items in several Broadway columns, spread rapidly. Again, the family was bombarded with mail and telephone inquiries from every section of the country.

"Who cares," wrote one newspaperman, "if the Waldorf-Astoria changes hands? But when a rumor gets around that Grossinger's is on the block, people everywhere start worrying. They seem to take a proprietory interest in the place—even total strangers."

Unable to squelch the canard completely, the entire Grossinger family once again signed their names to a joint statement front-paged in the *Grossinger News*, the hotel house organ, and mailed it to every guest on its mailing list—by then, more than seventy-five thousand names. It ended with this pledge: "As long as any member of the Grossinger family signing this statement is alive, Grossinger's will never be sold."

In the early Twenties, entertainment at Grossinger's was often provided by employes who doubled as bell-boys, busboys, waiters and waitresses. By the Thirties, however, Jennie decided to engage professional entertainers who would not be obliged to perform side jobs. She arranged to hire Don Hartman, a promising young Broadway actor and director, to head the hotel's first all-professional social staff. Hartman, who arrived with his attractive wife, Chick, had a unique talent for scrounging up theatrical supplies and equipment at low cost. When the Playhouse needed new sets or curtains, he would hurry to the Danziger Supply House to price their wares. If he found them too expensive for his anemic budget, he would try Cain's Warehouse, grave-yard for sets used in Broadway plays that had flopped. Usually he wound up at an establishment on West 55th Street run by I. Arthur Ganger, specializing in equipment abandoned by impecunious nightclub owners, who often found it easier to walk away from their cellars than to face unpaid bills. Ganger sold cheap and usually accepted a 25 percent down payment.

If Hartman wanted actors, he had only to pull up in front of the Palace Theater in a truck and mention "room and board." In ten minutes, the truck would be bulging. None may have heard of Grossinger's; few had even heard of the Catskills, but all were acquainted with hunger, an unattractive condition chronic in the acting professon. Girls who once had visions of playing

Lady Macbeth or Medea didn't mind playing in a chorus line as long as that all-important "room and board" was guaranteed.

If Hartman needed comics, he would drop into the I & Y All-Night Cigar Store off Times Square, patronized by the out-of-work nightclub and burlesque performers. You could hire comics by the pound in I & Y's during those years, and because they didn't eat much, they didn't weigh much. When this strange new breed arrived at the hotel, Jennie was a bit worried. Real actors? Night-club entertainers? Actresses? Would they be carousers and drunkards?

Not only did they work hard, but to Jennie's surprise many of them were Jewish, the sons and daughters of Orthodox parents. Jennie and Malke would beam when they saw a generous sprinkling of them at Sabbath services. Most were young, many had been brought up on the Lower East Side, in Brooklyn, or in the Bronx. They fitted in perfectly at Grossinger's once they overcame their initial distrust of such four-legged menaces as cows and horses.

Don Hartman put on nearly every type of show except a flea circus in the Playhouse. He even tried "Hamlet" and to everyone's surprise—including his—very few in the audience left before the Dane, after finishing his duel with Laertes, died dramatically.

"You know why they stayed to see the finish?" Hartman said to Jennie with a chuckle. "Not many of them ever read or saw 'Hamlet.' They wanted to see how it would end."

Don produced "The Taming of the Shrew," which the audiences loved, although one puzzled guest asked him,

"Why don't you pick a play sometimes by somebody who writes English?"

The producer-director-actor assured him the next play would include pratfalls, Yiddish songs, dances, music and pretty girls.

Jennie marveled at the ingenuity, energy and dedication of this young man who wrote skits and songs, directed and painted scenery. But she felt he worked too hard and suggested he hire an assistant. Don consulted a young friend named Moss Hart, social director at the nearby Hotel Flagler, in those days, the ranking Catskill hostelry. Hart enthusiastically recommended an even younger friend of his from Newark named Isidore (Dore) Schary, working at the Cedar Lake Camp which was operated by the Young Men's Hebrew Association. Schary wrote Biblical plays and songs, acted, recited poetry, put on an annual Fourth of July pageant and, like Hartman, built and painted sets and scenery.

Moss Hart told Hartman his friend Schary liked his job as social director at Cedar Lake except that he was supposed to double as a lifeguard. This was normal procedure in the Catskills, but Moss explained his friend was not a very experienced lifeguard. He wasn't even a very good swimmer. "To be perfectly truthful," Moss said dolefully, "Schary doesn't swim at all!" If Hartman wanted him as an assistant in writing, producing, acting, directing, as a stagehand, lighting expert, *toomler*, or carpenter, he was just the man as long as he didn't have to double as lifeguard, tennis pro, or riding master. And so the dark-haired, intense young man arrived at the hotel to help Hartman.

Dore Schary remained for only one summer. In addition to acting as Don's all-around assistant, he mimeographed scripts for distribution to the actors and he wrote a column called "At Liberty in Ferndale" for the daily hotel gossip sheet, the *Tattler*. Above all, Dore delighted in needling his friend Don when the latter tried to perform some role as ambitious as Hamlet. Dore wrote in his column that although he did the soliloquies well, Don's appearance left something to be desired. "In fact," Dore reported, "Mr. Hartman is built like no other Hamlet in history. The truth is that Mr. Hartman should never be seen in public wearing tights."

"You're just supposed to tell who's in the cast," Hartman said. "A drama critic for *The New York Times*, you're not. If I had any sense I would fire you."

"If you do, I will run you through my mimeograph machine," Dore countered loftily.

The mock feud amused them both and kept their hard-working staff good-natured. Don Hartman's infectious gaiety was good for the serious, introspective Schary. Years later, Schary would often give Hartman credit for teaching him how to handle humor on the stage.

Often Moss Hart would come to visit his two friends, and sometimes Jennie would listen to their excited talk of the theater and of plays they would write one day. She was fond of them all, but thought this was merely the exuberant expression of youthful fancies. She enjoyed their conversation—at least, that part of it she understood. When the trio argued as to why Iago hated Othello, they lost her. And when they discussed Chekhov's characters' inability to handle life's problems, they might as well have been speaking a foreign language.

Stubbornly, she would tell herself that some day she would learn about Chekhov, whoever he was, and about Ibsen, O'Neill, and Shaw.

Dore Schary had to leave before the season was over. When they learned the reason, Jennie and Don Hartman were the first to rejoice. Secretly, he had been writing a play and it had been accepted by a Broadway producer. It was this play which led him to Hollywood and to a meteoric rise to the top of the screen-writing profession. (He eventually became studio chief at MGM and a successful playwright with such hits as "Sunrise at Campobello" to his credit.)

Don Hartman and his wife stayed another year, and then he, too, went to Hollywood with a bundle of movie scripts under his arm. His rise was swift and soon he was selling every script he wrote. (Later, he became the production head of Paramount Pictures.) It might be added that even in those early years their friend, Moss Hart, was writing one unproduced play after another until he finally struck gold (aided by George S. Kaufman) with "Once In A Lifetime," one of the most successful comedies of its time. Jennie never lost the warm friendship of these three extraordinary men. All three played their part in the education of Jennie Grossinger.

When Hartman left, he suggested Jennie supervise the hiring of talent herself. She had learned a lot about entertainment from him, he said, but, more to the point, she had developed an instinct for knowing what her guests wanted. She accepted this new chore with some hesitation and usually ended up by asking performers, who had previously appeared at the hotel, to counsel her about new acts and productions. Among the neophytes she found were a knockabout burlesque comic, Hank Henry, and a young Italian-American songman named Robert Alda, who soon became mainstays of the resident entertainment troupe.

In conducting auditions, Jennie often allowed her heart to rule her head. If a comic auditioned nothing but scrupulously clean material and seemed to be "a nice boy," she would hire him and then was puzzled when he appeared on the Playhouse stage and "laid an egg"—to use an expression she learned from *Variety*.

Jennie was learning, but occasionally her inexperience led to beguilement by a proposition from some ingratiating stranger. Once, a night club was about to open in Monticello, only ten miles away. The owner of the establishment phoned her.

"I have a terrific show, but it doesn't open until next Saturday," he said, "I'd like my boys and girls to go through a dress rehearsal before a crowd. How about letting me put on my show in the Playhouse Wednesday night? It won't cost you a cent, and to be honest, it'll help advertise my place. So this will help both of us. I'll bring my own musicians—we won't even need an afternoon run-through."

Jennie, overjoyed at the opportunity of obtaining a professional show at no cost, was as excited as her guests on Wednesday night when the band struck up the opening bars. A phone call suddenly took her to the front desk. It wasn't until a half-hour later that she was able to return to the theater. As she went in she saw an angry man leading his reluctant young son away.

"Get to bed," the man said sternly. "I never should of

brought you in the first place!" The kid was crying lustily.

Jennie felt sorry for the youngster deprived of the chance to see the performance. She entered the Playhouse and sat down in the last row, relaxed, prepared to enjoy the proceedings. Three minutes later she was not relaxed; she was sitting bolt upright, furious at what she saw and heard. A line of very scantily clad girls was dancing and singing a song that made Jennie blush.

Helplessly, she looked around and saw Martin Starr, the Hollywood columnist, standing in the back of the auditorium. "You have to help me, Martin," she pleaded. "Get up there, draw the curtain, and apologize to the audience for me. Tell them I didn't know what kind of show this was and that this will never happen again."

The bemused columnist grinned. "Sure, Jennie, don't worry." He ran to the stage, motioned for the music to stop, drew the curtains, and made an apologetic announcement which placated the more puritanical members of the audience who had always equated Grossinger's with clean entertainment.

On another occasion in the Thirties, a young comic who played an engagement at Grossinger's used such risque material that Jennie made it plain he would not be re-hired. She had engaged him on the recommendation of Harry Brock, operator of several vaudeville houses, who told her the comic had been a smash hit at one of the theaters he owned in Newark. He neglected to mention that the theatrical emporium in question was a burlesque house. The comic's name? Jackie Gleason.

Years of living in the mountains had given Jennie's

cheeks a permanent rosy glow. Few believed her when she admitted to being past forty. She may have looked well, but actually years of constant hard work were beginning to take their toll. In addition to sheer physical weariness, she was worried about the future of the hotel. As the Depression deepened, business was falling off enough to hurt. There were still mortgages to be paid off, a large payroll to meet, and huge food bills appearing on her desk every week.

Again, Dr. Singer ordered her to bed for a week. He knew it was useless telling her to slow down, but he counted on his allies, Harry, and brother-in-law, Abe Friedman. Harry, Abe, and Dr. Singer stood at Jennie's bedside telling her she would have to curtail her activities. They made her promise to relinquish at least a few tasks, especially the arduous five-hour trips to New York to hire entertainers. She agreed that someone else should handle this; someone completely loyal to the hotel who would not be duped by bookers.

"You'd better take on the job, Harry," she told her husband. He looked astonished. "Me in show business? I don't know a thing about it, and I don't want to know anything about it. There's enough work around this place for me now. How about Abe?"

"Oh, no, Harry, don't look at me," Abe Friedman said, an expression of panic on his face.

The name of Milton Blackstone came up. In 1930, Blackstone left the hotel briefly to give Wall Street a whirl. As a customer's man he had done reasonably well, but he hated every minute of it. The world of finance didn't give his creative imagination enough scope. A short time thereafter, Blackstone tossed an idea to Harry and Jennie which they considered and finally accepted. He wanted to open an advertising-promotion-publicity office in New York. He suggested that Grossinger's become his first client. He would answer all queries sent to the hotel concerning rates and facilities. If there was no response, he would send a follow-up letter or make personal phone calls.

"In these days, hotels are luxuries," he told them. "A lot of people are eliminating the word 'vacation' from their vocabularies. We have to sell people on the idea that at Grossinger's they will get a lot for their money. The obvious answer is to advertise in the big New York newspapers, but we can't afford that. You *can* afford my kind of inexpensive letter-and-phone-call campaign."

After only a few months, Blackstone's campaign started to show modest but steady results. His phone calls to potential guests, sometimes as many as fifty a day, gave him new insight into the wants, problems and needs of vacationers and the prices they could afford. Blackstone was even more persuasive with his typewriter than he was on the telephone. "Even if you are coming by yourself we know you'll have a wonderful time," he would write to single girls. "You will meet a lot of fine, friendly people, and you can be sure that you will get our personal attention."

What Blackstone pioneered was a unique point of view that put the emphasis on the personal, homey touch —the "human element," as he liked to call it. It is a selling philosophy that has been retained at Grossinger's to this day of huge advertising and promotion budgets. Before Blackstone, the hotel had done some informal direct mail advertising. In the early days, loyal guests often pitched in helping to type and mail the letters. But Blackstone was the man who introduced a skilled professional approach without sacrificing the basic ingredients of warmth, unpretentiousness and directness.

When price seemed to be the barrier, the young adman wrote what he called his "three-hundred-acre letter." He would emphasize the vast size of the grounds, the many facilities, swimming, sports activities of all kinds, entertainment, nearly all of which were free. He suggested that even if a prospective guest had to take a shorter vacation, in order to keep within his allotted budget, the heightened enjoyment would be well worth it. If the doubtful head of a family was worried about price, Blackstone would tell of the cots for children that could be put in the parents' room at a reduced rate, and he noted special emphasis placed on the dietary requirements of children. Milton Blackstone was not only persuasive, he was absolutely honest. Grossinger's did, in fact, offer something for everyone; moreover, the prices charged would have seemed absurdly cheap in any but Depression years.

Blackstone's success and the fact that he was based in New York made him the obvious choice to undertake the added duty of finding entertainment for the hotel. He couldn't say he knew nothing about the business. Blackstone was a gregarious man who knew the Broadway scene well.

It wasn't long before he started to perform small booking miracles. One Saturday night, a headline performer he had hired, ambushed by the attractions of a roadhouse halfway to Liberty, failed to reach the mountains. Jennie phoned Milton at seven that evening to tell him his star had not yet appeared. He was calm as always. "I'll find someone else. Tell the guests after the preliminary acts are finished that we're trying something new this evening—a midnight show with a mystery headliner."

"Who will you send up?" Jennie asked.

He laughed. "Who knows? But I'll find somebody."

Blackstone went from one actors' hangout to another. At the Paramount Hotel Grill, he found a fire-eater and sword-swallower, whose night-club act he had once seen, swallowing not fire, but steak and bourbon. In five minutes, he persuaded the reluctant artist to go to his room, pack his props, and get down to the lobby. At least, it would be a different kind of act for Grossinger's, Milton thought. The fire-eater was in a cab before he knew what was happening and Milton was telling the amazed driver to go to Peekskill, go over the Bear Mountain Bridge, and keep on driving until he hit Route 17.

"Where we headin' for?" the puzzled cabbie asked.

"Grossinger's," Milton said.

"What's Grossinger's?"

Milton shrugged his shoulders. "Who cares? I'm paying you twice what your clock shows if you get us there by midnight. Here's twenty to start with." The driver made what was then a record trip to Liberty, arriving at the hotel fifteen minutes before the deadline.

By now the hotel was remaining open during the entire winter. Profit was a minor factor, because with the exception of holiday weekends you could fire a shotgun in the lobby without inflicting a wound on anything. Resort hotels constructed essentially for the summer months were not exactly designed to cope with zero weather.

JENNIE AND THE STORY OF GROSSINGER'S

Harry Grossinger knew what happened if you didn't allow a resort hotel to be "lived in" during the bitter cold months: kitchen paraphernalia rusted; expensive copper pipes burst at the seams; leaks in the roof made a shambles out of rugs and furniture; and snowdrifts destroyed the landscaping.

Determined to attract winter visitors, Milton Blackstone persuaded Harry and Jennie to lower the rates, but to offer the same food and to present entertainment on weekends. Since resident social staffs were a summertime staple, the off-season acts were hired for a single performance, the beginning of what was to become the usual pattern a decade hence.

Blackstone's telephone calls, letter writing, and a few inexpensive advertisements in the *Brooklyn Daily Eagle* and the *Bronx Home News* resulted in a trickle of winter weekend visitors. Except when weather interfered with trains and buses, which happened at infrequent but persistent intervals, he made good on his promises. The magnificent, weather-defying state highways which now bring New Yorkers to the Catskills in the time it takes to solve *The New York Times* crossword puzzle were still only a gleam in the prophetic eyes of state officials. They had managed to construct a few patches of isolated new roadway from New York to Sullivan County, and serviced them with snowplows and tractors in bad weather, but these were connected by unpaved country roads—definite hazards to the broad-beamed buses which took off periodically from Times Square.

Grossinger's actual beginnings as a certified winter sports playground are traceable to a day in 1933 when Jennie hired three-time Olympic champion Irving Jaffee as the hotel's first winter sports director. She met him at the old Iceland Skating Rink on West 52nd Street—now the Roseland Dance Hall—during a skating party for Grossinger guests. The youthful skating ace was to be the energizer who would introduce (in 1949) the first artificial skating rink in the Catskills; professional ice shows; a speed-skating team that won many major amateur titles; official Olympic trial events; and the world's barrel-jumping championships on skates.

In 1933, however, Jaffee found the winter sports scene in Ferndale primitive: skating on a pond, skiing over the golf course, and sledding and sleighing over the hilly terrain. Ever alert to publicity possibilities, Milton Blackstone immediately decided to capitalize on the Olympic champion's new connection with the hotel. In early February, he announced to the press that the New York-bred skater would attempt to break the world's twenty-five-mile speed record on the hotel lake with all proceeds going to a local hospital. The unusual event drew a crowd of over five thousand spectators. It also made a few sports headlines when Jaffee succeeded in shaving several seconds off the old record and establishing a new mark of one hour, 26.9 minutes racing around a one-third mile track seventy-five times.

One Saturday evening there was a fair-sized crowd on hand anticipating the expected group of Broadway entertainers. A severe storm made an Alpine drift of the swirling, deepening snow along the hundred miles between Times Square and Liberty. All trains and buses were put under warm shelters, but not even this defeated resourceful Milton Blackstone. He told the bus company he would buy chains for the tires of one bus to make the trip over the icy roads. He added, as a sure-fire inducement, that the bus company could keep the expensive chains after the trip.

As Grossinger's continued to grow in the years following Selig's death, one phenomenon never failed to amaze and delight Jennie: the intense loyalty and affection that the guests displayed for her, Harry and Malke. At first Jennie thought a larger hotel would mean a more impersonal hotel—that guests might soon become mere customers. How could guests possibly feel as close to the family now that there were so many? Yet, they did. One outgrowth of this was an institution launched in the early Thirties known as the "annual reunion." For many guests, Grossinger's was still essentially a summer hotel. They told Jennie that somehow friendships made during the summer season ought to be renewed. Jennie came up with the idea of a reunion dance to be held in New York each winter.

So overwhelming was the response, the reunions had to be staged in the largest hotel ballrooms available in the city—first, at the St. George in Brooklyn, and then at such landmarks as the Astor and Waldorf-Astoria in New York City. Once a year, the "Grossinger Reunion Dance" brought out at least twenty-five hundred frolickers for a rousing evening of dancing, entertainment, getting re-acquainted with friends from the previous summer, and, of course, saying hello again to Jennie and Harry.

Matching the fervid loyalty of guests were the warm feelings the Grossinger staff had for the family. All of the affection felt for Selig and Malke also belonged to Jennie and Harry. Leon Goldwater, a chauffeur in the Thirties, recalls: "When you worked for Jennie and

Harry, you felt like you were working for your mother and father. They treated everybody like their own."

This feeling of being part of the family was reflected in many unexpected ways. There was, for example, the matter of pay envelopes. With room and board taken care of, many employes would never even bother to claim their salaries on pay day. "Use the money, if you need it, for the hotel," they would tell Jennie. At one time, Jennie had to go around and literally plead with some staff people to pick up their money so that a newly installed payroll system could function properly.

As Jennie and Harry moved more into the forefront of the business, the no-longer-young Malke was required to do less and less. Yet she was everywhere and much beloved by everyone.

Once, a certain light-fingered employe was seen pocketing a handful of bills from an open cash register. One of his co-workers came running to the old lady, breathless with the news. Malke listened quietly, shook her head a few times, smiled sweetly at the informer and said, "Don't get so excited. So he's stealing. Maybe he needs the money. As long as he doesn't take everything! *A bissel fur ihm and a bissel fur uns.* [A little for him and a little for us.] So, it's not so terrible!"

Another time, an agitated chambermaid came to her with a tale of some departing guests blithely packing away towels, pillow cases and sheets along with their personal belongings. Again Malke remained calm and unruffled. "Don't be so upset," she said. "If it wasn't for the guests, both you and I wouldn't be here. As long as they don't take the buildings."

Chapter 12

During the late Twenties and early Thirties most of the material used by Catskill resorts presenting entertainment was, quite frankly, taken from Broadway shows. It was a custom hallowed by tradition (even if the tradition was quite young) and no one, least of all Jennie, felt that any law was being broken. After all, no author or producer of a Broadway show had ever protested. Every Wednesday, social directors accompanied by a pair of secretaries would attend Broadway matinees. While the secretaries, taking alternate scenes, jotted down every joke in shorthand, the social director would make notes of sets, costumes, entrance cues, and stage business. Few plays, except the classics, were published in those days. This made the job of the Catskill plagiarists all the more difficult. When the unholy trio returned to the mountains, all material they had accumulated would be typed, and then a Don Hartman, a Garson Kanin, a Moss Hart, or a Harold Rome would write a rough draft of the show, usually adding an original song or two and reworking some of the jokes.

Ben Silver, social director at Grossinger's on and off in the Twenties, was especially accomplished at bringing Broadway to the Catskills. He attended such musical hits as "Good News," "Five O'Clock Girl," "Follow Thru," "Sons o'Guns," and "Flying High" and promptly reworked them for performance in the Catskills.

George White, whose "Scandals" was having a successful run at the Winter Garden, was the first to protest, reasonably enough, that material he had either written or bought was really his property.

Evelyn Brown had become particularly adept at writing shorthand in a darkened theater; she had done it for so long that by now it was to her a perfectly legitimate activity. Evelyn usually bought a box seat because it gave her more elbow room. One matinee, while industriously taking notes in the midst of the first act of "George White's "Scandals," she was startled to feel a heavy hand on her arm and hear a stern voice say, "Young lady, come with me." It was George White himself. After confiscating her notes and giving her a lecture, he allowed her to return to her seat. Instead, she fled the darkened theater. "My heart was pounding so fast," she told Jennie, "I couldn't wait to escape."

She also informed her boss that if a letter arrived with the name George White on the envelope, it would not be a request for a reservation. Mr. White had told Evelyn his attorneys would get in touch with her employers very shortly. Actually, Mr. White did not prosecute, but he did make a complaint to the Authors League. Shortly thereafter, every hotel in the Catskills received a formal letter from a New York law firm stating that the next hotel to plagiarize theatrical material would be sued.

JENNIE AND THE STORY OF GROSSINGER'S

After that warning, Jennie bought scripts of plays from the French Company, which had recently gone into the business of purveying them legitimately once the Broadway run and the road tour had been completed. This was at best a stopgap. Much of the excitement generated at the Playhouse stemmed from the knowledge that guests could see the Grossinger versions of current Broadway plays—not those of two and three seasons back.

Show business actually discovered Grossinger's when Eddie Cantor first visited the hotel. He was then the outstanding radio personality of the day with three highly paid scripters to fashion his popular half-hour weekly show. Weary of working in a New York City hotel, one of the writers suggested they all take off for a quiet place he'd heard about in the Catskills called Grossinger's. Cantor was agreeable; he warmed to the idea of some peace and quiet in the country. They checked in without reservations registering under the name of the writer so as not to be recognized.

Cantor especially liked to take long morning hikes around the countryside before the hotel had awakened. That second morning, unshaven, dressed in old clothes, he was returning from an hour's tramp around the hotel grounds when he encountered Malke Grossinger. She peered at the skinny, perspiring, hungry-looking young man and mistook him for a tramp. Addressing him in Yiddish, she was delighted when he replied in kind.

"Are you hungry?" she asked eagerly.

"I am," he said honestly enough. He hadn't had breakfast.

"Good. Now you come with me to the dining room and have a good breakfast."

She beamed, happy because he was giving her an opportunity to do her daily *mitzvah* (blessing). The entertainer's new benefactress now led him to the dining room and sat him at a table with some plumbers who were installing a sprinkler system. She summoned Abe Friedman and told him to give the nice man anything he wanted to eat. "Let Abe order for you," Mom said. "He knows what a hungry young man would like for breakfast."

Abe smiled. "Leave it to me." In no time at all he returned from the kitchen with baked herring, scrambled eggs, coffee and toast. He was happy to see that the shabbily attired guest did justice to the food. Maybe he hasn't eaten for days, Abe mused. Then, as was his custom, Abe made the rounds to see that the regular guests were happy. He returned a few moments later to say to Malke's guest, "You want a laugh? A lot of guests think you're Eddie Cantor."

"I'm better looking than Eddie Cantor," the young man said solemnly. Just then a chant arose from some of the tables. "We want Cantor, we want Cantor," they cried, and now Eddie Cantor, his deception over, stood up and bowed to loud applause from the other diners. Abe Friedman looked incredulous, but when he peered closely at the "tramp" he realized he had made the same mistake as Malke. He hurried to the kitchen to tell her about the "tramp" she had picked up.

"Mom, do you know that the man you brought in for breakfast is Eddie Cantor, the famous radio star?" he asked excitedly.

"*Nu?*" Malke was always much too busy to listen to

the radio unless a Cantor Rosenblatt was singing "Eli, Eli."

"But Mom, he makes $10,000 a week," Abe said.

"*Ach*, Abe," she said with a smile, "you are always making jokes. You should be an actor."

From that day forward, Eddie Cantor visited the resort at least once a year, usually more often. And he always appeared in the Playhouse. At first, Jennie tried to pay him for his services as a performer, but he would always say, "You keep forgetting, Jennie, Mom paid me already. She thought I was a broken-down bum and she took me in and fed me."

Cantor was among the first to make Broadway conscious of a place named Grossinger's. It had no immediate economic effect, but it did make things a bit easier for Milton Blackstone, who was still trying hard to sell the hotel to potential guests and to hire Broadway entertainment at reasonable prices. Furthermore, Blackstone was becoming a master of the "gimmick"—a word indigenous to show business and press agentry.

In 1934, the fortuitous circumstance of being in the right place at the right time provided him with a gimmick that would put the name of Grossinger's on the sports pages of every newspaper in the country.

The place was Dave's Blue Room, a restaurant that attracted athletes, actors, sports writers, agents and sports promoters in the same manner that Toots Shor's does today. The time was lunch hour. Blackstone had asked Jennie to meet with him and Monte Proser, a knowledgeable theatrical publicity man and agent, to discuss possible attractions they could bring to the hotel.

A devout member of the cult known as the "night people," Proser generally did his soundest sleeping during
the lunch hour. He once slept right through a noontime
murder in a Times Square barber shop even though the
fatally wounded victim nearly fell into his lap. This
time, he remained sufficiently awake to notice a slim,
dark man in the crowd of celebrities at the Blue Room.

"There's a real nice guy," Proser remarked to Jennie.
"His name is Sol Gold and he trains fighters. If things
are going well with him, the big cigar he smokes is
always straight out. If things are bad, it droops down to
his chest. It's sagging now. Sol must be in trouble."

Monte beckoned. Sol Gold was introduced and sat
down. The reason for his unhappiness soon became evident. His fighter from Chicago was due in New York
within a month to train for a world's championship
fight, but Sol hadn't been able to find a suitable training
spot for him. Jennie hardly listened. Harry had often
asked her to attend the Madison Square Garden fights
with him, but the thought of two young men battering
each other for money dismayed her. She remained quiet
while Milton, Monte and Sol talked.

"Milton is always talking about getting something
different for the hotel," Proser said to Jennie. "You
know, some gimmick. Well, the gimmick is sitting right
here at the table."

Jennie looked bewildered and turned to Milton who
was obviously interested in Monte's suggestion. "Jennie,
remember a few years ago, a fighter named Sid Terris
from the East Side came to the hotel for a weekend?
Everyone made a big fuss over him." Jennie nodded.
"This kid of Sol's is named Barney Ross," Monte Proser

continued. "He holds two world championships and he's going to fight Jimmy McLarnin, another world's champion, in six weeks. Any place where either of them trains will get national attention."

Milton and Monte, caught up in the fervor of their own enthusiasm, kept on talking persuasively. Boxing was a foreign and distasteful word to Jennie, but she had great respect for Milton's judgment and for Monte Proser's winged imagination. Would the presence of a fighter hurt Grossinger's? Her mother would not like the idea, but fight fan Harry most certainly would. She finally agreed, if hesitatingly, and Sol Gold's cigar instantly levitated to a ninety-degree angle.

A week later, she and Harry returned to New York to work out the details and meet Barney Ross. Both were impressed by the warmth and graciousness of this good-looking boy from Chicago. Sam Pian, one of his managers, told them they would need plenty of room for sparring partners, trainers, managers, publicity men.

"Bring an army," Harry Grossinger said. "If we run out of rooms, we'll build a house for you."

And that is exactly what Harry did. He called it the Barney Ross Cottage. Barney and his entourage moved in followed by a corps of sports writers who were just discovering Grossinger's. Jennie had to learn an entirely new vocabulary. She found out that in terms of boxing a "stable" did not mean a place to park a horse; it meant a bunch of fighters a manager had under contract. Nor was a "hook" something only used to catch fish. A "towel" was a fabric that, occasionally, managers, as well as housewives, threw in; and a "ring" was not necessarily something that girls yearned for.

In no time at all, Harry and his boys built a regulation ring—it always puzzled Jennie that the ring was square —and serious training began. Each afternoon, Barney Ross and his sparring partners would flail away at each other with heavy gloves. Every guest in the hotel wanted to see the world's champion in action. Milton lost no time in renting folding chairs and charged fifty cents for each admission. Within a week, the cost of constructing the boxing area was repaid. Jennie was also worried that Ross would attract a lot of questionable types whose drinking and brawling would annoy the regular guests. She soon discovered that the drinking was confined to the sports writers who were as experienced at the bar as they were at their typewriters. One veteran writer said to Jennie, "Mrs. Grossinger, I've never seen a training camp like this. In forty years of covering fight camps, this is the only one you could take your mother to." Jennie decided that she would. She tried to persuade Malke to attend one of the afternoon sparring sessions.

"What?" Malke said in horror. "Watch two boys hitting each other?"

"It is more like a dance than a fight, Momma," Jennie responded defensively. Malke gave her daughter a dubious look.

A few days later, while Harry was showing the lightweight champion through the kitchen, he introduced Ross to Malke.

"This is the box-fighter?" she asked incredulously. "He was Friday night in the synagogue."

She was amazed that a fighter could chant Hebrew prayers and join in the choir to sing Hebrew hymns. The fact that he was a world's champion meant nothing to her; the fact that he was an observant Jew gave him the proper *yichus* (status).

"A glass of tea, maybe?" she inquired.

Ross nodded and accepted the offer. Malke had picked up many English phrases, but she spoke Yiddish most of the time. Barney understood her easily. She still hated the thought of this nice young man fighting and she would say sadly, "Enough fighting already. You could be better a doctor, a lawyer, or a dentist."

When Barney's Yiddish-speaking mother arrived at the camp to watch the training, Jennie was startled by the enthusiasm Mrs. Rasofsky (Barney had shortened his name when he took to the ring) displayed as her son ferociously pummelled his sparring partners and was, in turn, just as fiercely pounded by them. She explained she had seen Barney fight many times and he always assured her the punches didn't really hurt. If her son said so, that was enough for this simple, trusting, uneducated woman. To Jennie, wiser in the ways of the world, the spectacle remained a brutal one. She rarely watched the workouts and, when she did, every blow made her wince.

The gimmick that Milton and Monte Proser dreamed up paid off handsomely. The best-known sports writers of New York, Chicago, Philadelphia and the wire services were all there. With a nudge from Milton Blackstone, instead of datelining their daily stories "Liberty" (home of the nearest Western Union office), they datelined them "Grossinger, N.Y." When rain canceled Barney's workout, they would write feature stories on the hotel, about Jennie, about how it all began back in 1914, and about the invigorating air of the Catskills.

This kind of publicity, which no hotel in the world

could afford to buy, probably marked the beginning of the national eminence of the place. It was no longer just another Catskill resort; it was, as *New York Daily News* sports columnist Paul Gallico wrote, "The Big G."—a handle that everyone soon began using when referring to "Jennie's Place."

After Barney Ross defeated Jimmy McLarnin and became the first man in the history of boxing to hold three world titles, he returned to celebrate (on herring, *holapchis, cholent* with *knaidel, kreplech,* potato *kugel, tzimmes, hamantaschen,* and *strudel*). It seemed to Jennie as though all of Broadway followed him. Abe Lyman, young Milton Berle, the Ritz Brothers, song writers Gordon and Ravel, Belle Baker and many others joined Barney in celebrating. Almost overnight, Grossinger's became "big time." Once Broadway adopted a place, the daily columnists followed, and the resultant publicity could make an anemic resort robustly healthy in no time at all. When Damon Runyon dubbed the hotel, "Lindy's with trees," Broadway knew Grossinger's was in.

Abe Lyman, one of the better-known band leaders in the country and an important star on the airwaves, was particularly enchanted by the hotel—and Jennie.

"Why," he asked her, "don't more people know about this place? The show biz mob would eat it up."

After the maestro left, he wrote an extravagant letter of praise to his hostess and gave Jennie permission to use it in ads. He added a postscript suggesting that Jennie listen to his next radio show. Although Lyman broadcast from a studio each week, he created the illusion that his program was coming from Cannes, Biarritz, Monte Carlo,

Palm Beach, or some other smart-set playpen. This evening, while the entire family, staff and every guest listened eagerly, he announced that his show was coming from "beautiful Grossinger's in the beautiful Catskill Mountains of New York State." The message was beamed to countless millions of listeners across the country who had never heard of Grossinger's before.

New York newspaper columnists, having discovered the hotel, kept coming back year after year, writing about the place and bringing still more vacationing Broadway entertainers in their wake. Grossinger's in the mid- and late Thirties became the place to go. To Jennie's delight, a liberal sprinkling of non-Jewish actors, politicians, professional athletes, writers as well as ordinary businessmen also began patronizing her establishment.

The first non-Jewish guest to become a so-called "regular" was an extroverted Italian-American named Jimmy Mirabito, a young official with the Metropolitan Life Insurance Company. Self-conscious about his alien identity, Mirabito invariably checked in using the pseudonym, "Jimmy Meyers." In later years, when Gentile guests began arriving in large numbers—first in convention groups and then on their own—Mirabito switched back to his real name, but Jennie, to this day, still kiddingly calls him "Jimmy Meyers."

Barney Ross continued to train at The G. until May, 1938, when Henry Armstrong administered a savage beating to the plucky Chicagoan to wrest the welterweight title away from him. Ross, who retired soon after the Armstrong bout, was the first of a glittering roll of champions to drill at the hotel followed during the next three decades by Max Baer, Billy Conn, Lew Jenkins, Joey Maxim, Randy Turpin, Rocky Marciano, Ingemar Johansson, Gene Fullmer, Bob Foster, Dick Tiger and Nino Benvenuti.

Ansel Hoffman, manager of Max Baer, came up to inspect the resort as a possible training site for the handsome California playboy-fighter who won the heavyweight crown in 1934 by stopping champion Primo Carnero and then lost it to Jimmy Braddock the following year. Paul Grossinger, now old enough to start learning the hotel business, showed Hoffman the Barney Ross Cottage. "Downstairs is fine," he said. "What about upstairs? I want a bedroom higher up." Mystified, Paul took him upstairs to another bedroom.

The manager opened the window and leaned over the sill. He nodded happily. "This'll do," he told Paul. "Maxie can never jump from this height."

Happy-go-lucky Max Baer, a strapping, six-foot three-inch, 220-pounder who could hit with the force of a hydraulic press, had a zest for living and a marked distaste for training. Dedicated to the philosophy that training should always take a back seat to fun and females, the jovial gladiator became known as "the Clown Prince of Boxing."

He would rather slip out than work out, and Hoffman had to watch him every minute. When he arrived at the hotel, everyone was captivated by his charm and anything-for-a-laugh attitude toward the world. When he did his roadwork in the morning, his pockets were always filled with chocolate candies which he would toss to any youngster who crossed his path. The word went out and Max Baer became a Catskill Pied Piper with a huge following of kids who accompanied him every morning on his long runs.

Max had a huge, 250-pound Negro sparmate named Elza Thompson, as he drilled for what was to be a losing bout against Lou Nova. One afternoon, Jennie escorted a well-known magazine writer to the daily workout. It was a lively session. Baer, who had a devastating right hand, was in good shape and battered Thompson at will.

"That poor, poor boy," Jennie said sympathetically, "Max is very rough with him."

"Thompson?" the writer said. "The guy is getting $50 a day plus room and board for being cuffed around. If he wasn't a sparring partner what would he be doing? Working as a grease monkey in a gas station, or as a laborer on a construction job, or as a bouncer in a Harlem night club. Listen, Jennie, he never had it so good."

"I know," she said. "It's just that men of his color don't have the opportunity the rest of us do. No matter how good and fine they might be, they are thought of as Negroes—not people. It's not right."

"So, he won't have to pay the kind of income taxes you have to pay," the writer said.

"Things haven't been so good that we're paying such big taxes," she responded. "I hope things get better and we have to pay twice the taxes we pay now. Living in this country is a privilege. I can't understand why people complain about paying taxes."

This was a refreshing viewpoint to the writer accustomed to hearing well-to-do New Yorkers damn Franklin D. Roosevelt for increasing taxes. He led Jennie away from the ring to relate to him the story of how she and her family had emigrated to this country and how grateful all of them were for the liberties and privileges they were enjoying. In fact, Quentin Reynolds was so impressed he forgot about doing a story on Max Baer; instead, he did one on Jennie Grossinger and called it "One Hundred Percent American." It was the first magazine story ever written about Jennie and a legend was aborning.

Jennie always had a special affection for the huge, amiable Baer, although the clowning clouter gave her one of her more embarrassing moments. Some years later in Miami Beach, Jennie was walking down Lincoln Road accompanied by a group of prominent local ladies serving on a committee with her for a charity affair. Suddenly, she felt a set of massive hands around her waist and her unwilling feet leaving the ground. As she was lifted skyward, a familiar gruff voice boomed from behind: "It's me, Jennie, sweetheart! Maxie boy!" Baer whirled her around while her face grew redder and redder.

Each boxer who trained at Grossinger's had his own style. There was the late Rocky Marciano, a stolid, courtly man whose gentle manner out of the ring belied his ferocity once the gloves were on and whose capacity for rigorous training was matched only by his fierce determination to win. He would happily endure as long as six months of Spartan self-denial while preparing for a bout. He was never in less than flawless physical condition. Serious, dedicated, purposeful, Rocky was the very model of the clean-living good guy, obeying all the rules. He emerged triumphant in every one of his ring encounters starting with an impressive thirteenth-round knockout of champion Jersey Joe Walcott in Philadelphia's

Municipal Stadium on the night of September 23, 1952, to annex the heavyweight crown. Rocky kayoed forty-three of his forty-nine pro victims before he bowed to his wife's wishes and quit the ring, undefeated.

In startling contrast to the "Brockton Blaster," Swedish heavyweight Ingemar Johansson, who came to this country to challenge champion Floyd Patterson, set a colorful new mode for training camps that generated reams of copy for the sports journalists and confounded the experts. Ingemar was probably the first fighter in the history of pugilism to bring his entire family—mother, father, brothers, and sister—along with him to a fight camp. Suspicious of American cooks, the Swedish battler imported mama to prepare all of his meals. Even more irregular, not to say scandalous, he insisted upon having his girl friend, a pert smorgasbord named Brigette, with him during the entire five-week training period. Women in a fight camp were unheard of; a sexy girl friend was absolute heresy. Marciano rarely saw his wife during his lengthy training stints. Johansson never let Brigette out of his sight and, often as not, spent his evenings in the hotel night club dancing and making merry. Ingemar, undisputed master of his camp, succeeded in breaking just about every training rule in the book. Evidently, this somewhat original approach to the business of conditioning for a major fight did little damage to his fistic abilities. On a warm June night in 1956, the rugged, confident Swede stepped into the four-square at Yankee Stadium and handily dispatched Mr. Patterson to become the new world's heavyweight champion.

In addition to the glamorous aura provided by boxing personalities, people were beginning to identify Grossinger's with "show biz" and its biggest names. During the late Thirties and early Forties, Blackstone's policy of hiring performers who had potential "star quality" produced such entertainers as Shelley Winters, Robert Merrill, Betty Garrett, Beatrice Kaye, Kay Medford, Sam Levenson, Gene Barry, Jan Murray, Billy Reed, Red Buttons, Hank Henry, Phillip Reed, Everett Sloane, Robert Alda, Jan Peerce, Jerry Lester, and Phil Foster— most of whom worked on the resident social staff. Legend has it that all of these glittering names plus many more were "discovered" at Grossinger's—a pleasant myth, only half true.

Many young talents did reach stardom via the Playhouse, but not all. One legend has it that Jerry Lewis received his start at The Big G. Actually, it was Jerry's father, Danny, an able song-and-dance man, who was on the hotel staff. His young son, who was born Joseph Levitch, was doubling as busboy and comic at the hotel owned by Charles and Lillian Brown in Loch Sheldrake. One day his father brought him to Grossinger's to watch a rehearsal. Jennie sat with the youngster and said to his father, "He's an adorable little boy."

"He's more than that," the boy's father said proudly. "He's a great talent and one of these days he's going to be a star."

Jennie laughed. "All of you doting fathers are the same," she said, and walked away from what could have been one of Grossinger's greatest discoveries.

When World War II broke out, recruiting large resident social staffs became more and more difficult, forcing Grossinger's to abandon the hallowed institution. Show bills began featuring "name acts" signed for one performance and a new era in the Catskill entertainment industry was under way. A newcomer would still be hired for the small resident social staff—Robert Merrill in 1944; Buddy Hackett in 1946 (actually, he joined the athletic staff following his discharge from the Army); and Eddie Fisher in 1947; but most of the entertainment was now purveyed by high-priced variety artists—singers, comedians, dancers, novelty artists—who came up for a single evening.

Along with the stars, there were also many young unknowns on the bottom half of the bills, or even head-lining during slow periods when budgets were smaller. All were waiting for the big break—to be heard by some important agent or talent manager in the Grossinger audience. Opera star Robert Merrill (Merrill Miller in those days) got his first career boost when theatrical agent Moe Gale heard him singing at The G. Impressed by the young man's resounding baritone and virile good looks, Gale decided to place Merrill under his manage-rial wing. Within a year, the young singer was signed for the Met roster.

Soon other Catskill hotels were following Grossinger's lead in hiring top Broadway talent. Most of the hotels presented elaborate entertainment only on Wednesday and Saturday nights, with lesser performers filling in the rest of the week.

Another popular if less polished form of entertain-ment that caught on during those days were the annual "staff and guest shows." These were elaborate amateur extravaganzas put on each summer—one by staff, the other by guests—that involved long afternoons of work and rehearsals. With original songs, lyrics and books, the productions were always highlights of the summer season, making up in enthusiasm and spontaneity what they lacked in professionalism. Occasionally though, Blackstone would hire a fledging young sketch writer or tunesmith to work with the amateurs in shaping the original material. That's how Jerry Ross and Mel Brooks became members of the social staff in the early Fifties. Jerry left The G. to co-author the score of two of Broadway's biggest musical smashes, "Pajama Game," and "Damned Yankees." Mel Brooks became a top TV writer for Sid Caesar and later won an Academy Award for his comedy film, "The Producers."

Blackstone was perhaps the first to advise young (or unemployed) talents to head for the mountains and travel from resort to resort. No matter how little the pay, he told them, one would always be well fed on this circuit. It was Abel Green, editor of *Variety*, who dubbed this phenomenon of show business the "Borscht Belt." Every menu in the Catskills featured *borscht*, which in Russia had been as aristocratic a soup as *petite marmite* had been in France or *gazpacho* in Spain.

The soubriquet caught on and brought quick attention to the Catskills. In more recent times, with the great number of luxury hotels that blanket the area, local chambers of commerce have taken a dim view of the term. With virtually no success, they've tried to gain acceptance for what they regard as a much more appropriate rubric, "Champagne Circuit." But "Borscht Belt" clings tenaciously to the Catskill Mountains.

It was during these years just before Europe was to explode in another cataclysmic war that Jennie came to realize that there was a very large and important world outside of the Catskills. The newspapers and radio brought harrowing news of Hitler's Germany. Friends like Eddie Cantor, anticipating the holocaust that would eventually descend upon the Jews of Germany, were raising money to spirit thousands of Jews out of the country to Palestine. Once arrived, they had to be fed, clothed and taught trades which would enable them to support themselves in a new country.

Each winter, the annual reunion of Grossinger guests continued to be held in New York. Jennie decided to organize these gatherings on a larger scale and donate the proceeds to one of the charities whose purpose it was to alleviate the sufferings of European Jews. "Youth Aliyah" was one organization very close to Eddie Cantor's heart.

Smuggling adults out of Germany was becoming more and more difficult unless they were willing and able to pay what amounted to heavy blackmail. It was easier to get children out of the country, and "Youth Aliyah" was organized for that purpose. Jennie told Milton Blackstone to pull out all stops in his promotion campaign. This he did. On the night of the reunion at the Hotel New Yorker, the Grand Ballroom was crowded. So were the lobby and the corridors. The management, bowing to the rules of the fire department, had to close the doors. The event was both a social and financial success. The next morning, Jennie phoned Cantor to tell him that Dave Kriendler and his helpers had counted the receipts which came to a little more than $3000.

"I'll send you a check, Eddie," she said happily.

"Every minute counts," he said. "Bring the cash over to my hotel now."

Most of the money was in bills of small denomination. Jennie and Milton crowded it into two shoe boxes and a hotel laundry bag and headed for the Essex House. They were met with curious glances from people in the lobby and from the elevator operator, but when they entered Eddie's suite, the reaction was different. Cantor threw his arms around Jennie and kissed her. They opened the shoe boxes and the laundry bag and the money spilled out on the table.

"Jennie,"—Cantor's eyes reflected his delight—"it costs about four hundred dollars to get a child out of Germany and take him to Palestine. This is enough to save the lives of at least eight children!"

This was a deeply moving moment for Jennie. She had always donated generously to charities, but she was merely doing her duty, she felt. Now she sensed the satisfaction that her father and mother must have had so often when they actively helped others. From that day on, Jennie decided to divide her time equally between the hotel management and worthy charities. She did not merely contribute; she became an active organizer and indefatigable worker. Her bounty and her energies were behind Jewish, Catholic and Protestant charities.

Jennie's health remained a cause of constant anxiety to her family and her doctor. Torturous headaches assailed her constantly. One day, after a thorough examination, Dr. Singer said in despair: "Jennie, these short rests you take just aren't good enough. You've got to turn your back on business and everything connected with the hotel and go away for a long, long rest."

"Perhaps," she said half-heartedly, "I might take a month off."

The doctor shook his head and said bluntly, "I mean a long rest. I mean you should leave the hotel for a year."

"A year!" Jennie looked at him in amazement. "You couldn't be serious. What would I do?" she asked.

"Well, to begin with, take a long sea trip. You'll be away from the telephones and all the problems of running the hotel. And, Jennie, you must learn to relax."

For the first time in her life, Jennie was really concerned. No, she wouldn't take a year off, but she would at least take a trip.

A month later, she and Evelyn Brown were on a gleaming ship bound for California via the Panama Canal. After the first few days, Jennie actually began to enjoy herself. It was the first extended vacation she had ever taken. She spent hours lying on a deck chair, and gradually her headaches became less intense. By the time the ship reached California, they had almost disappeared. She chided herself for not having taken the doctor's advice sooner.

Don Hartman, now head of production at Paramount Pictures, and his wife, Chick, were waiting for her. She lunched at the studio dining room and met cinema giants like Cecil B. DeMille and Gary Cooper. Jennie was thrilled to discover that many of the film stars she met knew of her and of Grossinger's.

The next day, the Hartmans arranged to take Jennie to Agua Caliente for a few days. It was apparent that Hartman had been talking to Harry Grossinger and that Harry had said, in effect, "Don't let Jennie worry. Everything is going fine at the hotel. Make her relax."

The prescription was a good one. At Agua Caliente, Jennie saw her first horse race and first gambling casino.

She even ventured a few dollars timidly at the roulette table and was amazed to find it was fun. Don Hartman's prescription worked almost too well. After two weeks of the serene Mexican life, she felt so good, she wanted to return home. After all, she was a hotel-keeper by trade. She also felt guilty about being away a long time.

In Ferndale, everyone was delighted to see the returned traveler looking so well, though Dr. Singer expressed disappointment that she'd cut her vacation short. He checked her blood pressure and said it had improved, but cautioned her again to take things easier. Jennie was happy to be flitting again from the front desk to the kitchen, the kitchen to the lake. She was back bringing order to the chronic Sunday afternoon chaos, checking out six or seven hundred guests while simultaneously checking the same number in. She rarely finished a meal. Someone or something always required her attention. Business was booming, and she loved being a part of the exciting scene again. Always at her side was Abe Friedman who never missed an opportunity to bring her optimistic reports about how well things were going. Jennie would listen and then invariably say, "I'm pleased to hear all these nice things, Abie, but that is not what counts. I want to hear the complaints. Just tell me what our guests are not happy about." Jennie's business instincts remained unerring.

At last the long struggle for economic survival was over. Jennie and Harry had done something few mountain resort hotels were far-sighted enough to do—they put their profits back into the hotel. They bought more land and more cottages and installed more private bathrooms. Harry Grossinger was now also making two trips a week to the Washington Market in New York City to buy all the meat, vegetables and fruit for the kitchen (poultry and eggs were bought locally). As meticulous as Selig in selecting only the best, he had received his basic training as a waiter in the dining room, carefully assessing both the praise and the complaints of guests about the food. Harry, too, learned from his guests.

There was an unwritten law at the Washington Market: buyers could touch and feel, but they could never cut into fruit.

"They look good, they feel good," Harry would say, handling a melon, "but I can't tell if they're good until I cut one open." An exception was made and he was allowed to cut open anything he wanted. Harry's orders became so large, produce men just couldn't afford to displease him. Besides, they were fond of him. He had bought a single-bladed knife for $3 in Liberty, and, for fifteen years, he used it to scoop out a piece of melon, grapefruit, or orange.

Harry Grossinger had the same reputation in Liberty that Pop Grossinger had enjoyed during his lifetime. He was made a director of a bank and allowed unlimited credit. He personally hired all the outside and kitchen help. If they proved efficient, they found a firm supporter in him, but he was impatient with incompetence. Though slow to anger, once he lost his temper, his rages were monumental. "Look out for the boss if you see his neck getting red," the men in the kitchen or on the construction crew would say.

When a certain distant cousin came to work as a busboy and carelessly let a glass slip off a tray and break on the cement floor, Harry delivered a mild rebuke. The man became upset, tilted the entire tray, and watched helplessly as the full load came crashing down. Presuming on his fragile kinship with the boss, he announced airily, "So what, Harry, there's plenty more where they came from!" "You—you *trumpvinik!*" Mr. G. roared. "Go to the timekeeper and get your pay!" Mr. G. seldom swore. The word *trumpvinik* was his favorite epithet when he had to upbraid someone. *Nudnik* is a Yiddish word which means pest or incompetent; *trumpvinik* could be roughly translated as *nudnik* raised to the nth degree.

In 1936, Paul Grossinger graduated from the Cornell University School of Hotel Administration. Armed with his diploma, he went directly into the business of helping to run the hotel. Ever since he was old enough to lift a plate, he had worked summers as a busboy, bellboy, waiter or behind the front desk.

This practical experience, plus studies at Cornell, made it easy for him to move into the job as a junior executive. It also took away some of the burden from his mother. Jennie was at last convinced that her frequent headaches were the symptom of chronic high blood pressure and, insofar as her nature would allow it, she began to delegate time-consuming tasks to others.

Dr. Singer, anxious about her blood pressure, had been urging her to spend a month or two in Florida each year during the winter months. It wasn't easy for a woman who knew only long hard hours of work since the age of twelve just to lie in the sun doing nothing, but she made the attempt. She would call the hotel two or three times a day and ask Harry how things were going; ask Paul who had checked in; talk to her daughter, Elaine, now a tall,

pleasant teenager; and to query Abe Friedman, who had
become more and more her indispensible right hand.

Miami Beach is a winter playground, but it was also
the headquarters for many fund-raising activities. The
presence of Jennie on the dais at these functions always
attracted many Grossinger alumni. Jennie would never
refuse any such request. This was hardly the sort of rest
her physician had in mind. Soon, the piercing headaches
returned.

In 1940, Miami Beach was in the midst of a boom;
there were simply not enough hotel rooms to take care of
the mounting waves of refugees from the harsh northern
climes. One day, Leon Miller, a Miami Beach hotel
owner, noticed Jennie talking to a lawyer-realtor who
had some beachfront property on 18th Street and Col-
lins Avenue. Miller concluded the Grossingers must be
planning a Miami Beach hotel and immediately leaped
into action. The Grossingers coming to Florida was an
event of some consequence to the resort industry.

He asked a mutual friend, Leo Robinson, to call Jennie and mention two friends of his, Joe and Frieda Edell,
who owned an even choicer piece of property on 17th
Street. "If you want to build a hotel," Robinson told
her, "Seventeenth Street is the spot."

Jennie, honestly protesting that she had no such
thoughts, eventually yielded to his entreaties that she "at
least meet" the Edells. She did and was instantly taken
by the couple's warmth, sincerity and openness. The
Edells, she found, were eager to form a partnership and
build a new hotel. Jennie argued she was not well and
could not work hard. The couple said that didn't matter.
They had admired Jennie for many years and wanted to

be associated with her. They would do everything, they vowed. (Unfortunately, it didn't quite work out that way.) Jennie called Harry in the Catskills and discovered he liked the idea. A deal was completed in only a few days and the building began to rise rapidly—an eleven-story structure with a hundred-and-thirty-five rooms.

With twenty-six years of hotel experience under her belt, Jennie now took an active role in the planning and design of the new edifice. She had, indeed, learned a great deal from her guests and made many valuable architectural suggestions. Inspecting the blueprints, she immediately overruled the original specifications for the closets, insisting they be made twice as large.

She told the architect, "I've learned there's something just as important as the size of the room and that's the size of the closets. Make the rooms a little smaller if you have to, but the closets must be large." To compensate for a foot taken off the width of each room for additional closet space, Jennie ordered extra-large picture windows which would, she said, "let the outside come inside and make the rooms appear much bigger."

Just about this time, a certain guest checked out of Grossinger's in the Catskills, complaining, "It's impossible to get any sleep around here with all this construction going on." (A new dining room wing was being added to the Main House.) The next day, he entrained for Miami Beach "to get some peace and quiet." After checking into the Dorset Hotel on 16th Street, the displaced traveler went to bed immediately. Early in the morning, he was awakened by the shrill sound of saws and the pounding of hammers. Furious, he picked up the phone and demanded the front desk. "Don't blame us for the noise," the clerk explained. "The Grossingers from the Catskills are building a new hotel next door and they start work early."

Paul Grossinger was named assistant manager of the new Grossinger-Beach Hotel, and it is likely that he still has nightmares over it. In the Catskills, when Harry ordered new rugs and furnishings from the New York wholesale firms, they always arrived on time. It was different in Miami Beach, where one firm monopolized the hotel-and-restaurant equipment field. With the upswing in new hotel construction, the company was doing turnaway business. The owner promised Jennie on three different occasions that all the furnishings and equipment for the new hotel would arrive in time. "Don't worry," he assured her. "You'll have everything before the carpenters are even through. I give you my word."

Jennie, still dubious, said she would be willing to pay storage charges to guarantee early delivery. A full house was booked for the opening of the hotel Christmas week and she wanted to be positive everything would be ready. The owner of the company again informed her there was nothing to worry about.

Evidently, the gentleman's word was something given freely and meant little. With the season's bow only a few days off, the furniture and equipment still had not materialized. Two days before the scheduled opening day, Jennie was told the order could not be filled for two more weeks. She was incredulous and angry. Had not the owner of the company given his word? Faced with this unexpected crisis, the Grossingers scurried about Miami Beach, picking up makeshift furniture and equipment wherever they could, mostly from retail shops and other hotels. The delinquent supplier finally woke up to the crisis and turned everything available in his warehouse over to Jennie. They were out-of-date pieces, but at least they were something.

On opening day, nothing worked but the telephones and these carried only complaints. Yet, once again the special loyalty inspired by the Grossinger family saved the new business from failing right then and there. Long-time guests like Irving Streit—head of the Streit's Matzoh Company—and his wife, Mary, willingly slept on mattresses placed on the floor the first night. Some disgruntled guests left, but the majority remained.

For a week or so, things were very hectic on the Miami beachfront. Not unexpectedly, the strain and the tension again sent Jennie's blood pressure rocketing. This time, she was hurried to Kellogg's Sanitarium in Miami Springs for ten days of total rest. When she returned, the Grossinger-Beach Hotel was in good shape. Paul and Joe and Frieda Edell told her every room was filled and that the desk was piled high with reservations.

Leaving the hotel in the competent hands of Paul and her new partners, Jennie returned to New York to see Dr. William Hitzig, a cardiac specialist on the staff of Mt. Sinai Hospital. Dr. Hitzig was to become the guardian of Jennie's health for the next quarter of a century. This man, who cared for a small army of renowned patients and was responsible years later for bringing Japanese atomic bomb victims to America for treatment, soon became much more than Jennie's doctor. He was, Jennie said, "a beloved friend, guide, teacher, and inspiration to me." One reason she saw a specialist of the stature of Dr. Hitzig was a troublesome new symptom worrying her. As she explained it to him: "It's not only headaches that bother me, I also have the feeling that swarms of ants are crawling over my back and shoulders. I know this sounds peculiar." Dr. Hitzig did not take patient's complaints lightly. "You're going into Mount Sinai immediately for some tests," he said. By now, hospitals were a familiar second home to Jennie.

The results of the tests were not encouraging. Her sinuses had become infected causing toxicity throughout the body which produced the "crawling-ant" sensation. Only surgery could alleviate the condition. She had no choice but to submit to the doctor's directive and spent five pain-wracked weeks recuperating from the operation. Jennie left the hospital in early December of 1941, as the world was convulsed anew by Japan's treachery at Pearl Harbor.

Chapter 13

Miami Beach was quickly put on a wartime basis. Thousands of regular soldiers and Army Air Force personnel began descending on the city. By the spring, several Miami Beach hotels—including the Grossinger-Beach— were requisitioned as Air Force installations. Jennie returned to the Catskills to meet with Harry, Paul, Abe and Milton and discuss ways in which the hotel could help the war effort. As a result, bond raffles were soon held every week at the hotel. Admittance to special shows in the Playhouse was by war bond only.

Within a year, nearly $1,000,000 worth had been sold. Grossinger's was selected as one of the few institutions other than banks to be named a direct government sales agency for war bonds. The Army Air Force wrote that inasmuch as Jennie and her guests had "paid for" a bomber, they could have the privilege of naming it. The stipulation was that the name had to be geographic. Guests were asked to vote for a suitable name and they selected "Grossinger Lake." Before the war was over, more than $10,000,000 in bonds would be sold at the hotel.

All during the war, a steady parade of wounded servicemen came to Grossinger's as guests of the family from Army and Navy hospitals in the East. On one Friday evening, a tall young man of serious mien, dressed in the uniform of a staff sergeant of the United States Army, sat himself down at the grand piano in the main lobby and began playing familiar classical music. Walking by, Jennie paused for a minute at the piano and said, "I hope you don't mind, but I wonder if I might ask you to stop playing. It's the Sabbath eve, you know, and guests are requested not to play. Come back tomorrow evening, if you like."

The next day, she bumped into the soldier again, introduced herself, apologized for not allowing him to play, and asked, "By the way, what is your name, young man?" The sergeant responded softly, "Emanuel List." Mr. List was, of course, one of America's most brilliant young classical pianists enjoying a major reputation on the concert stage before he was drafted.

Jennie found there was much that could be done to make the lives of the men in uniform easier. One service was unintentionally suggested by Private Alvin Kaplan, a former staff member taking Air Force basic training in Miami Beach. He sent a card which merely said, "They don't serve pickled herring for breakfast here any more." The card pictured the former Grossinger-Beach Hotel. A jar of pickled herring was dispatched to Private Kaplan instantly. Harry, Jennie, Abe and Milton then decided to start the Grossinger "Canteen-by-Mail."

At its peak, the Canteen-by-Mail went to over two thousand servicemen and women who had either worked or been guests at Grossinger's. The financing of the gift packages came in part from the family, in part from guests' contributions, and in part from the proceeds of special shows and sports exhibitions at the hotel. Those in basic training received shoe-shine kits. When they were shipped overseas, they were sent soap and cigarettes. Chocolates went to GIs in cool climates. Those in the tropics received nonperishable fruitcakes and other goodies. Whenever possible, jars of pickled herring were shipped. The packages were always acknowledged with gratitude. Often the GIs asked for news of Grossinger's. This prompted Jennie to ask staff member Lee Rogow (later to become a well-known magazine writer and critic) to publish a special Grossinger's newssheet, the *Bugle*, shipped overseas along with the packages. When Rogow left to command a Navy PT boat, Paul Zousmer, an aide of Blackstone's, took over. In addition to hotel news, he wrote about movies and shows that were playing in New York and a "Where Are They?" column including overseas addresses that brought about many a reunion. And he printed letters which the GIs sent, some hilarious, others heart-breaking.

It wasn't always easy to ship pickled herring to combat areas, but a jar did get through to a Marine in the midst of the most bitter fighting on Guadalcanal. Marine Sgt. Barney Ross wrote his thanks saying, "I'm not suggesting this for the hotel menu, but pickled herring goes great with C Rations."

A by-product of the Grossinger Canteen-by-Mail turned out to be the celebrated slogan, "Grossinger's Has

Everything." When food treats were shipped to service-men, fudge often went to those stationed in northern regions. Because fudge would spoil in the South Pacific and Southeast Asia, Paul Zousmer looked for a substitute that would hold up in hot climates, finally settling on a fruitcake.

When Sgt. Herbert Feldman in Burma, got his cake loaded with an endless variety of fruits and nuts, he wrote back in appreciation, "The fruit cake reminds me of Grossinger's—it has everything." The line "Grossinger's Has Everything" appeared in the very next hotel ad.

Although he was unable to read the eye chart with his right eye during his physical, Paul Grossinger was inducted into the Army in March of 1944. When Paul was a youngster, the child of a guest accidentally shot him in the right eye with a bee-bee rifle. The sight in the eye had been seriously impaired ever since. Because of the disability and his extensive knowledge of the culinary arts, Paul was assigned to the Quartermaster Corps and put in charge of the Officers' Mess at the Fort Dix Army base in New Jersey.

One day an old friend, Captain Joe Gould (the one-time manager of heavyweight champion Jim Braddock) arrived for dinner. When it was over he said to Paul, "I don't want to offend you, but the food here isn't as good as the food at Grossinger's."

"I know," Paul said sadly, "but I couldn't persuade them to draft our cook."

Paradoxically, the war was not hurting business at the hotel. People couldn't buy new cars or new homes, but they could buy reasonably priced vacations. One of the guests who made a profound impression, not only on

Jennie but the staff, was the world-famous statesman, Dr. Chaim Weizmann, who would become the first President of the new State of Israel. A mutual friend, Meyer Weisgal, now head of the Weizmann Institute of Science in Israel, first suggested Grossinger's to the famed Zionist as an ideal retreat for convalescence after he underwent major eye surgery.

Dr. Weizmann, accompanied by his wife, Vera, a physician who was able to nurse him, lived for eight weeks at the Ross Cottage. During those turbulent days, he was more the scientist working for the common war effort than the revered leader of Zionism. The girls at the telephone switchboard had to get accustomed to hearing a voice say crisply, "This is No. 10 Downing Street telephoning Dr. Chaim Weizmann," or, "The White House is calling Dr. Weizmann."

In 1944, Jennie's blood pressure soared to astronomical heights. She had read in *The New York Times* of a revolutionary new operation designed to reduce blood pressure. Doctors called it a "radical sympathectomy." At that time, it was still in the experimental stage and many surgeons counseled against it. Now, she was told by Dr. Hitzig, that the operation was being performed successfully at the Mayo Clinic in Rochester, Minnesota. Jennie decided to go to Rochester. She announced to the family she was going for a checkup. In her heart, she prayed the Mayo doctors would tell her they could operate. She had been living too long with high blood pressure and oppressive, unrelenting headaches. She was willing to grasp at any straw for relief.

While still at home, a small abscess developed under Jennie's right arm which she chose to ignore as trivial. By the time she reached Mayo, it had enlarged into an ugly egg-sized lump. The doctors would not even discuss an operation; they were interested only in treating the infection. For seven weeks, she lay in her hospital bed. The infection was cured, but the battle weakened her.

Once recovered, she looked confidently toward the blood pressure surgery. But the word she finally received from the consulting surgeons was disheartening. "We've decided this operation is not for you," her doctor told her. "We don't feel you'll be able to stand the shock right now."

"Will I be able to have the surgery when I'm stronger?" Jennie asked, almost desperately.

The doctor hesitated then said, "I'm afraid not, Mrs. Grossinger. I'm afraid your condition is something you'll have to learn to live with."

The doctor's tone was gentle, but firm. The verdict staggered her. She had convinced herself she could be operated on and the result would be a complete deliverance from pain. The sudden realization that this was not to be left her faint. For a few minutes she sat engulfed in self-pity. Then, unbidden, the familiar words she had heard her mother intone so often came to her: "God will help you all the time. Remember, God is the greatest doctor of all. The others are only his assistants." Her mother had always lived by this faith and it was a good one. Jennie resolved not to let herself drift into hopelessness and invalidism.

She knew she could not go back to work right away. She decided this might be the ideal time to indulge her long-standing passion for self-education. She would devote herself to learning about the world of art. Author

Irving Stone had once taken her to the Metropolitan Museum of Art where she had been overwhelmed by the world of color and form that Stone and his wife knew so well. She confessed her ignorance to the couple, but also confided a determination to learn something about art "when I get the time." She decided the time was now, while she recuperated.

Eddie and Ida Cantor had been singing the praises of Palm Springs, where they had a home, for a long time. She had promised them that one day she would see it for herself. This seemed as good a time as any. In Los Angeles, she was met at the train by Sam and Pauline Golter, who arranged to take her to Palm Springs. Sam Golter was a boyhood friend of Harry Grossinger's from Chicago. Moving to the West Coast at the same time Harry returned East, he eventually became the administrative head and guiding spirit of the famed City of Hope Hospital in Duarte, California, one of Jennie and Harry's favorite philanthropies. Their contributions financed the main food preparation center at the institution, still called the "Grossinger Kitchens."

Perhaps it was the extreme dryness in the desert oasis that caused her health to improve; more likely, it was simply that here she allowed herself a really long vacation with complete relaxation and afternoon naps every day. This was the kind of idleness both Drs. Singer and Hitzig wanted her to enjoy years earlier. She spent five full months in the picturesque resort and seemed to gain strength with every passing day.

Eddie and Ida Cantor's concern for her was touching and deeply gratifying. She saw them two or three times each week; spoke to them by phone every day that she didn't see them; and, indeed, did much of her relaxing at their charming home. She also found in Palm Springs the opportunity to study art. Soon after her arrival, she leafed through a copy of the *Desert Sun* and saw an advertisement which made her wonder if destiny hadn't sent her to the Springs. It read: "Jon Gnagy, artist, interested in private pupils." She phoned Mr. Gnagy.

The next morning, a pleasant-mannered young man knocked at her door. He looked exactly like her conception of an artist, complete with neatly clipped Van Dyke beard. (It wasn't until some time later that she learned this beard was not a mark of his profession, but a custom of his Mennonite religion.)

"I've never had a lesson in painting," she warned him.

"And I have never given a lesson," he said a bit solemnly. "You're my first pupil."

The following weeks were exciting ones for Jennie. She grew fond of the warm and witty Jon, his wife and their child. When they took sketching trips to the desert, she realized that for fifty years she had had eyes, but had never seen. Jon Gnagy pointed out the multihued beauty of the desert, and, even if she didn't become a proficient artist, she did develop an appreciation of the art in nature.

She enjoyed the lessons so much she thought the guests back at the hotel would enjoy them, too. She broached the subject to Gnagy. Even though he had never heard of Grossinger's, he promised he would visit her the following summer at the hotel.

As a result, he started the hotel's first art program, and then, after three years, left to open his own studio on New York's 57th Street.

While still in California, Jennie visited a widowed cousin by marriage employed in the posh Beverly Hills salon of the noted women's hat designer, Mr. John. This effervescent, Viennese-born lady, the very embodiment of Continental charm and chic, was known professionally as "Mme. Savonier." In fact, her name was Karla Grossinger. The moment Jennie met her, she decided that Grossinger's and Karla were made for each other. "Now that Evelyn Bittker has left to open her own place in Arizona, we could use someone like you around the hotel," she told Karla. "And, after all, you are a member of the family." It took persuasion, but the bubbling lady finally agreed to chuck the sophisticated world of haute couture for the rustic life.

To say that Karla brought Old World class and elegance to The G. would be an understatement. Outgoing, witty, radiant, polylingual, extravagantly gracious, this Grossinger-by-marriage eventually took on the job of social hostess. With her familiar "Allo, Allo," greeting, she became a cherished adjunct to the social life at Grossinger's. After a decade, homesick for Europe and the world she knew in her youth, she left America to take up residence in the Italian spa of Montecatini where to this day she reigns as a *grande dame* and local personality basking in the title, "Donna Karla."

Jennie not only felt physically improved when she departed Palm Springs, her mental attitude had changed. She knew she could not expect a miraculous cure for her high blood pressure, but she now felt she had learned to endure it until such time as medical science might provide new ways to help her. Life in the serene desert environment, so unlike the hurly-burly of her demanding daily existence at the hotel, had given her a new inner calm and fortitude. She had also made up her mind to delegate more and more of her duties to others, promising herself to keep as free from nervous strain as was humanly possible.

It was a promise she found difficult to carry out. Back in the Catskills, there were important business decisions to be settled. The death of Joe Edell in Florida made it imperative that the Grossingers think about the future of the Grossinger-Beach Hotel. All agreed they did not want the responsibility of running it on their own. With Harry so busy, Jennie decided to return to Florida to arrange a sale in April, 1945.

She had barely completed the final details when Harry phoned her with the suggestion that she inspect another hotel, the sprawling Pancoast Hotel, then on the block. Harry still had not abandoned the idea of maintaining a Florida base as a complement to their Catskill resort.

Another factor: he now had a new associate, restaurateur Harry Horowitz, someone he had known since East Side days. Mr. Horowitz, who once owned a cafeteria on Broadway in mid-Manhattan, was naturally anxious to invest with the Grossingers and share ownership of an important Florida operation.

The hotel was old, with an air of elegance. It was one of the original landmarks built by Carl G. Fisher, the visionary tycoon who literally dredged Miami Beach out of a mangrove swamp and single-handedly developed it as a resort mecca. After the city was incorporated in 1915, Fisher, a man with a Barnum streak, who made his original millions manufacturing Prest-O-Lite auto lamps, used every kind of ballyhoo to promote the area—from circus elephants to bathing beauties. He built the Beach's first hotels, put in polo fields and glass-enclosed tennis courts, and enticed his millionaire friends to build lavish homes there.

The Pancoast had three-hundred-and-thirty feet of beachfront, a Spanish-Moroccan motif, two-hundred-and-sixty rooms, and a superb location on 29th Street. The Grossingers decided to buy. They took over ownership during the summer of 1945. Paul flew down to take active charge, along with his wife, the former Martha Rothkrug, a striking-looking, dark-haired girl whom he had met when she was a Grossinger guest. And Jennie soon had her first grandchild, Richard. The Pancoast, used as an Army Air Force Hospital throughout the war, required considerable remodeling and refurbishing before it could be formally launched as the Grossinger-Pancoast.

There was one awkward episode prior to its opening on January 10, 1946, which made it seem like the Grossinger-Beach all over again. Using the direct-mail approach which had been so successful in the Catskills, they sent thousands of new brochures to all the former Pancoast clients. The accompanying letter emphasized that dietary laws would be strictly observed at the new Pancoast.

One recipient wrote back with obvious bafflement: "I was pleased to learn that you have taken over the Pancoast Hotel and you have my best wishes, but I am puzzled by your reference to dietary laws. Do they have anything to do with dieting?"

The Grossingers, it developed, were unaware that the Pancoast was once a restricted hotel—one of many high-priced Miami Beach hostelries where metal plaques with the legend, "Gentiles Only," were prominently displayed. It would take several decades before this ethnic line would be effectively cracked. During the mid and late Thirties, Jewish businessmen who survived the Depression and saw the potential of the sun-splashed beaches, began investing heavily in oceanfront real estate —and their money was more than welcome. When columnist Walter Winchell discovered the Mediterranean style Roney-Plaza Hotel and began to sing the praises of the sunshine-and-orange land in his widely syndicated pillar, the flight southward became fashionable for a new set of affluent citizens. They were Broadway and show business types, most of them Jewish, who began to transform the face and life style of Miami Beach.

The Grossinger-Pancoast prospered from the start. Once it was operating smoothly, Jennie returned to the Catskills and again spoke of "really slowing down" and "living sensibly." But it was just talk. The idea of Grossinger's without Jennie just didn't make sense. In 1946, after more than thirty-two years, the two were inseparable. Instead, Jennie continued to work as hard as ever and, not surprisingly, her headaches returned. During this period, another rankling matter aggravated her stress. When Selig died, he and Harry each owned 50 percent of the Grossinger stock. Pop Grossinger knew his son-in-law well; he knew that Harry would always take good care of Jennie. He decided to leave his 50 percent share to his daughter, Lottie Grau, and his mute son, Harry—12½ percent of his holdings to Lottie and 37½ percent to Harry. This would insure both families' security. In 1931, the resort was not yet a national institution, but it was clearly on its way to becoming a financial success.

Fifteen years later, the value of the stock had multiplied many-fold. Lottie's children were now married. Some of these new relatives felt they were entitled to join in the management of the hotel's affairs. Though all received a considerable share of the annual Grossinger income, they still felt like outsiders and envied the recognition enjoyed by Jennie and Harry. Their complaints were more a matter of ego and power drives than simple dollars and cents. Little Harry, the second largest stockholder in the hotel corporation, found himself in the middle of the tug-of-war between the Grau forces and the Grossingers. His first child, a boy named Selig after his grandfather, was also born without hearing or speech. But good fortune eventually smiled on the handicapped couple. Their second-born, Mary Ann, was completely normal in every way. Strong and compassionate, she developed early a powerful sense of responsibility and protectiveness toward her afflicted parents and brother. Mary Ann literally became their voice and ears to the outside world.

For his part, Harry Grossinger, a man of resolute will, was unalterably opposed to any interference in the hotel's operation from his new relatives. He and Jennie were knowledgeable professionals (just as Paul and Elaine were now emerging as competent hotel executives), and he disliked the thought of amateurs, even if they were in the family, tampering with a successful business so laboriously built. Some of the arguments with the minority stockholders were acrimonious, causing Jennie considerable mental anguish. She knew her husband was right, but she hated controversy. The unpleasantness of family strife left an open festering wound that had, sooner or later, to be bound.

Feeling that she could no longer endure her oppressive headaches, difficulty in speech, and even lapses in memory, Jennie's thoughts turned again to the operation which had been denied her at the Mayo Clinic. In Miami Beach, she sought out Dr. Emil Isberg, formerly of the staff of Dr. Max Peat of the University of Michigan, the physician who specialized in the difficult sympathectomy surgery. Dr. Isberg strongly recommended that Jennie have the operation. Dr. Peat personally flew south for a brief visit, examined Jennie, and agreed to accept her as a patient.

Before making her final decision, Jennie consulted Dr. Hitzig who had originally urged the operation several years back. "Afterwards, I can convalesce in Miami Beach," she pointed out. "Dr. Isberg knows how to handle cases like mine."

"You must understand, Jennie, this is extremely dangerous," Dr. Hitzig cautioned.

"I know that, but I'm living in torment. If there is the slightest chance this operation will help me, I want that chance."

Just after the 1946 summer season ended, Jennie left for Ann Arbor, Michigan. She told everyone she was merely going for another checkup. The truth, she confided only to Paul and to Barney Ross. The former world's champion had only recently returned from Guadalcanal with medals for heroism on his chest and a monkey on his back.

Barney's boxing style was all guts—and so was his style

as a U. S. Marine on that bloody Pacific Island in 1942, where he killed twenty-two of the enemy while guarding three wounded buddies and nursing his own wounds. That action earned him a Silver Star. Badly wounded, he battled a long siege of malaria for which large doses of pain-killing morphine was standard treatment. The malaria finally ran its course, but now his body screamed for the morphine on which it had become dependent. Barney voluntarily committed himself to the government hospital at Lexington, Kentucky, for the long, agonizing cure.

The stalwart champion had a nobility of spirit that lifted him above the common man. "You'll beat it, Barney, and so will I," Jennie assured him.

"We'll meet here at the hotel in sixty days," he said solemnly and each took comfort from the confidence of the other.

But they didn't meet in sixty days. Each went through a much tougher ordeal than either had anticipated. Jennie's operation was a success, but she hadn't foreseen the dreadful post-operative agony. One night, a week after surgery, she awoke in acute pain. Though repeatedly cautioned to remain in bed, she thought a walk to the window might help ease the cramps. Carefully, she sat up and just as carefully moved to the edge of the bed. She took a step, another step, and then a fit of dizziness seized her and she fell heavily to the floor.

The fall delayed her recovery for months. Several of the sutures had been ripped and additional surgery became necessary. Back in New York, she had to enter Doctor's Hospital for many more weeks. The pain was unrelenting. Some two months after the operation, she left for Miami Beach where doctors thought the sunshine and continued rest would help. She and Harry now owned a comfortable Spanish-style house on Pinetree Drive with a spacious patio shaded by palm trees. Jennie tried to walk up the steps to her bedroom, but found she could not. She literally had to be pulled up each day by her nurse. For the first time in her life, depressed and in almost constant pain, Jennie harbored suicidal thoughts, although self-destruction was an act totally alien to everything she had ever been taught.

One afternoon, she had a visit from a devoted friend, Link Scheffres. Jennie's depressed mental state alarmed him. He tried to comfort her by telling of the recovery of an acquaintance who underwent similar surgery a year before. Jennie smiled appreciatively, but she felt that he was only trying to be kind. When Scheffres returned to New York, he called the man, Phillip See, owner of a textile mill in New Bedford, Massachusetts, and told him about Jennie. A few days later, she received a five-page, hand-written letter obviously composed with deep feeling and sincerity. The sympathetic stranger's comforting words had an instantaneous therapeutic effect. This letter, from someone who had gone through much the same agony as Jennie, was a rallying point for her, physically and mentally. Years later, she confided to Link Scheffres, "You know, your friend Mr. See really saved my life!"

When, at long last, Jennie returned to the mountains, she found the headaches came with less frequency and less intensity. Her mind and memory were sharp again and she felt a freedom of body and spirit that she had not known for years.

Events moved rapidly in those days. Back in civilian life, the enforced separation of wartime placed an insuperable barrier between Paul and Martha. They agreed to an amicable divorce. On June 17, 1947, Paul married Ricelle "Bunny" Persky, a vivacious brunette, originally from Hartford, Connecticut. Two months later, daughter Elaine married David Etess, a hometown boy from Liberty, entering his junior year at the University of Syracuse Medical School.

With Jennie back as the symbol of Grossinger's and its grand lady, Harry once again retreated into the background. His desire for anonymity was a ruling passion with him, yet he was always at the center of power. He directly supervised all construction and maintenance work; went to New York to do the buying; prowled through the massive freezing rooms below the kitchen; and kept an eye on financial matters. He was essentially a private man, shy and withdrawn. Many of the guests who saw him walking around the grounds did not even know who he was.

His closest friends were the men who had worked with him for years, like purchasing assistant Lubo Tudor who would move mountains for the boss. Except on Saturday evenings when he appeared at the weekly hotel cocktail party, Harry seldom showed the warmth of his personality or his dry sense of humor to strangers. But when you were his friend, it was different. Then, his affection and generosity overflowed. Often, when he spoke to someone he liked, he would good-naturedly jab that person in the ribs. It was his way of saying someone was a *menseh*, someone he could respect.

No matter how successful the business became, Harry

never could quite believe it. Schooled in the old-fashioned hotel virtues of hard work, fresh air, good food and a comfortable place to sleep, he never completely lost his underlying distrust of some of the new-fangled ideas that competition and progress demanded. Long after the Grossinger family had any need to worry about such matters, he would be upset by an electric light left on unnecessarily and testily flick it off.

Nepotism was another activity that Harry looked upon with open suspicion, especially when he encountered self-styled "relatives" whom he'd never heard of before. Once the name of Grossinger became well known, long lost "relatives" from Europe turned up in an unending procession. A much repeated story about Harry concerned a young public relations assistant hired by the hotel. One morning, Harry saw him eating at the staff table in the dining room and called Abe Friedman over to inquire, "Abe, who is that sitting over there with the staff? He doesn't look familiar to me."

"He's the new public relations man," Abe replied brightly.

"I don't care what kind of relation he is," Harry snapped. "We have enough relatives around here already! Get rid of him!"

For all these occasional outbursts, the employment records at Grossinger's show that it took a great deal to get anyone fired. No matter what happened, there was always Jennie as the last "court of appeal." It was almost an automatic procedure: whenever an employe would be sacked, for whatever cause, he would instantly seek Jennie out and plead his case anew. Nine times out of ten, he would be back on the job the next day!

For her part, the venerated Mom Grossinger had evolved into a kind of dowager empress, albeit an empress who also could not accept the idea that she was a wealthy woman. She consistently refused to open a bank account. Jennie and Harry insisted that she draw at least $100 a week from the cashier. (Had she asked, she could have had a great deal more.) Every Monday, she drew the money, always in small bills. By Thursday, she was broke and would borrow from the busboys and waiters. The family wondered where Mom spent her money. No merchant in Liberty would accept money from her; instead, they would send the bills to the hotel. But these bills were small, usually for fabric to make herself a dress or an apron.

Mom had a favorite waiter, Sy Abrams, whom she spoke of proudly as "my secretary." For a long time, he was the only one who knew what happened to Mom's $100 in small bills. Mom received many letters—the major part from Europe—written by children and grandchildren of people she had known in Galicia when she was very young. Nearly all were pleas for financial help. She never turned anyone down.

One day, Governor Thomas E. Dewey, scheduled to speak at a dinner at the hotel, arrived early. As he entered the lobby, someone pointed him out to Mom Grossinger. Mom, who was never abashed at meeting the great or near-great, volunteered to take the Governor on a tour of the grounds. He smilingly accepted her offer. They walked for a half hour and guests who saw them were amazed at the rapt attention the Governor paid to everything Mom said. Occasionally they stopped and seemed to be discussing something of great interest to the state's highest official. When they returned to the hotel, Mr. Dewey went directly to the dining room. Curious guests rushed up to Mom.

"What did you and the Governor talk about?" one asked anxiously.

"But what would we talk about?" Mom shrugged her frail shoulders. "About Moses and King David and King Solomon we talked. He is a very religious man, you know."

The trip to Albany was no longer a burdensome automobile ride; it was now a swift half-hour airplane flight. Soon after the war, an ex-Army Air Force pilot named Vernon Wright stopped at the hotel. He and a partner owned a small charter airline and were looking for a spot that could be converted into a landing field around Sullivan County. In fact, Milton and Jennie began thinking about the feasibility of air travel to the hotel more than a decade before, back in the summer of 1936. At that time, an amateur pilot named Sam Barish, cruising around the area, decided to see Grossinger's. He flew into a small airport at Monticello, ten miles south of the hotel, and phoned ahead about landing at Grossinger's. Milton Blackstone, who took the call, suggested he land his Travelaire bi-plane on the golf course. When Mr. Barish's small craft dropped out of the skies for a perfect three-point landing on one of the fairways, he was greeted by a cheering, applauding throng. Virtually every guest in the hotel turned out for the landing which had been heralded on the hotel loudspeakers. The amused pilot remarked to Jennie, "I feel like a Jewish Lindbergh."

Milton and Jennie, with their unfailing vision, foresaw

even then that air travel was the wave of the future for the Catskills.

Ten years later, Milton Blackstone drove Vernon Wright around the countryside. The only level fields they found were either too expensive or not for sale. But Wright had planted a seed in the nimble brain of Blackstone. The next morning, Milton drove to a "hill" adjoining the Grossinger property three miles from the hotel. Two brothers, Tom and Will Nicholson, lived in a small farmhouse on the hill, which was really a fairly flat plateau. They were sitting on their porch when Milton arrived. Both had been born in this house and for fifty-seven years had farmed the land they owned. Milton discussed the question of buying the land and making an airport of it.

Tom said: "Too many trees."

Will shook his head: "Awful lot of boulders."

Milton warmed to the subject: "The trees could be cut down. The boulders could be blasted. This could make a nice little airfield. Would you be interested in selling?"

"Maybe," Tom said.

The property was finally bought for $50,000. Within six months, planes were landing on the plateau which was called Grossinger Field—one of the first airstrips ever built exclusively for the use of guests of a resort hotel.

Now, Grossinger's did have just about everything, including a small synagogue presided over by Rabbi Harry Z. Stone, who was a great favorite with staff and guests. Not only did he reign as resident intellectual, but his unique personality and wit seemed to be ideally suited to the role of a "resort rabbi" whose view of the world was gently mocking and comic. One of Rabbi Stone's minor vexations, he confessed, was some difficulty in rounding up a *minyan*, the ten-man quorum necessary for an Orthodox Jewish service. "Even those who pray back home," he would say, "have too many distractions around here. How can God compete with a golf course?"

Change is the life blood of an institution catering to the public and Grossinger's, though steeped in tradition, had necessarily "to keep up"—or fall behind. The years immediately following World War II brought much ferment to the American social scene and a few radical changes to the style of life at Grossinger's. One change stemmed from the need to modify restrictive religious practices that impinged on the activities of vacationers who did not hold rigorous beliefs.

As late as 1948, the Sabbath was a somber period of low-key activity at Grossinger's. For thirty-four years, the seventh day of the week had been scrupulously marked by the total absence of any form of diversion once the sun descended on Friday evenings. During the summer, the Playhouse—some distance from the Main House— could be used since it was considered a separate entity. With the onset of cold weather, however, all activities were moved to the Main House and the Sabbath eve became a subdued time of religious observance. By 1948, most weekend guests were not notably pious, with the result that the local movie houses in Liberty became the immediate beneficiaries. A new clientele was also beginning to come to Grossinger's—assimilated young suburban couples who had abandoned the strict Orthodoxy of their parents. They would no longer continue to patronize a resort that failed to offer some kind of diversion every evening of a brief weekend away from home.

The hotel's rabbinical advisor agreed that an acceptable arrangement might be worked out that would not violate the ancient Talmudic law. What was necessary was legal transfer of the ownership of the premises to a third party—not a Jew, of course—for the period of the Sabbath. The Talmudic sages anticipated this modern-day dilemma when they evolved a doctrine known in Hebrew as the *Shtar M'Chirah,* which directs an observant Jew to divest himself of all "incidents of ownership" during the Sabbath as a means of adhering to the law while insuring the continuity of a business enterprise. Malke listened attentively to the rabbi, but her piety was too deep-rooted to allow for such a radical change. It remained for Abe Friedman to win her over.

Abe patiently spelled out to the pious matriarch that strict observance of the dietary laws or *kashruth* (her prime concern) was not in any way involved. They would be adhered to just as before. But, he asked in his kindly way, was it really fair to impose a person's convictions and practices on guests who spent hard-earned money for a vacation and who did not necessarily share those ideas? Moreover, he pointed out that guests who were Orthodox did not have to attend any of the shows or listen to the dance music if they chose not to. His most effective argument, however, focused on a more immediate and humane consideration: the livelihoods of many of the staff whom Malke loved were being threatened. If there was no weekend business, many would have to be laid off.

"Mom," he explained, "before long we will have to

close up on the weekends in the winter if we have no music or entertainment on Fridays. It wouldn't be right for all the people who make a living with us."

The old lady could not resist this last argument. She relented with a sigh. It was unanimously agreed that Hans Behrens, the veteran stage designer at the hotel, would be asked to become the official purchaser of the Main House just after sundown every Friday night, and all the legal documents were properly drawn. The ritual re-sale would take place the next day after sundown. And so, having duly transferred the deed and consummated the ritual "sale," a variety revue was presented for the first time on a Friday evening, in May of 1948, in the dining room. To this day, the ritual sale, *Shtar M'Chirah*, is performed each Friday.

This symbolically significant leap forward took on even added importance the following year when one of the nation's most prestigious magazines, *Holiday*, which normally chronicled such high-toned tourist attractions as the Riviera and Newport, decided that Grossinger's merited elaborate editorial coverage. A nine-page, illustrated article written by Al Hine for the August, 1949, issue imparted to Grossinger's the kind of cachet that clearly established it in the front rank of America's leading resort playgrounds.

Increasingly, too, the hotel became the site for special dinners, celebrations and functions with Jennie spotlighted as the "Queen Lady" on the dais. The feelings of inferiority which plagued Jennie for most of the early years of her adult life rarely asserted themselves now. These days, she exuded confidence and seemed to have a natural affinity for a microphone.

As she continued to gain strength, Jennie began to preside over the many charitable and social affairs held at Grossinger's. She had developed into an adroit toast-master and a lively public speaker though she was sometimes guilty of malapropisms which caused guests (and herself) to howl with laughter. One night, the world of popular music gave a dinner at the hotel. Eddie Fisher, Fred Waring, Sammy Kaye, Perry Como, Irving Caesar and many other musical greats were present.

Jennie was asked to introduce Hugo Winterhalter, musical director of RCA-Victor Records. She began, "And now, ladies and gentlemen, I would like to introduce my very dear friend, Mr. Victor Hugo." Pandemonium broke out.

Another time, called upon to introduce Florence Chadwick, soon after the swimmer of the English Channel negotiated the equally treacherous Catalina Channel in the Pacific Ocean off the California coast, Jennie blithely announced, "Ladies and gentlemen, I'm so proud to welcome back that courageous lady, Miss Florence Chadwick, who has just returned from swimming the Pacific Ocean!"

In the Mid-Fifties, a syndicate of realtors made a very attractive offer to lease the desirable waterfront land on which the Grossinger-Pancoast Hotel stood in order to build a new luxury hotel to be called the Seville. Paul Grossinger had been bringing a great deal of convention business to The Big G., filling in what had formerly been the slack season. He also had a pretty good idea that the day of leisurely hotels like the old-fashioned Pancoast was about finished. Enormous, very luxurious inns were beginning to spring up all over Miami Beach. The charming old resorts were no longer in demand.

A tragic event occurred some months before the leasing of the Pancoast which also strengthened Jennie's resolve to quit Florida. One February morning, she was horrified to receive a frantic phone call from Ferndale telling her that one of the staff cottages had burned to the ground with the loss of many lives. Earlier that morning, an employe had made some coffee on an electric hot plate. Apparently, a short circuit developed, sparking a flash fire. Jennie knew every one of the victims well. She was in a state of shock for days. Unreasonably, she felt that the tragedy might have been averted had she not been away. This deepened her grief. For a time, she could not bear the thought of returning to the mountains to meet the friends and relatives of those who perished. There were also many who had suffered severe burns and were recuperating in Maimonides Hospital in Liberty.

Finally, an anguished Jennie forced herself to fly home. Her first stop was the hospital. Hesitantly, she entered the ward where some of the injured women were being treated. Anxiety and uncertainty paled her face. But the moment the patients saw Jennie, they spontaneously shouted greetings and sat up in their beds, eager to kiss and embrace her. To Jennie's amazement, she found the girls were consoling *her*. The special bond between Jennie and those who worked at Grossinger's had never been more poignantly expressed. Still, she resolved that henceforth, she would spend all of her time in the Catskills.

Chapter 14

Of the galaxy of show business stars whose names are intimately associated with The G., Eddie Fisher's is the one the public thinks of most often—and with good reason.

The story of Fisher's discovery at Grossinger's is almost the classic tale of how entertainers used the hotel as a stepping stone to fame and great fortune. One day in 1947, Jennie received a phone call from Milton Blackstone, who asked if she would mind doing Monte Proser a favor. Proser was handling publicity and booking talent at the Copacabana in New York. He was high on a seventeen-year-old singer from Philadelphia using the professional name Dick White, but the boy needed experience before an audience. Jennie told Milton to send him right up. Jennie also liked the sky, skinny youngster, who arrived by bus because it was a little cheaper than the train. When he sang in the Terrace Room, dancers paid him the ultimate compliment: they stopped dancing and gathered around the bandstand. Though Julie Karson, the master of ceremonies, was enthusiastic about the boy's voice, members of the band disagreed.

"Nice kid," they said, "but he can't sing a rhythm tune. He can't keep the beat."

At the end of the week, Morty Curtis, who was hired by Blackstone to book entertainment for the hotel, tried to get Eddie work at some of the other resorts. Their bookers came, heard and shook their heads.

"You can have him for $35 a shot," Morty said.

"At that price, what can you lose?"

"Our clients," they replied. "The kid doesn't have it." Next, phoning several resort owners, Curtis asked them to book Eddie as a favor to Milton Blackstone and himself. Since some of them owed Blackstone favors, two or three half-heartedly agreed. The same thing happened. The musicians shook their heads, but the dancers invariably clustered around the bandstand to hear him. When Eddie had exhausted the possibilities of other resort hotels, he came back to Grossinger's and was put on the staff at $50 a week. He shared a room under the Playhouse with a lifeguard, a masseur, and a waiter, but this didn't deter Eddie from taking in boarders. Joey Forman, a Philadelphia chum of Eddie's, who later became a successful TV and film comedy character actor, hitchhiked to the hotel to see his friend. He slept on the floor of the already-crowded bedroom, and each night Eddie smuggled food from the dining room to Joey.

Eddie had been singing with the hotel's house orchestra for three summers when Milton Blackstone decided he was ready for bigger things. He arranged for young Fisher to perform on the same bill with Eddie Cantor who was booked to headline the 1949 Labor Day show.

"I've got a boy I think you'll like," Milton told Cantor.

The show that Labor Day eve was emceed by a popular figure around the hotel in those days, suave Bob Weitman, then managing director of the famed Paramount Theatre in New York. (Today, Bob Weitman is chief of all studio production at Columbia Pictures in Hollywood.) When Fisher sang, Cantor listened closely. After the young man finished, Cantor walked out to the microphone and said, "Ladies and gentlemen, I've heard many young singers in my time, but no one quite like this kid. I'm starting a vaudeville tour across the country next week and I'd like to take him along as part of my act. What do you think about that?" There was a roar of approval from the audience. Cantor smiled broadly and said to the young performer, "Well, Eddie, I'm opening next week in your hometown of Philadelphia. Are you coming along?"

From that day onward, it was a series of spectacular triumphs for the curly-topped boy crooner. Under Blackstone's managerial wing, he soon moved into the front rank of recording stars with a succession of hit platters; his own three-times weekly network TV show; and headlining appearances in most of the nation's top night spots and theaters. Included were periodic stints at Grossinger's, the place he always referred to as home. It was during one of these visits that the gaiety of the occasion was shattered by the death of Malke who passed away in her sleep on the night of August 16, 1952. The emotional shock was great, yet Jennie bore up well.

"This time," she said to Harry, "at least we are prepared."

The old woman had been failing for many years. Four years before, she suffered a severe stroke and became bed-ridden for the first time in her life. Jennie brought specialist after specialist from New York, but they all told her Malke would never be the same. Her brain cells had been seriously damaged and her mind retrogressed until, once again, she was living on the little farm in Galicia. Jennie would sit by her bed for hours listening to Malke retell tales of her girlhood as if they had just taken place.

The loss of her mother and still-painful memories of the hotel fire robbed Jennie of any real peace of mind. As the 1954 summer season approached, she had great difficulty sleeping. She also found it impossible to concentrate for any lengthy period. Everyone agreed she should get away from the hotel with its constant reminders. A long-thought-about, but oft-deferred trip to Europe and Israel was now urged upon her by Harry and the children. Jennie protested she could not possibly leave in the middle of the summer season. Only after much cajoling did she relent and agree to make the second transatlantic crossing of her life.

Traveling aboard the luxurious *Queen Mary* seemed a few centuries removed from the spring of 1900 when Jennie, her mother and sister sailed in the steerage class of the *Potsdam*. As the ship passed now-deserted Ellis Island, slowly moving down New York Bay, Jennie looked out from the rail toward the open sea and the ensuing fifty-four years seemed to roll back. She saw again the trembling little girl huddled close to her mother on the crowded deck of the *Potsdam*.

Meyer and Regina Pesin accompanied Jennie on the trip to Israel. For years, she had worked hard for the new state and now, at last, she was going to see some of the tangible results of her efforts. In Israel, the happiness she saw on the faces of those survivors of the Nazi terror who had built a new life in a Jewish homeland sent her spirits soaring. From Israel, the trio went on to Italy and France and learned that no matter how far you get from Grossinger's, you never really leave home. Though Jennie was by now accustomed to being regarded as somewhat of a minor celebrity in America, she was honestly amazed to discover that she and the hotel were known in Europe, too; that people reacted emotionally to the magic name Grossinger.

A few months after her return home, Jennie was honored at a $100-a-plate testimonal dinner at the Waldorf-Astoria Hotel in New York. The Jewish National Fund earmarked the receipts to build a Jennie Grossinger Recreational and Convalescent Home on a hilltop in Safed, Israel, overlooking the Sea of Galilee. More than one thousand guests were on hand as well as dozens of Broadway's biggest stars—all Grossinger "alumni."

Jennie became more active than ever in charity efforts. She extended aid freely, from the "Fight for Sight" drive to the National Association to Help Mentally Retarded Children; from the Deborah Tuberculosis Hospital in Browns Mills, New Jersey, to the Leo N. Levi Memorial Hospital for Arthritic Patients in Hot Springs, Arkansas. The Hebrew University in Jerusalem was another favorite beneficiary of her philanthropy, reflecting a life-long dedication to the ideal of education. Meanwhile, the hotel began donating thousands of free vacations as raffle and door prizes to countless worthy charities.

Like many people who have a reputation for charity,

JENNIE AND THE STORY OF GROSSINGER'S

Jennie was constantly being solicited by total strangers asking for money, mostly from older folk who claimed they were distant relatives or else grew up in the same *shtetl* in Austria-Hungary that she did. She rarely said no.

As her philanthropic and charitable duties took more and more time from the business, Paul Grossinger began exercising the managerial responsibilities he had been preparing for almost since childhood. One of his first accomplishments was guiding Grossinger's into the rapidly expanding group and convention area. Business and professional conventions and trade shows soon became an important source of income. A sales manager and staff were hired to attract conventioneers and The G. began playing host to such blue-chip companies as IBM, Metropolitan Life, General Electric, Eastman Kodak, and Dupont, as well as key trade associations and an assortment of prestigious professional societies in law, medicine, dentistry, science and education.

One of the reasons for this immediate success with convention-goers was that same cozy, familial atmosphere that appealed to the individual guest. At Grossinger's, men could bring their wives. While they conferred and made speeches, the ladies would be royally entertained.

As Paul assumed greater executive duties so did his sister, Elaine, who took up permanent residence at The Big G. with her husband, Dr. A. David Etess, upon his discharge from the Navy Medical Corps with the rank of Lt. Commander. The young physician opened an office in Liberty for general medicine while Elaine became increasingly involved in hotel affairs. With two children of her own now, Susan and Mark, Elaine inclined naturally toward young folk.

Although Grossinger's opened its first children's camp in the Twenties, it was Elaine who spearheaded a major expansion of children's and teenage activities. She also assumed full control over all decorating and design work. Jennie's relationship with her two children grew closer as they took on more and more duties of management. If Paul and Elaine had once resented the fact they had to share their mother with all of Grossinger's guests, they now came to fully appreciate how jealous a mistress the resort business could be.

The hotel kept growing, for there was plenty of room on the 1,300 acres. New fourlane highways now linked New York City and The Big G. The trip, once a torturous seven hours, now took but two from the George Washington Bridge in New York. Fast buses had replaced the slow-moving, uncomfortable Ontario and Western railroad trains. The little railroad station at Ferndale was just a memory.

Sports continued to play an important role in the hotel's growth. America had taken winter sports to its heart, and Grossinger's was one of the resorts nearest to New York.

There were not many skiing facilities in the state to compare with Grossinger Ski Valley and no comparable outdoor skating rink. All in all, Grossinger's was becoming a Sun Valley of the East. During weekends and holidays, a thousand winter sports fans dotted the ski slopes and the rink and hurtled down the toboggan slide.

Warm weather sports, too, were booming. Babe Didriksen Zaharias, America's foremost distaff golfer, and Joe Turnesa of golfdom's "royal family," were hired as resident pros. Some of the mightiest names in tournament golf came to play on The G. fairways—Gene Sazazen, Lloyd Mangrum, Sammy Snead, Vic Ghezzi, Byron Nelson, Ed Furgol, Doug Ford, and Mike Souchak (who became the hotel's first "traveling pro" on the big-time money circuit). A glittering line-up of tennis royalty— Don Budge, Vinnie Richards, Pancho Gonzalez, Bobby Riggs, Ellsworth Vines, Jack Kramer, Frank Kovacs, and Dick Savitt—gave exhibitions on the local courts.

While boxing and boxers provided most of the sports news coming out of the hotel, Grossinger's soon became a mecca for big league baseball and football stars. The G. made headlines, too, in 1951 when English Channel swimmer Florence Chadwick elected to train in Grossinger Lake for her second successful crossing. A few years later, she became The G.'s first fulltime aquatic director.

The sport of basketball also contributed a great deal to Catskill—and Grossinger—lore. Friday night basketball games, featuring some of the best collegiate stars in the country, were a staple in the Forties. The players usually took jobs as waiters or athletic staff members. That's how Lou Goldstein, the present resident *toomler*, first came to Ferndale. In 1950, the sporting world was rocked by a major gambling scandal involving several New York college stars who worked at Grossinger's. When Jennie read about the scandal and recognized the names of some of the players implicated, she called Lou Goldstein and asked him to stop the Friday games. Few mourned their demise, for the entertainment tastes of guests were becoming more sophisticated, and basketball didn't fit the new image of "big-name" nighttime performers.

By the Fifties, dozens of entertainers, whom Jennie had known as struggling youngsters, were coming regularly to the hotel as celebrity guests. Some were old friends and former staffers such as Dore Schary and Moss Hart, now married to Kitty Carlisle. Others, who had been guests for years, opened homes nearby. Irving and Ellin Berlin purchased an estate in Livingston Manor and had their children learn to ride, swim, skate and ski at Grossinger's. Playwright-director George Abbott bought a home in Monticello, only a few miles away.

Another celebrated face that showed up with welcome frequency was that of funnyman Milton Berle, riding high as comedy king of the television lanes in those early days of the new sight-and-sound medium. The popular clown would arrive to visit with his long-widowed mother, Sandra Berle, a season-long guest every summer for years until her death. Berle was absolutely devoted to this colorful, extroverted woman and she, in turn, doted on her famous son. When they got together at Grossinger's—the irreverent, anything-for-a-laugh jokester and the flamboyant, quintessential "stage mother"—the ensuing merriment was unfailingly explosive.

In the post-war period, if you stayed at The Big G. long enough, the world would come to you. Political, charitable and purely social banquets brought the illuminati. When United Nations Day was celebrated there, Eleanor Roosevelt presided. This marked the beginning of a warm friendship between the immigrant innkeeper and the widow of the wartime President.

Jennie welcomed many other U. N. notables to the

hotel including Dr. Ralph Bunche, the distinguished Under-Secretary; Arthur Lall, then head of the Indian delegation to the international body; Ghana's Alex Quaison-Sackey; Dr. Abba Eban, Israel's chief representative; and A. Matsui, Japan's permanent ambassador.

Mrs. Roosevelt heads the illustrious pantheon of celebrated women whom Jennie says she has admired most, women from whom she drew inspiration in shaping her life and ideals. The others: Marie Curie, Clara Barton, Florence Nightingale, Helen Keller, Annie Sullivan, Golda Meir, Marian Anderson, and Malke. Of Helen Keller, Jennie once noted that her saintly expression was identical to that which Malke showed the world. "She always reminded me of my mother," Jennie said. She also told the same interviewer that of the hundreds and hundreds of famous personages she has hosted at her hotel, the one she felt most honored to meet was Dr. Jonas Salk, discoverer of the anti-polio vaccine.

Eddie Fisher remained a constant visitor. One September, he brought a lovely-looking girl named Debbie Reynolds. Jennie had already met Debbie and her mother on a plane en route to California and had prophetically observed to Barney Ross, traveling with her to the West Coast, that "she's the kind of girl I'd like for Eddie." When Eddie brought the vivacious actress to Grossinger's, the press suspected they were getting serious and recorded their every move.

When the couple decided to wed in the fall of 1954, Debbie's mother called Jennie and asked if the ceremony could be performed at the hotel. Eddie had the sentimental idea that he should be married at the place that gave him his start. Debbie agreed. Jennie and Harry thought they would hold the ceremony in their own Joy Cottage, but the living room proved too small to accommodate the wedding party. Instead, it was performed in the adjoining home of Elaine and David Etess. Judge Lawrence Cooke of Monticello did the honors while newspapermen, television cameras and radio microphones covered the event with the kind of frenzied attention usually devoted to a national election.

Four years later, the pattern was repeated when Eddie, whose marriage to Debbie was disintegrating, brought the widow of his closest friend, Mike Todd, to stay at Joy Cottage. She was, of course, Elizabeth Taylor. Once again, thousands of words poured out around the world via press association wires, each story carrying the dateline, "Grossinger, New York."

Jennie retained the friendship of both Debbie and Elizabeth after each girl's marriage to Eddie ended in divorce. It was with the first Mrs. Fisher, however, that Jennie maintained a particularly warm friendship. Debbie did not hesitate to visit her at the hotel in the years following the divorce, although Grossinger's must have been filled with poignant, perhaps painful, memories to her.

A great deal had been written about Jennie in the nation's press making her a reasonably celebrated individual—particularly in show business circles and among her co-religionists. But it took television to turn her into a nationally-known personality. In December, 1954, an unsuspecting Jennie was the guest star of Ralph Edwards' "This Is Your Life." The popularity of the program, seen by an estimated forty million viewers, was largely due to the fact that the guest had no idea of what was to happen.

Friends and relatives were contacted and sworn to secrecy; then came the complicated business of getting the main figure in the drama to appear at the television studio on some plausible pretext. In Jennie's case, it was Eddie Cantor and Milton Blackstone who persuaded her to attend a "preview" of a Cantor film. This was not very difficult considering the affection Jennie felt for Cantor.

They took her to dinner in Hollywood and then walked with her the two blocks to the El Capitan Theatre. It seemed natural for Jennie to enter by the stage door, but it didn't seem natural to be led onto the stage of a theater where a thousand applauding spectators were sitting. And it was startling to see the familiar grin of Ralph Edwards and to hear him cry: "Jennie Grossinger, this is your life!"

One by one, Edwards introduced her family and then old friends like Fisher, Cantor, Jackie Robinson, James G. MacDonald, first American ambassador to Israel; and Father Fred Gehring, the famed Guadalcanal Padre, who told how Jennie had helped support his missionary work in the Far East.

Cantor recalled his first visit to Grossinger's and his memorable meeting with Malke: "When I asked if all this land belonged to her, she replied, 'No, it belongs to God. I'm just watching it for Him while I'm alive.'" And so it went.

Until then Jennie Grossinger had been a name; she now became a recognizable figure all over the country. For the first time, total strangers stopped and asked, "Aren't you Jennie Grossinger?"

Because her interfaith activities and charities had been emphasized by Edwards on the program, Jennie was deluged by requests for help from organizations as well as individuals. Father Gehring had said: "She has helped pay off mortgages on churches—both Catholic and Protestant—and only on condition that her identity be kept secret. Jennie Grossinger, of the Jewish faith, is also one of the finest Christians I know."

As these requests mounted, she threw up her hands helplessly and turned them over to Paul.

"You'll break us yet, Mom," he said cheerfully.

But The G. didn't go broke. It just kept expanding. In 1958, a sixty-room addition was built onto the Main House, and adjacent to it, an imposing million-dollar, glass-enclosed Olympic-sized indoor pool. Beneath it sat two elaborate health clubs complete with dry rooms, steam rooms, exercise rooms and masseurs. These new luxury additions were all constructed in the same Tudor style which had always characterized the resort. From the very beginning, Jennie insisted upon this consistency of architectural style. Hardly one of the thirty-five buildings on the property seems alien to the dominant motif of the whole.

The Fifties came to a moving conclusion for Jennie on November 9, 1959, when the immigrant girl from Galicia, with only a few years of formal schooling, was awarded an honorary Doctor of Humanities degree by Wilberforce College in Ohio, the nation's oldest independent Negro institution of higher learning. (In 1966, she was to receive a second honorary degree, Doctor of Humane Letters, presented by New England College.)

Not long afterwards, a second testimonial was tendered Jennie, this time to a sellout audience in the Grand Ballroom of the Hotel Astor. Over 1,500 of New York's most prominent political, theatrical, and financial figures attended the dinner. Enough money was raised to spearhead the drive to build the three-story Jennie Grossinger Medical Center in Tel Aviv.

During all these apparently good years, the frictions between the Grossinger and Grau branches of the family continued to exacerbate. When an impasse had been reached, Harry Grossinger felt the situation could no longer be tolerated. The wrangling between the contending parties was taking its toll on the business as well as doing great psychological harm to everyone, especially Jennie. Seeing no other possible solution, Harry, with the aide of a substantial bank loan, agreed to buy out both Lottie and Little Harry's interest in the hotel. Not many weeks after the final papers were signed and sealed in early 1962, Lottie succumbed to a heart attack at the age of sixty-seven. Feelings of remorse and guilt assailed Jennie anew. She and Lottie had been very close as children. The estrangement of their adult years now seemed vain, foolish and unnecessary. Jennie's smiles to her guests in the weeks following her sister's death masked a heavy heart.

When, in 1964, Grossinger's celebrated its fiftieth anniversary, the town of Liberty expressed its appreciation of the warm relationship that had always existed between the community and the members of the family. A plaque was presented to them by the townspeople during a ceremony at the local high school. At the top of the plaque, which now hangs at the hotel's main entrance, was inscribed a line from a poem by Sam Walter Foss:

"Let me live in my house by the side of the road
And be a friend of man."

It was typical of Harry to insist that Jennie accept the honor on behalf of the family. Jennie found it difficult to speak that night, for her mind overflowed with the memories of fifty years. Her whole family was seated on the stage of the Liberty High School auditorium and old friends had come from New York to participate in the ceremonies. It was the last joyous gathering the Grossinger family was to have.

During the winter and spring of 1964 Harry was busy building an eight-story addition to the Main House. He had suffered two mild heart attacks—if a heart attack can ever be called mild for a man in his middle seventies. His doctors pleaded with him not to climb up and down the skeleton of the new building, but he ignored them with a shrug.

"I've been a builder all my life," he said stubbornly.

He had capable assistants, but, like Selig before him, he hated to delegate authority. Wearing his hip boots and broad-brimmed Stetson, he continued to scale the steel skeleton, no matter how raw the winds. One day he returned to his bedroom with a severe chest pain. The next day he ran a high fever and was rushed to New York's Mount Sinai Hospital with pneumonia.

After a month of confinement, he was allowed to return to the mountains, laughing with good nature at his doctors. He looked fine and his eyes twinkled behind his steel-rimmed spectacles. It was warm now and he sat comfortably in a large chair on the lawn in front of Joy Cottage viewing the nearly completed new wing of the Main Building.

Late one night, about three weeks afterwards, complications developed. Harry was taken to Maimonides Hospital in Liberty, with his son-in-law, David Etess, at his side. But it was too late. He died of cardiac arrest at one o'clock on the Wednesday afternoon of July 22, 1964, barely two months after he had sat smiling so happily, while Jennie accepted the plaque on the stage of the Liberty High School.

A stunned Jennie, away in Washington, D. C., received the news on the telephone from Abe Friedman. She had gone to the capital to testify at a Federal Aviation Agency hearing on the proposed new jetport planned for Sullivan County which she had championed for so long.

She knew that Harry's heart condition was serious, but his doctors reassured her he was doing fine. Her eldest grandson, Richard, a nineteen-year-old Amherst undergraduate, had accompanied her to Washington. Both in their hotel room and on the plane to New York, Richard proved a source of great comfort and strength to Jennie. A week later, the young man wrote an eloquent epitaph for his grandfather which was published in a local newspaper. Jennie was to read and re-read it many times for solace.

In the Orthodox tradition, funeral services were held the following day in Monticello. The mortuary was crowded early and still people came to pay their last respects: Irving Berlin and his wife, Rocky Marciano, Eddie Fisher and a host of others. They weren't all famous. There were men from the Washington Market in New York and there were farmers from whom he had bought eggs and poultry. Since there was no room to hold them all in the funeral home, more than five hundred stood on the lawn outside listening to the brief services over a loudspeaker. Never had so many people attended a funeral in Sullivan County.

A long cavalcade of cars followed the funeral cortege to the Congregation Ahavath Israel Cemetery on the Loch Sheldrake Road off Route 52 near Liberty. Harry was buried on a gentle hill that overlooked the country-side as far as the hotel. The family, all of whom had presented a dignified front during the long day, returned to Joy Cottage.

There were over 1,300 guests in the hotel, but all understood when it was announced there would be no music or entertainment that evening or the next in re-spect to Harry's memory.

When the mourning period was over, Paul was chosen president and chief executive officer by the board of directors and moved back into his office to assume heavy new responsibilities. So did Elaine who was named secre-tary-treasurer, and Abe. Jennie now showed herself to be the strong and indomitable woman her mother had been when Pop died so long ago. Dry-eyed though pale, she went from the front office to the kitchens to the dining room. She was much more than a symbol of the hotel now, for this small empire had been bequeathed entirely to her by her husband.

After the funeral, Jennie's first instinct was to leave everything in Harry's bedroom permanently intact, in-cluding his clothes and personal effects. This was, friends reminded her, an unhealthy throwback to her mental state after Pop Grossinger died—an unwillingness to accept fully the reality of death. Jennie had to admit to herself that this was no way to cherish her husband's memory. Instead, Harry's room was converted into a library.

It was this same insight and maturity that gave her much-needed strength less than ten months later when her brother, the younger Harry, passed on at the age of sixty-three, victim also of a heart ailment. Jennie was now the only surviving member of the remarkable little family that came to the New World at the turn of the century poor in everything but hope, love and humanity.

Chapter 15

What is Grossinger's like? To begin with, it covers close to 1,200 acres of rolling countryside which makes it just twice the size of the principality of Monaco. In all, there are thirty-five structures on the property and the population during the peak summer months approaches 2,300, close to one thousand of whom are permanent, or semi-permanent, staff members. Unlike Monaco, it is not a principality, although Jennie Grossinger is generally accepted as its sovereign queen.

A resort hotel that never closes its doors is no less than a microcosm of the larger world. Children have been born at the hotel while the elderly have died. People have fallen in and out of love. Marriages have been performed. Major decisions affecting a lifetime have been made. Celebrated artists—from Irving Stone, the novelist, to Paddy Chayefsky, the playwright—have come to work or re-kindle creative energies. Man's communion with God is often celebrated. The hotel theater, the Playhouse, where some of the most glamourous names in the entertainment world have appeared, has also been used as a synagogue, a Catholic church, a Methodist meeting hall, and a Seventh-Day Adventist prayer site.

In a material sense, however, to say that "Grossinger's Has Everything" is not strictly true. It does not, for instance, have a standing army or navy, the power to make treaties with foreign countries, or a launching pad capable of projecting a space capsule to the moon. But it does have just about everything that any fairly prosperous suzerainty of its size and population has. Its private airstrip is no longer called Grossinger Airport; it is now known officially as Liberty Airport. The hotel does not have a supermarket, but it does have a drugstore, jewelry shop, a beauty salon, barber shop, gift shop, art gallery, coffee shop, portrait artist, staff photographer, Federal post office (Grossinger, N. Y.), a well-equipped infirmary, an apparel shop, a fleet of buses and limousines, a security force, a fire department, and a number of other community services very few towns with a population of 2,300 can afford. Grossinger's, as such, is a self-contained Catskill community.

But Grossinger's is also much more than a resort hotel. It has, in a very real sense, become an authentic institution—symbolic representation of an affluent life style for an entire ethnic class that rose from the ghettoes to positions of wealth, power, and importance during the first half of the 20th Century. Particularly in the post-World War II decade, to many an upward-striving individual, coming to Grossinger's was indisputable evidence of having "arrived"—of having "made it!"

What is generally called the Catskills these days comprises all of Sullivan County and parts of neighboring

Ulster County—approximately one thousand square miles of green, hilly countryside about one hundred miles northwest of New York City. In point of very strict fact, the entire vacation belt is actually in the Shawungunk Mountains with the real Catskills to the north, but only geographers and some old-time settlers seem to be aware of this territorial distinction. Most of the pilgrims of pleasure en route to the world-famous fun mecca simply refer to the entire area as the "mountains"—a term that can only mean the Catskill Mountains.

Although Grossinger's is the undisputed aristocrat of the mountains—and Jennie, the area's First Lady—there are a number of other major hotels in the area with which Grossinger's enjoys spirited, good-natured competition; notably, the Concord, twelve miles south in the town of Kiamesha Lake. The late Arthur Winarick, an ex-barber, made a fortune in the hair tonic business before discovering greener fields in the resort industry.

The 1,500-room, glittering Concord is today a much larger caravansary than Grossinger's, though its total acreage is smaller. The intense, if good-natured, rivalry between the two hotels has, inevitably, been catnip for Catskill comedians. Grossinger's *toomler*, Lou Goldstein, started it years ago by stubbornly refusing to mention the Concord by name. He dubbed the rival hotel, *dorten*, a Yiddish word meaning "over there." The Concord has been known as *dorten* ever since.

Lou has a bulging repertoire of sly sallies about the Concord ("They had a beauty contest over there last week. Nobody won!"), but despite the jokes and sharp competition, the Grossingers and Winaricks have remained friendly and cooperative through the years. Jennie has maintained the same close friendships with scores of other hotel pioneers who came to the Catskills just as her family did to escape the oppressiveness of Lower East Side existence: the Holders of Youngs Gap, the Sussmans of the Windsor, the Dans of Sha-Wan-Ga Lodge, the Rosenthals of the Waldmere, the Levinsons of Tamarack Lodge, Ike Evans of the Evans Hotel in Loch Sheldrake, the Posners of the Brickman Hotel, Charles and Lillian Brown of Brown's, and many others.

Most, like Jennie and her family, arrived with a vision of a new life on the soil. Some had their roots in the East European *shtetl*, towns where Jews often kept cows and maintained vegetable gardens, though they were usually not permitted to farm. Others were consumptive or fearful of consumption. Continued work in the sweatshops for them, as for Selig, seemed like a death warrant. And so they came to the Catskills to wrestle with an inhospitable land and, ultimately, to make ends meet, take in boarders.

Not all of the original farm settlers decided to assume the mantle of boarding house operators. The Yasgurs in Bethel (of latter-day "Rock Festival" fame) eventually developed one of the largest independent dairy operations in the state while the Brender family in Ferndale built a poultry empire on a spot not too many miles from Grossinger's. But they were the exceptions.

When Jennie is in residence—which is most of the year—she confers daily with Paul and Elaine. But the nerve center of the hotel during the daytime hours is Paul Grossinger's office in the Main Building of the sprawling hotel. As chief executive officer, Jennie's only son is directly responsible for day-to-day operations.

While consulted on all policy decisions of any consequence, Jennie has by and large turned over daily operating decisions to Paul. As former two-term president of
the New York State Hotel and Motel Association, and a
nationally known and respected figure in the $2 billion
hotel and resort industry, he's been a prime innovator at
Grossinger's. Under his creative stewardship, up-to-date
business techniques have been introduced without sacrificing the traditional warmth and informality of a small
family enterprise. As a direct result, business volume at
Grossinger's nearly doubled during the past decade.
Paul's wife, Bunny, though not directly involved in the
hectic activity of the business, is often around to assist
when needed, and she pitches in willingly. (Her brother,
Bill Persky, incidentally, is the Emmy Award-winning
writer of the "Dick Van Dyke" television comedy show.)

Occupying an office alongside that of her brother,
Elaine is intimately concerned with a wide range of
management duties, from financial affairs and internal
public relations to interior design and decor, and, of
course, supervising all youth and children's activities. In
her spare time, the attractive mother of three serves as
president of the Liberty Board of Education, directing
educational programs for 2,500 students in the elementary and secondary schools of the area. Increasingly, as
Jennie finds it a bit tiring to make dining room rounds
and meet and greet as many guests as she used to, Elaine,
who has inherited all of her mother's natural warmth
and love for people, takes over that role, too.

The typical Grossinger guest mix is a potpourri—except for periodic "All Singles" weekends and weeks—
comprised of unmarrieds of all ages, young and middle-

aged couples without children, and couples with children. In this respect, the people design approximates the normal population pattern. This sort of natural arrangement leaves both married and single guests feeling more comfortable. There are times, too, notably between school terms, when the hotel seems more like a college campus with huge influxes of undergraduates paying special low rates and also periods when groups of senior citizens (also at discount rates) are strongly represented.

Older unmarried folk—spinsters, widows, widowers, mature bachelors—seem to feel a special sense of kinship to Grossinger's where they find a familiar, protective environment that shields against the pervasive loneliness and impersonality of urban life.

Still another category of habitué are those who consider the hotel their second home and think of themselves as part of management. After a confrontation with one, Harry Grossinger would always say wryly: "In this hotel we have no guests—only partners!" They rarely have to be coaxed to offer suggestions on how to run the establishment more effectively.

Men in uniform are also always in evidence. Ever since the start of World War II, Jennie has been inviting servicemen up for long holidays. To this day, the policy is maintained with four Army, Navy, Marine, or Air Force personnel on hand every week—generally boys just back from overseas duty or recuperating in base hospitals. In the past few years, large groups of foreign militarymen, taking special training in this country, have also been added to the roster of on-the-house guests.

Grossinger's has its full complement of "characters," too—off-beat, colorful guest personalities. One of the more conspicuous eccentrics is white-bearded David Newman, an affluent bachelor in his middle years who has been spending every summer and holiday—some four months in all—at the hotel for two decades. The flamboyantly attired Mr. Newman holds court royally at a table in front of the dining room where he takes his meals in solitary splendour only occasionally inviting an attractive female guest to join him. And there's Jack Blatt, a retired New Yorker who decided he'd had enough of the city's noise, dirt and crowds and checked into Grossinger's for an "indefinite stay." He's been around since 1965, contentedly settled down to the life of a permanent guest. Nor will old-timers forget the irrepressible Sammy Hamlin, unofficial Mayor of Grossinger's in the Forties and early Fifties. A garment salesman who wanted to be a comic, he did not miss a single weekend in years always finding a ready audience for his zany antics.

Businessman George Geiger, an exuberantly amiable, very familiar face around The G., also belongs in this company. George consistently disdains the society of his co-vacationers for that of the staff. He eats with staff; selects his friends from among them; and conducts himself as a sort of *ex-officio* member of the staff. He delights in being privy to what's going on behind the scenes at the hotel and, by now, most of staff people consider him one of their own. The only difference—and not an insignificant one—is that instead of getting paid, George pays!

Whenever "Uncle" Henry Bunin arrives—which is very often, indeed—the service employes at the hotel break into big smiles, for the courtly, elderly, well-fixed gentleman is second to none when it comes to dispensing extravagant tips. "Uncle" Henry's favorite pastime, however, is gathering up all the unattached, more mature ladies in the house and inviting them to share his table and largesse in the night club rather than sit alone. Friendly and amusing, he operates like a one-man escort service entertaining as many as a dozen appreciative damsels who can always stop at his table for a drink and pleasant chit-chat.

Any resemblance between a Catskill resort hotel of forty years ago and that of 1970 is purely geographical. Grossinger's today is a luxury hotel run exclusively on the American Plan with accommodations to suit a wide spectrum of incomes. It is not at all unusual for the $100-a-week stenographer and the head of a large company to share the same dining room table; or for the college boy paying his special low rate to exchange volleys on the tennis courts with a millionaire realtor. Both skilled workingmen and high-income executives, office personnel and business tycoons can enjoy the delights of a Big G. holiday. Except for the type and location of one's room, everything else offered guests is identical, whatever the rate.

A typical August day at Grossinger's is quite different from a typical day in a town its size. To begin with, the hotel awakens early. Rachel "Mom" Tuchman is usually the first to appear, although a skeleton crew is on duty all night. She arrives in the kitchen at six-thirty, just after the eggs have been delivered. (She came to this country over thirty-five years ago from Bialystok, Russia, and has worked as an egg candler in the kitchen ever since.)

First, the eggs are candled by X-ray, the generally

accepted method of guaranteeing the freshness and the absence of blood spots which violate the Orthodox dietary tradition. Several hundred eggs are left whole to be used for boiling. But Mom Tuchman, slightly suspicious of this new-fangled invention called the X-ray, inspects all eggs in the time-honored way; that is, she breaks the shell, separates the white from the yolk, gives a penetrating glance at the yolk, then deftly drops the yolk into one huge bowl and the white of the egg into another. Each morning she handles fifteen crates of eggs (thirty dozen in each box), which means that she personally breaks and inspects 5,400 eggs a day.

Meantime, the kitchen staff starts trooping in. Henry Gern, the dairy chef, arrives about six-thirty with his assistant, Foo Shing. (More than a dozen of the higher-ranking culinary artisans at The G. are Chinese.) Quickly and efficiently, they prepare the baked herring, which is a favorite breakfast dish. Jars of jellies and preserves are removed from the icebox and put on an aluminum-topped table, easily accessible to waiters. Busboys and waiters begin to stream into the kitchen. Three men assigned to squeezing oranges get to work; every morning fifteen crates, each crate holding one hundred and fifty oranges, are turned into juice. Early-morning golfers are served in a small separate dining room. They are usually men with hearty appetites who like to start the day with two double-orange juice orders.

The literal meaning of kosher is "fit and proper" for the Mosaic laws of kosher food processing are basically a strict sanitary code keyed to hygienic concepts. In terms of Jewish dietary laws, this means certain foodstuffs and cooking methods are prohibited: animal hindquarters, shellfish, pork, scavengers, etc. Slaughtering must be performed according to ritualistic techniques by specialists. Preparation of meats must be in conformity with certain "purifying" methods—notably, *kashering* which is the process of removing blood. Meat and dairy products must not be served at the same meal, cooked in the same kitchen or stored in the same areas. Kosher embraces three categories—meat, dairy, and parve. Parve, a term meaning neutral, indicates the absence of both meat and dairy ingredients and may include foods like bread, cookies, crackers, candies and fish products which can be eaten with meat or dairy products. There is also a special classification of products without leavening, used only at Passover.

At Grossinger's, there are two completely separate kitchens—one for the preparation of meat dishes; the other, the dairy kitchen, where dishes made with milk and its derivatives are prepared. Each kitchen has its own dish-washing and silver-cleaning equipment, steam soup kettle, walk-in freezers and refrigerated storerooms.

Pop and Mom Grossinger were adamant in following the dietary laws. These are observed just as strictly today at Grossinger's. Luncheon is the dairy meal, at which butter, milk, cheese, sour cream, fish, vegetable casseroles, apple pancakes, and egg dishes are served.

At dinner, the meat meal, no dairy products are served. Butter and cheese are not available, nor is there cream for coffee. Another tradition of Orthodoxy still followed in the dining room is the ban on smoking on the Sabbath. Ash trays are removed Friday evening not to be returned until sundown Saturday. Besides improving the appetite, the restriction on smoking is an Orthodox interpretation of the command to do no work on the "Sabbath of the Lord thy God." Among nomad Biblical tribes, the kindling and maintenance of fires was one of the cardinal items of household drudgery. Hence, a specific injunction of Exodus (XXXV, 3) holds that, "Ye shall kindle no fire throughout your habitations upon the Sabbath day." Thus kitchen stoves and ranges are turned on before sundown Friday and kept burning all night at a low flame, and, naturally, smoking is prohibited since it is manifestly impossible to smoke without kindling a fire.

The regular dining room opens at eight-thirty A.M. By this time, the kitchen crew of one hundred and fifty is ready. Many are not concerned with breakfast; they are already preparing lunch. A few are absorbed with dinner preparations. Most of the kitchen helpers are specialists in their jobs. There are twelve men who do nothing but make salads, two who make sandwiches and four who prepare only the vegetables. Even the dishwashers are specialists; some handle only glassware, others devote their energy to pots and pans; and three do nothing but wash, dry and shine silver. There are ten porters whose job is to clean the kitchen floor and dispose of the refuse. Malke always boasted, even when supervising the cooking at the Longbrook House, that hers was the cleanest kitchen in the world, a tradition vigorously upheld to this day. Jennie often strolls through the kitchens just to be certain that Malke would still be proud of them. Hyman Plinner and Ephraim Singer, the resident *meshgiachem* (dietary law inspectors), are constantly prowling the kitchens to make sure that dishes, pots and silver used for dairy meals are kept separate from those used at meat meals. Both work under the supervision of Rabbi Chaim Dov Chavel who supervises the *kashruth*.

Lengthy service is a hallmark of the kitchen help. Head Chef-Steward Henry Speckhardt has been on the job for nearly thirty years; Assistant Chef-Steward Jack Vidas started thirty-three years ago; China-born John Yuen, chief salad man, is another thirty-year man; Head Baker Benny Noecker arrived in 1947; Meat Chef Henry Poehlmann and Dairy Chef Henry Gern are relative neophytes with about twenty years service between them.

Roman Tarasuk, who worked in the pantry continuously until his death last year, was the unquestioned "dean" of the Grossinger culinary corps. He began in 1919. Ten years ago, Jennie spoke to him about retiring. Roman protested: "How can I retire? Where would I go? This is the only home I have." Jennie took his hand and said, "Roman, as long as you live, you will have a home here and a salary, whether you work or not." Sadie Moroz, who took a job as a waitress more than forty-five years ago, is another G. *ancienne*. Now, too old to work, she is officially retired, but comes to the dining room every day to putter about and gossip with the girls. She, too, like all other long-time employes, will have a home at Grossinger's as long as she lives. That is a Jennie promise—made many times.

Because of the unique nature of the business with its great number of skilled and semi-skilled jobs, every resort hotel also seems to have a large floating population of employes who come and go quickly. Most end up working in the kitchen. These transients are sometimes people in flight from personal crises or down on their luck. Uncertain in the direction of their lives, they gravitate toward the protective sanctum of a resort where food and shelter, as well as a job, can be had and the pressures and decisions of normal existence are momentarily cast off. A kitchen porter who was once a Shakespearian actor; a handyman who held a university professorship; an athletic staff member who argued cases before the state's highest court are just a few of the unlikely types who found an interim haven at Grossinger's through the years.

But many more are careerists who came intending to stay. For all that and despite years and years of service, an image of impermanence seems to attach itself to everyone working in a resort environment. There is scarcely an employe around for any length of time who does not repeatedly hear the refrain from a returning guest: "Are you still here?" Perhaps because all Catskill hotels were, in the first instance, only summertime operations, it is difficult for many guests to realize fully how The G. has evolved into a major business enterprise with a small army of steady employes. These days, it even has a full-time personnel director, Alex Dana, to hire new workers.

Four bakers have toiled all night preparing the 3,000 pieces of breakfast pastry and the 4,500 rolls—both soft and hard—which will be consumed at the morning meal. Hundreds of *challahs* are made Thursday evening and Friday for the Sabbath evening meal that night. Since 1954, no rye or pumpernickel has been baked in the Grossinger bakeries—only white bread. That was the year the General Baking Company bought out the first two products in its new Grossinger Bread Division—a rye and a pumpernickel enclosed in a wax wrapper decorated with Jennie's smiling face and the slogan, "Hearty Appetite." The hotel bakeries do, however, produce a rich variety of pastries, cookies and desserts.

Handling and processing the tons of meat and poultry put away each week—1,100,000 pounds of meat, 59,000 pounds of delicatessen meat and 142,000 pounds of poultry are the annual G. consumption—is the responsibility of four butchers under Benny Reiss, who began working at The G. nineteen years ago. One of them is called a *shochet*, a butcher licensed by rabbinical boards to perform ritual animal and poultry slaughter.

During breakfast, the athletic staff is preparing for the guests who will soon be flocking to the outdoor Olympic pool (if it is raining, the indoor pool gets the play), the golf course, the tennis courts and the lake. Hundreds of reclining chairs are arranged for those who want to bathe in the sun rather than splash in the water.

At ten-thirty A.M., tall, fast-thinking Lou Goldstein, who learned his comedy craft over a period of twenty-five years before hundreds of thousands of guests, takes over to the shrill delight of hundreds who seem to come to Grossinger's just to be amused by him. His formal title is director of daytime activities, but he is really the most celebrated *toomler* in the Catskills. A comic and game leader of the old school, he collects big crowds in the lobby or on the shaded lawn and, relying solely on wit and audacity, entertains for hours on end, five days a week. Brash, but never offensive, he keeps up a steady bantering with his delighted audience.

It was Lou who popularized the adult comedy version

of that ancient children's game, "Simon Says." The idea of the game is to do whatever Simon says. If Goldstein calls out, "Simon says put your hands on your head," and a few luckless participants put their hands on their hips, they are out of the game. Between giving his orders, he tells jokes and exchanges barbs with hecklers. Actually, "Simon Says" is merely a springboard for Lou's endless quips. In the classic Jewish tradition, the bulk of Lou's humor is good-natured jibes at the foibles and excesses of the guests. With the possible exception of the Irish, no other group is more prone to mocking, exaggerated self-deprecation than Jews. It is almost a life style.

Typically, Lou might say: "This is probably the only hotel in the world where the food is kosher and everyone eats like a pig!"

Although Goldstein never stops talking, he seldom repeats himself. A woman will protest that she is too old to play "Simon Says." He'll say, "Nonsense. Yesterday we had a seventy-five year old *bubba* [grandmother] from New York playing. When I asked her, 'What do you think of sex?' she answered, 'I think it's a fine department store.'" An old joke, but the delivery is flawless and the laughter explosive.

At Grossinger's, no idea holds sway as powerfully as that of love, with the hotel functioning as a vast and verdant marriage mart. "Providing social opportunities for out-of-towners particularly is a genuine service," observed a well-known sociologist in an article about Grossinger's. "People in small cities and towns, as well as those in fixed occupations with limited access to new friends, who fail to marry in their early years, face increasingly difficult chances of doing so thereafter. A resort like Grossinger's, fed by hundreds of communities all over the country, significantly—and often fruitfully —widens that range of opportunity."

It would be impossible to state with any degree of accuracy the actual number of married couples who first met at The G., since no records are kept. Jennie estimates the figure may be as high as 10,000, with occasional instances where both mother and father, and then offspring, met their mates at the hotel.

Grossinger romances are indeed many, varied, and, sometimes, wholly unpredictable. One of the more celebrated—if brief—encounters was a widely publicized liaison between skimaster Tony Kastner and film glamour queen, Kim Novak. She came to The G. to learn to ski and, instead, found a headline-making romance with a ruggedly handsome, Rumanian-born ski instructor that provided choice morsels for Hollywood gossip columnists for many months.

Nowadays, to insure even broader possibilities for nubile men and women, the hotel sets aside special periods —about one every six weeks—as "Single Weekends" plus two "Singles Weeks" in the summer, assuring quantity as well as (hopefully) quality. Since they were first launched eight years ago, these "Single Weekends" have been emulated everywhere and have become an authentic part of the Grossinger folklore.

During lunch, Lou Goldstein announces the activities of the afternoon. It may be a pro-amateur tee tournament arranged by resident pro Phil Galvano on the hotel's new golf course (twenty-seven holes in all), using name professionals partnered with guests; or an exhibition tennis match. (There was a time when handball and softball were the major sports at The G., but the more sophisticated, affluent guests of today prefer the links and the courts. There are still four handball walls, but finding an opponent often rivals the search for the proverbial needle in the haystack, while a baseball diamond is favored mostly by youngsters and the staff.)

At poolside there may be a hypnotist practicing his art, or a free group dance lesson. Sometimes Lou announces he will take them on a tour of the kitchens (once the dishes are done). This is a treat that very few women can resist. Other times, he offers a one-hour walking tour of a good part of The G.'s 1,200 acres. There are always repeaters on this tour who go mainly because of Goldstein's amusing running commentary.

In his comedy antics, Lou is abetted by a trio of professional funsters, Larry Alpert, Mac Robbins and Emil Cohen, who are more or less comics-in-residence all summer long. Evenings, they play other spots around the mountains, but during the daylight hours, they are on hand to do impromptu bits, sketches and routines with Lou. More than twenty years ago, Emil stayed at Grossinger's simply as a guest. He was then a real-estate man from Wilmington, Delaware, who told funny stories to anyone who'd listen. It wasn't long before fellow-guests convinced him to switch from mortgages to mirth-making full time.

Not infrequently, there will be a lecture by some noted speaker. It was Jennie's intense preoccupation with culture that led to the establishment of these programs. They have since become one of the resort's most popular features. The speaker might be Max Lerner, Art Buchwald, Leo Cherne, Abba Eban (when he was Israel's U. N. ambassador), Harry Golden, former Senator Wayne Morse, Clifton Daniel (Associate Editor of *The New York Times*) or William Shirer. Sometimes a forum is held under the guidance of a professional psychologist, Dr. Nathan Fleischer, the discussions ranging from pop art to drug use, civil rights to the sexual revolution. These are generally held outdoors on the lawn or, on rainy days, in one of the large lounges, with half of those listening usually sprawled comfortably on the deep-carpeted floors.

Regularly, Lou will announce an art class with portrait painter Sampson Sanger or that beauty specialist Bruce Deidre is conducting a make-up class, which sends eager women scurrying to wherever he sets up his demonstration paraphernalia.

If a guest is not interested in any of these planned activities, he will be left alone. When the weather is nice, many like to take walks. There are trails through the woods that border the lake and paddle and row boats on the lake. Others like to use the palatial health clubs on the bottom level of the indoor pool presided over by Robbie Mosler.

If any guest has not been surfeited by the herring, halibut or whitefish in the dining room, he can grab a pole and try for a sunfish or perch. Or he may swim. Grossinger's is big enough to get lost in without the slightest difficulty. This applies even to the dining room where most people prefer to sit at large tables for ten and eight and make new friends, but where secluded tables for one, two and three are always available.

Many guests pass up lunch in the dining room for hamburgers and roast beef sandwiches served in the golf house or at an outdoor pool-side dining pavilion. Each has its own kitchen and, because each serves but one meal a day, it can be meat without violating the dietary code.

Meanwhile, all kinds of things are going on in "back-of-the house" which few guests know about: there are construction men under Tom Mangin; electricians supervised by Conrad Slaver; gardeners headed by Louis Perez; thirty-five bellman taking orders from Superintendent of Service Jack Greenberg and his assistants, Sam Plotsky and Ernie Levy; twenty-five laundry workers led by Maximo Fernandez; four printers under Joe Halpner; twenty traffic men directed by Val Hammer, all utilizing their special skills to enable the hotel to run smoothly.

Chief Housekeeper Rose Friedman, supervising a staff of one-hundred maids and porters, is a busy figure from eight A.M. to ten P.M. Rose always has an anxious look on her face—not only because of the great responsibility she has as housekeeper for this huge establishment. She also worries about the astronomic number of towels, toilet paper rolls, kleenex boxes, and such which souvenir-hunters make off with each year—a time-honored occupational hazard of the hotel business.

During the afternoon, nurse Harriet Feldman stays in her first-aid room to treat the bruised shins and scraped knees of guests who play too hard. Sometimes she has something more interesting to take care of. One day, Broadway and Hollywood director Joshua Logan and his wife, Nedda (daughter of the late Irish singer, Bill Harrigan), hurried into her sanctum with songwriter Harold Rome and his wife, Florence. They had been walking past the golf house when a large dog, owned by the gardener, leaped at Nedda and took a nip at her well-formed leg. Harriet examined the leg and said fortunately the skin had not been broken.

"That old dog doesn't have any teeth," she said. "He never tried to bite anyone before. I wonder why he picked on you?"

"That's easy," friend Harold Rome said gravely. "He just couldn't resist the sight of some non-kosher meat."

Unknown to many a frolicking guest are the hard-working white-collar employes. Maurice Karliner, who used to manage a hotel in New Delhi, India, has been running the reservations department of twenty clerks since 1950. With aides Webb Blue, Lippy Berkowitz and Howard Weiner, he fills one of the more nerve-wracking jobs at the hotel. Booking rooms is also the concern of a crew of girls in the telephone reservations department under Carol Weiner, answering six direct lines from New York and other parts of the country. Elizabeth Reilly is the spunky lady in charge of the nine girls who man the hotel's regular switchboard with over 1,200 extensions in operation twenty-four hours a day. Other key white-collar personnel are found in the large accounting, cashier, and payroll departments under controller Bernard Roth and assistant Ann Ash, and payroll chief Rebecca Kaplan, who employs six girls just to handle the bi-weekly outlay of salaries.

Equally removed from fun and games are such hard-working executive types as Howard Bern, Jim Murray, Mary Goodwin and Alex Frankel in the sales and convention operation. General Manager Morton Sunshine sits at the apex of these varied specialties.

The afternoons pass quickly at The Big G., and now it is time to think of what lies ahead. By five o'clock, single girls are thinking about that new mini-skirt they bought just last week or having their hair set in the House of Albert beauty emporium. Properly coiffed and decked out, they set off for the gala cocktail party for single men and women held at the beginning of each week in the Terrace Room where Ruby Linner, the head waiter, oversees all preparations. The single men, who may have been mere girl-watchers all afternoon at the pool, are anxious not only to sample the free drinks and hors d'oeuvres, but to get acquainted with the girls. When the party is over, many will drift into the bar in the adjoining lounge. It is crowded only in the evening. Guests at Grossinger's are very modest tipplers.

It is almost impossible to spend more than a few hours at the hotel without having your picture taken by Ted Howard, who has been snapping his shutter around Grossinger's since 1945. When Whitey Ford checks in, Ted's eyes light up because he knows he is in for a few profitable days. "Hey, Whitey, come over here, I need you," Ted will shout, and good-natured Ford always obliges. He will pose with anyone for friend Ted, and many a guest will order a dozen pictures to send home. Ted is perhaps the most original character on a staff that boasts a small army of raffish types. Resorts traditionally afford a tolerant environment for these fascinating fauna. Among other things, human eccentricity adds up to good business. Ted's greatest gift is *chutzpah* or brash nerviness. State governor captain of industry, man of the cloth or movie glamour queen, all are regarded as long-lost friends and bosom pals only seconds after he meets them. Nearly all the entertainers and sports personalities who come to the hotel are as amenable as Ford. Few can resist Teddy's bear-hug charm.

Another certified G. character is taxi driver Henry Young, who's been piloting guests to Grossinger's in private limousines, or "hacks" as they are known throughout the mountains, for over three decades. Voluble, faintly cynical, and spontaneously amusing, he has passengers howling with laughter long before they arrive at the hotel. The trip northward from New York is a succession of hilarious anecdotes and reminiscences. Henry protests, "I never tell jokes. I just tell about all the crazy people I meet in my hack."

Gone some years, but still remembered is Joey Sugarman, a big bear of a man. An extravagantly mustachioed bell captain often mistaken for Jerry Colonna, he was without peer when it came to the audacious put-on—especially double-talking. Joey would say the wildest, most outrageous, even insulting things to guests, but in a fractured manner that always left the listener puzzled. Working his verbal specialty at every opportunity, Joey was a consummate artist and justly notorious around the hotel for more than a decade.

Nearly every evening, friends of Jennie walk to Joy Cottage for a drink before dinner. There is a bar in Jennie's living room, but Jennie still doesn't know the difference between a martini and a Shirley Temple cocktail. Terrace Room Maitre D' Phil Manos often comes over personally to handle the mixing while the kitchen dispatches enough hors d'oeuvres to feed the population of Luxembourg. During the day Jennie has said, "Stop by the cottage before dinner for a drink—and bring any friends along you like." This may be eight guests or eighty.

Dinner is definitely the main event at Grossinger's. All the day's activities are mere preliminaries to this nightly battle against malnutrition. Anyone who doesn't gain weight at the hotel just isn't trying. But most guests do their best.

The doors of the dining room, presided over by Abe Friedman, Maitre D' Dave Geiver and Head Waiter Hy Hoffer, open at seven P.M. Aided by four captains, they must combine the tact of a diplomat with the insights of a psychologist, as they make instantaneous decisions deploying people in suitable table arrangements.

There are approximately two-hundred-and-fifty tables seating as many as 1,600 and serviced by eighty-two waitresses, six waiters and forty-five busboys. (There are also eight regular room service waiters and a total of eighteen waiters and busboys who serve employes exclusively.) Ever-watchful captains Johnny Barna, Bill Goldwasser, Joseph Siedlecki and Joe Van Meur have very strict orders to note carefully if any guests appear to be unhappy with their fellow diners. If so, they will instantly move the unhappy one to another table. A spirit of familiarity lightens the air since many of the dining room staff are senior employes. It is not uncommon for guests when making reservations to ask for a favorite waitress.

Along with the year-round "professionals," the usual contingent of college kids is hired as busboys and waitresses during the summer. The dining room, service and athletic staffs continue as a kind of undergraduate haven. Although most people tend to think of The G. as a training ground for show business hopefuls or future hotelmen, the number of successful doctors, lawyers, teachers, dentists, accountants and business executives —both men and women—who financed their educations with Grossinger summer jobs during the past half century could easily supply the needs of a small city—literally thousands. Among Jennie's closest friends are some of these G. "alumni" like Dr. A. Harvey Neidorff, a nationally renowned allergist who was the sparkplug of the dining room staff more than three decades ago. She likes to tell guests there isn't a city she might visit that doesn't have at least one of her "boys" as a well-established physician.

Not every G. "graduate" has gone into the mainstream of the business and professional worlds. A few have earned a measure of fame and/or fortune in more esoteric callings—men like Irving Lazar, the famous literary agent who makes those well-publicized, million-dollar-plus deals for a string of leading literary lights, from Truman Capote to Alan J. Lerner. In the Thirties, he was a fast-talking, on-the-run busboy from Brooklyn with big ideas and a ready eye for the main chance.

William Graham is another. In the summer of 1951, a young Korean War veteran came to Jennie and asked for a job. Jennie sent the ex-Marine to Dave Geiver who agreed to hire him as a busboy. Today, as anyone under thirty can probably tell you, Bill Graham is the world's No. 1 rock music impresario as owner of the celebrated Fillmore East and West Theatres. That same summer, Chester Stern was a trumpet player in Eddie Ashman's house orchestra and already pathetically hooked on hard drugs. His departure from the hotel was an inglorious one, handcuffed to a local sheriff. Chester Stern received a long sentence in the county jail. For the past five years, he has been the top official of the nation-wide Synanon Movement, which has had such extraordinary success rehabilitating drug addicts.

True enough, working at The G. proved an invaluable apprenticeship for many who did, in fact, achieve notable success in allied fields: the Kriendlers of "21," El Morocco's Billy Reed, Jack Entratter of the Sands Hotel in Las Vegas, or Ash Resnick of Caesars Palace, another Vegas landmark. But the college kids are the ones Jennie has a special affection for. Most, still personify the old-time egalitarian spirit, establishing personal friendships with guests and adopting characteristically irreverant attitudes toward the "bosses."

The menu at every meal is merely a suggestion. Though overflowing with choices for each course, hard-to-please guests can order anything in season and get it. The captains are happiest when they can persuade a guest to have a second steak or to order several different desserts.

There is an axiom at The G. that many go to the hotel "to taste, not to eat." The Big G. is one of the very few resort hotels in the country which does not have a food-checker. If someone wants a steak, but also wishes "to taste" the broiled halibut, the liver, or the stuffed chicken, that's quite all right with the dining room staff. They are also delighted when non-Jewish guests discover what the kitchen help calls "K rations." These consist of three ancient and honorable dishes brought from Europe more than a hundred years ago—*kugel* (baked potato pudding), *kishka* (stuffed derma), and *kreplech* (a ravioli-like dish with meat stuffing).

JENNIE AND THE STORY OF GROSSINGER'S

The international cuisine is not only superbly varied, it is a gourmet's delight. In no time at all, even the first-time guest completely forgets his meals are guided by dietary laws. Recently introduced at meat meals, mocha mix (a soya-bean derivative) is an undetectable substitute for cream while margarine (a vegetable product) serves handsomely in lieu of butter. In cooking, however, *schmaltz*, which despite its current show business connotations is nothing more than chicken fat, is still preferred as a butter substitute during meat preparation. When boiled and strained, chicken fat is an excellent frying oil and shortening. There is even available a bacon substitute, "bac-o-chips," also made from soya. Guests who wish to sample G.-style delicacies back home often stop at the hotel's Mon Ami Book Shop for a copy of *The Art of Jewish Cooking* by Jennie. Originally published by Random House, it has become a cookbook best-seller in a paperback edition from Bantam Books with world-wide sales over the half-million mark.

If you happen to be a head-hunter, you can bag a dozen or more celebrities any night at dinner. Irving Berlin and his wife, Ellin, occasionally drop in from their house just a few miles away. If the Yankees or Mets have a day off, chances are that Elston Howard, Ed Kranepool, or Jerry Koosman, with their wives and children, will spend the day in G.-town. Jackie Robinson is another frequent visitor, as is syndicated newspaper columnist Leonard Lyons. In 1945, Lyons came to Grossinger's with a rare gift for Jennie—the handle from the front door of Hitler's mountain retreat at Berchtesgaden which he appropriated in Germany just weeks before. To celebrate the occasion, Leonard took his first drink that night after a lifetime as a teetotaler. Sylvia

Lyons, Leonard's wife, and the mother of their four sons, used to come to Grossinger's with her parents long before her marriage to the columnist.

Other guests you may see include Herman Wouk, Erich Leinsdorf, Rod Steiger, Norman Cousins and Eli Wallach. You might brush elbows with Senator Jacob Javits or Frank D. Roosevelt, Jr., as you walk to your table or notice that those two serious-looking men at the next table are Sid Caesar and Milton Berle. Dr. Selman Waksman, who received a Nobel Prize for discovering streptomycin, has been a visitor several times. Even Salvador Dali and Mrs. Vincent Astor have been to Grossinger's! If Jennie meets someone she likes she always says, "Please come and see our place and be my guest."

A quick glance at the hotel registration cards shows as many as forty-five states represented with the majority hailing from the East and not a few from foreign countries. Thanks to its international reputation, Grossinger's has welcomed visitors from almost every European and South American nation as well as Asian countries as distant as Japan. The hotel is a particular favorite with Canadians, Englishmen and South Africans.

When King Baudouin of Belgium came to the United States, Grossinger's was among the places he asked to see. Baron Edmund de Rothschild of France, reputed to be one of the richest men in the world, also put the hotel on his itinerary during an American tour. The G. has even hosted such unlikely guests as an Archbishop of the Syrian Orthodox Church, fully caparisoned in the long scarlet robes of his office, and an African tribal chief seeing America under the auspices of the State Department.

JENNIE AND THE STORY OF GROSSINGER'S

Under Jennie's guidance, Grossinger's has struck an effective blow against the parochial, illiberal tradition of vacationing in rigidly defined, ethnically "pure" enclaves. Though strictly kosher in diet, and exuberantly Yiddish in ambiance, it is heavily populated with non-Jews. Without fanfare, interfaith amity is nurtured and encouraged in uncounted ways that demonstrate the essential brotherhood of all humankind. Grossinger's has become a kind of microcosmic social laboratory where the simple coming together of different races and religions has proved a more powerful antidote to bigotry than thousands of high-sounding words.

A not untypical week in February of last year showed a guest profile comprised of 100 members of the Sisterhood of the Beth Chaim Synagogue of Philadelphia; 250 undergraduates, mostly black, from Manhattan Community College; 450 clerics and their wives attending an annual retreat of the New York area, United Methodist Church; and a diverse delegation of businessmen here for a sales parley—all co-mingling harmoniously with easy, natural, spontaneous mutual acceptance. A fortnight following, a national convention of the Yeshiva University Women's Organization was immediately followed by 700 young members of the Catholic Youth Organization of the New York Archdiocese.

This deeply felt commitment to universal brotherhood and understanding is at the core of Jennie's personal credo, learned from her parents. Jackie Robinson, a friend for many years, summed it up in a television interview when he said, "To Jennie, people are people! It's about as simple as that—no matter their skin, their place of birth, or where they happen to pray."

Jennie's visits to the dining room remain her brightest moments. When she goes from table to table to greet guests, it is always with affection. On Saturday night, it has become her custom to sit on a high chair near the entrance of the dining room and exchange a few words with virtually every guest as he or she leaves.

Jennie still never takes a drink, but there was one occasion when she momentarily stepped out of character. Making her dining room rounds, she stopped at a table with four unfamiliar men. She smiled, said hello, asked if they were having a good time, chatted briefly and moved on. Before she was out of earshot, Jennie heard one of the men ask, "Who was that nosey dame, anyway?" Still smiling, Jennie quickly retraced her steps and announced, "I owe you gentlemen an apology for not introducing myself. My name is Jennie Grossinger." Startled by this revelation, the foursome blushed and laughed nervously. Jennie sensed their discomfort and promptly said, "Come, gentlemen, let's all have a drink to toast our new friendship." The tension instantly dissolved. The men applauded their new friend as Jennie proceeded to hoist one.

This open approach to total strangers is a characteristic of Jennie's that often amazes first-time visitors to the hotel. Having heard and read a great deal about this legendary lady, they are understandably awed when she approaches unannounced, extends a hand and says simply: "I'm Jennie Grossinger—and I'm so happy to have you here as my guests."

On the other hand, like most people in the resort hotel business, Jennie also has to cope with the embarrassing problem of not remembering everyone. Tributes galore have been paid to her phenomenal powers of recall, but once in a while someone will walk up and announce confidently, "You remember me, Jennie, don't you?"—and Jennie will probe in vain through the recesses of a memory filled with thousands of names and faces. Often as not, the person is someone Jennie hasn't seen in twenty-five or thirty years. Faced with such a situation these days, she will apologize to the unrecognized guest and say something like, "After all, I don't exactly look the way I did thirty years ago, either, and if you didn't know I was Jennie Grossinger, I'll bet you'd have difficulty recognizing me."

On each dining room table, guests will find the *Grossinger Tattler*, a mimeographed paper published each evening at the hotel since the Twenties. If you stay at Grossinger's more than a day, you are sure to see your name in the little sheet. Its editor drifts from table to table jotting down the names, occupations and hometowns of guests. Sometimes there are as many as two hundred names in the paper. Every male guest is either "urbane," "genial," or "handsome," and every female guest is either "charming," "lovely," or "fascinating." If a two-headed woman with a third eye in the middle of each forehead were to be in the dining room, it would not faze the resourceful *Tattler* editor. He would probably refer to her as "distinguished and unusual."

An enterprising public relations department also publishes a breezy, four-page, tabloid-size house organ, the *Grossinger News*, circulated to a mailing list of over 100,000 former guests. The *News* features stories of hotel happenings, profiles of staff members, gossipy chatter, and profuse photographs of celebrities. Some of the successful writers who apprenticed on the sheet during the past two decades include: Jack Shor, public relations vice-president of the Clairol Company; comedy writer Arnold B. Horwitt; magazine scribe Howard Eisenberg; television critic Barbara Delatiner (Long Island *Newsday*) film publicist Bud Rosenthal (Columbia Pictures); former *New York Post* city editor Bernard Lefkowitz; New York public relations executive George Bennett; novelist Jonathan Baumbach; and the author of this volume.

The *Tattler* always announces the entertainment for the evening. At eight-thirty, there is a recorded hi-fi concert of classical favorites at poolside. Strolling around the brilliantly lit pool under a starry sky while strains of Vivaldi or Verdi fill the night air is a rare treat even if you aren't a votary of long-hair music. For those who don't wish to venture outdoors, resident staff pianist Henry Woode is always at the big Steinway in one of the lobbies playing musical comedy favorites for a sing-along session. If it's Friday night, many will attend the traditional "Oneg Shabbot" service when Sabbath, Hebrew, and folk melodies are sung under the spirited direction of Cantor Shalom Gruen. This is a G. tradition that dates back to 1914 and now honors the memory of Malke.

On many Monday nights during the summer, the evening's divertissement centers at the huge floodlit outdoor pool where an aquacade and diving show, featuring top professional water stars, is held. Other nights of the week are devoted to "music festivals," an occasional Broadway play presented by touring companies, and at least four variety shows staged in the Playhouse. They are emceed by Julie Karson, a suave, highly articulate gentleman of twenty years service. He might introduce such stars as Red Buttons, Roberta Peters, Jackie Mason, Vic Damone, Joan Rivers, Peter Nero, Tony Bennett, Gordon MacRae, Diahann Carroll, Alan King or any other headliner Jerry Weiss has signed for a single appearance.

Quick thinking and absolute stage presence are probably the greatest assets of the never-ruffled Mr. Karson. Introducing a host of variety offerings every week over a period of two decades has placed him at the center of innumerable onstage crises—forgotten lyrics to unintentional nudity.

He had one of his finest hours the night a young lady contestant in a Champagne Hour dance competition, apparently carried away by the frenzied tempos of the mambo, suddenly lost control of one of her natural functions and found herself surrounded by an ever-widening puddle. As the audience began to snicker and murmer, the resourceful Julie blithely waltzed onstage from the wings, looked down on the big circle of liquid, looked up at the ceiling, extended his right hand, palm upward and dead-panned: "I thought I told the plumber to fix that damned sprinkler." The resulting audience screams instantly bridged the poor woman's embarrassment and another crisis was weathered.

Jerry Weiss, who began as a night clerk in 1943, is in charge of all evening entertainment, sometimes booking as many as seven different shows a week using two and three acts each. With musical director Eddie Ashman, he also supervises the two bands in the Terrace Room nightclub, two combos appearing in the adjacent

Lounge, and a rock-and-roll group playing for teenagers in their own haunt, the Night Watch Room. The bands play until around two-thirty A.M. G. guests, as a rule, are not night owls; there's too much to do in the daytime to go to bed at dawn.

Many drift to the Coffee Shop supervised by Ben Geiver (Dave's brother) for cream chesse and lox on bagels or a double strawberry banana split buried in hot fudge. If the night is cool—and nights are usually quite cool in the Catskills—couples go walking in the moonlight. At this late hour, Milton "Top" Friedman, chief security officer, and his assistants patrol the corridors to assure that all is well.

Real trouble is unknown at Grossinger's, but sometimes a few frolicsome souls think that four A.M. is an ideal hour to engage in an impromptu songfest at the piano in the darkened main lobby. Gently, but firmly, they are advised that some of their fellow guests are eccentric enough to want to sleep. A night manager, room clerk and three auditors remain on duty at the front desk while several members of the fire department, headed by Len Hayes, are patrolling every corner of the hotel grounds to see that all is well. Throughout the nocturnal hours, an army of porters vacuum, scrub, polish and wipe carpets, rugs, windows, furnishings and walls of the hotel's many lobbies and public rooms. Because immaculateness is a way of life at The G., a dusty window sill or dirty ashtray is as hard to come by as an order of ham and eggs.

By now Mom Tuchman is about to enter the kitchen for her daily rendezvous with 5,400 eggs. Another day is about to start at The Big G.—all because fifty-six years ago Jennie went to the country.

Epilogue

"You're crazy," George Jessel said. "How can you write a whole book about Jennie? A book about Jennie would have no conflict. I've known her for over forty years and I know she never had an enemy. She's been pouring out her love for humanity all her days. And she's received nothing but love in return. No one will believe it."

"Maybe so," I agreed, "but, anyway, Georgie, she did have two enemies—poverty and bad health."

"So what?" he said. "The truth is, she never knew she was poor when she was a kid and today she's rich. Bad health? She's always managed to beat that, too."

"I know, Georgie," I countered, "I've talked to more than two hundred people who've known her as long as you have and not one has put the rap on her."

"Jennie is undoubtedly this country's best-known innkeeper," Jessel said, and I listened, because, like so many comics, Jessel is a serious man. "But that isn't good enough to carry a whole book. Of course, Jennie is an unusual personality. She's a quiet, humble woman, but when she walks into a room, she lights up the place. She's got a touch of magic in her makeup. I'll tell you what I mean.

JENNIE AND THE STORY OF GROSSINGER'S

"A couple of years ago, I think it was 1964, I attended a $100-a-plate dinner with Jennie at the Waldorf sponsored by the American Committee for the Weizmann Institute of Science. The principal speaker was none other than the President of the United States, Lyndon Johnson, and the dais overflowed with some of the most famous names in American public life—Supreme Court Justice Arthur Goldberg, Assistant Secretary of State Averell Harriman, General David Sarnoff, Nobel Prizewinner Isador Rabi. Because the program was long, Ben Grauer, the master of ceremonies, asked the audience of over 1,500 not to applaud as the luminaries took their seats at the dais. The crowd obliged and maintained a respectful silence. But the moment our Jennie walked in, the assemblage began applauding spontaneously and soon everyone was on his feet giving the bewildered gal a standing ovation that lasted while she walked the entire length of the table, found her place, and sat down. I can't explain it. But that's how people react to Jennie."

Although many have tried to explain Jennie, it really isn't too difficult. One of her guests once observed, "Jennie cares about people—so people care about Jennie." And by people, he meant everyone—the big and the little, the famous and the obscure, strangers and friends. To her, everyone is someone. As that same guest added, "She knows how to make a person feel he matters. With Jennie, everybody counts."

Today, approaching seventy-eight, Jennie is slim, chic, looks at least fifteen years younger and has her eyes steadfastly on the future.

A few years ago, she entered the recondite realms of high finance and banking when she was elected a direc-

tor of the Marine Midland National Bank of Southeast-
ern New York, replacing her late husband. Each fall, she
spends some time at Duke University Hospital on a rice
and salt-free diet, and at the Leo N. Levi Memorial
Arthritis Hospital in Hot Springs, Arkansas, to treat the
arthritic pains that have plagued her in recent years. At
the Hot Springs Hospital—she is one of its principal
benefactors—Jennie is a beloved figure. Each day of her
stay—about three weeks—she never fails to visit the
patients confined to their beds. In the dining room for
ambulatory patients, she goes from table to table just as
graciously as if she were back at Grossinger's offering a
greeting here, an embrace there, a few comforting words
to each. She is "Jennie" to everyone.

She devotes the rest of the year (except for a three-
month winter sojourn in Miami Beach) to the hotel and
its future. Above all, she has an abhorence for wasting
time. "It is our most valuable gift—the gift of life. Why
do so many people squander it so?" she often asks ruefully.

Jennie's quest for self-improvement continues una-
bated. Books and records stacked high in her bedroom
attest to the lady's unquenchable thirst for knowledge.
In one of my many talks with her, Jennie confided: "I've
been lucky and have few regrets in my life. But if I had
to do it over again, I would have spent much more time
as a student. Education is the one thing I have missed
the most."

One of her greatest pleasures these days is simply to
reunite with families who have been loyal guests down
through the years. Grossingerites of four decades and
more are numerous. Most of the old-timers usually re-

turn during the Jewish holiday seasons—Rosh Hasha-nah, Succoth, or Passover. Some treasure a relationship with Jennie that goes back to the early days at Long-brook House.

Jennie's hopes for the future of the hotel now rest with the younger grandchildren. She was elated when Mark (Elaine's eighteen-year-old son) and Jimmy (Paul's seventeen-year-old) both began showing an avid interest in the business. Not long ago, she took the two youngs-ters, and nineteen-year-old Michael, Paul's middle son, for a stroll around the grounds. The boys talked as though they were about to take over the entire opera-tion.

"I'll tell you one thing, Grandma," Mark said as they walked near the lake. "There are too many tree stumps around here. We ought to cut some away and make more walks people can use in the summer. Right, Jimmy?"

As they chatted on, Jennie listened quietly. The hotel business was in their blood and their words exhilarated her. Jennie would not have to worry about the future. Paul would train these boys as she and Harry had once trained Paul and Elaine. Maybe Elaine's twenty-year-old daughter, Susan, and her eleven-year-old youngest, Mitchell, would come into the business, too.

But she felt there was one small lesson she should teach the boys. She led them back to Joy Cottage. Then, pointing to one of the dozens of plaques and citations on the wall, she said: "A resort isn't buildings and kitchens and lakes or nightclubs. The real hotel is the people who work here. Do you see this plaque? Please read it, Mark."

The boy read: "A few weeks ago, a distinguished committee on the West Coast named Jennie Grossinger one of the ten outstanding women of the world. To those of us who have worked with her during the years, she is far more than that. To us, she is the architect who poured her soul into the creation of this fabulous resort. She is the humanitarian who has helped endow hospitals, nurseries and schools in Israel and elsewhere throughout the world. She is the benefactor who made it possible for countless young men to go to college and become physicians, lawyers, engineers and teachers. She is the patroness who nurtured fledgling entertainers on their way to stardom. She is the friend who always listens with a sympathetic ear and an understanding heart to the woes of even the humblest of us. She is a woman of great social genius and magnetic warmth. To us, she is the No. 1 woman of the world! We want, at this time, to wish her a long, long life, filled with further opportunities to give aid and comfort to her fellow-men."

The scroll was signed by nine-hundred-and-fifty Grossinger staff members.

"That is our hotel—those nine hundred and fifty men and women," she said. "This is the finest award I've ever received—the one I cherish most. Always remember, these people are the real Gossinger's."

The relationship between Jennie and her staff, which she always calls my "larger Grossinger family," is close and authentic. Almost every day that she is at the hotel, she visits the kitchens, the reservations desk, laundries, the greenhouses, the traffic control center, or the security office to say hello and inquire about her employes' health and their families. She is not there to inspect, just to see how they are getting along and is always on a first-name basis. Usually, a warm embrace will follow the greeting.

Such outpourings of affection are as natural to Jennie as breathing—and she seems to inspire the same kind of response in others. Withdrawn, unemotional types experience sudden personality transformations in her orbit. She is one of those human beings who manage to transmit to others her own particular emotional atmosphere without apparent effort or design. It just happens! And these displays are more than a smile, a handshake, or a friendly word. Jennie may be one of the kissingest and most-kissed woman in America. She greets everyone with an affectionate buss and everyone responds in kind, especially children.

Stories about Jennie's unaffected humility abound. A few months back, while peregrinating around the dining room, she stopped at one of the executive tables to chat with Jerry Weiss. Seconds after she sat down, a worried-looking busboy, hired only the day before, rushed over, tapped her on the shoulder and said: "I'm sorry, lady, but you can't sit here! That's Lou Goldstein's seat—and he told me he doesn't like anyone to sit in his place!" Jennie turned, smiled at the boy, and, before Jerry or anyone else could protest, was on her feet. Without a word, she moved to an empty chair at the far end of the table!

A central theme in Jennie's life has been chronic serious illness, met and overcome. Such afflictions have challenged and spurred rather than handicapped her. Even as this book was being written, she was the victim of a cerebral stroke while at her Miami Beach home. Within months, she was up and around doing the things she always did although now her cautious doctors insisted she have a nurse with her at all times.

When word of the stroke got back to Liberty, a group of Sullivan County citizens launched an informal campaign to rename that portion of Route 17 known as the Quickway, leading directly to the Catskill vacation belt, in her honor.

From the germ of an idea originated by Abe Friedman, the project snowballed and soon won enthusiastic approval from thousands of public figures across the state including many prominent legislators. The drive was climaxed on January 23, 1968, by New York State Assemblyman Ferdinand Mondello, who rose in that legislative body to introduce a formal resolution requesting the New York State Commissioner of Transportation to re-name the Route 17 expressway from the Harriman Interchange to the northern Sullivan County line (sixty-two miles) the "Jennie Grossinger Quickway."

When the cumbersome, slow-moving legislative machinery kept the resolution from coming to the floor for a vote in that Assembly session, an impatient Governor Nelson A. Rockefeller sprang into action in behalf of his old friend. On June 16, coinciding with Jennie's seventy-sixth birthday, the Governor issued an official New York State Proclamation designating the twenty-four hour period as "Jennie Grossinger Day"—the first time such a Proclamation had ever been issued to honor a living woman in the Empire State.

Last New Year's Eve, there were over 1,600 people in the dining room. Jennie was with them until midnight, but as soon as the crowd sang "Auld Lang Syne," she slipped into the staff dining room in back of the kitchen. "Now, let's have a family party," she said, beaming. Dave Geiver produced champagne and pastry. Within a few minutes, most of the staff drifted into the big room. Jennie, nursing her usual ginger ale, remained with her old friends until one A.M., the latest she had stayed up in many, many months.

George Jessel once said to her: "You'll never get the hotel business out of your system, Jennie."

"That's right," she replied happily. "And do you know something else? When I die, wherever I go, I hope they have a hotel there, too. And I hope they'll let me run it. I'll find a lot of our early guests there and I'll remember what they liked to eat. And my mother will be there to do the cooking and Poppa . . . and Harry. . . ."

Index

317

INDEX

INDEX

INDEX

INDEX

INDEX

INDEX